CONTACT CHARLIE

CONTACT CHARLIE

THE CANADIAN ARMY, THE TALIBAN
AND THE BATTLE THAT SAVED AFGHANISTAN

CHRIS WATTIE

KEY PORTER BOOKS

Library and Archives Canada Cataloguing in Publication

Wattie, Chris, 1961-
    Contact Charlie : The Canadian army, the taliban and the battle that saved Afghanistan /
Chris Wattie.

ISBN 978-1-55470-084-4

1. Canada. Canadian Army. Princess Patricia's Canadian Light Infantry.
Battalion, 1st. Company, C. 2. Panjwaii, Battle of, Afghanistan, 2006.
3. Afghan War, 2001- —Participation, Canadian. I. Title.

DS371.4123.P36W38 2008   958.104'7   C2008-902209-2

ONTARIO ARTS COUNCIL
CONSEIL DES ARTS DE L'ONTARIO

The publisher gratefully acknowledges the support of the Canada Council for the Arts and the
Ontario Arts Council for its publishing program. We acknowledge the support of the Government
of Ontario through the Ontario Media Development Corporation's Ontario Book Initiative.

We acknowledge the financial support of the Government of Canada through the Book
Publishing Industry Development Program (BPIDP) for our publishing activities.

All photos not otherwise credited were provided by the soldiers of 1 PPCLI. A donation will
be made on their behalf to Boomer's Legacy. Established in remembrance of Corporal Andrew
James Eykelenboom, a Canadian military medic who was killed by a suicide bomber in August
2006, the foundation works to help aid the women and children of Afghanistan. For more
information, visit www.boomerslegacy.ca.

Key Porter Books Limited
Six Adelaide Street East, Tenth Floor
Toronto, Ontario
Canada M5C 1H6
www.keyporter.com

Text design: Marijke Friesen
Electronic formatting: Alison Carr
Maps: Richard Johnson
Printed and bound in Canada

09 10 11 12 5 4 3

For Shorty, Kevin and Bill

*"Good old Charlie Company: leading the charge again . . .
After about an hour-long fight the Company broke contact
but lived up to the nickname the soldiers had given us,
'Contact Charlie'."*
—Captain Andrew Charchuk
Forward Observation Officer, attached to C Company
1st Battalion, Princess Patricia's Canadian Light Infantry

*"These guys saved Kandahar, which means they saved
Afghanistan and probably saved NATO."*
—Brigadier-General David Fraser
General commanding Regional Command South
Kandahar, Afghanistan

CONTENTS

Foreword by J. L. Granatstein   11
Introduction   15

Prologue
"Where do these guys keep coming from?"   21

PART 1: Prelude to Battle, Winter 2005–2006

Chapter One
"No shortage of fighters."   31

Chapter Two
"Kick the door in, throw in the grenade and
'Follow me, boys!'"   47

PART 2: Bayanzi, May 16–17, 2006

Chapter Three
"The Taliban are coming."   71

Chapter Four
"An unattractive target."   88

Chapter Five
"My Sunray's down."   102

Chapter Six
"Be careful what you ask for."   120

Chapter Seven
"Spread the word, motherfucker."   144

PART 3: Seyyedin, June 12, 2006

Chapter Eight
"Nowhere to squirt." 157

Chapter Nine
"Do I look Afghan to you?" 174

Chapter Ten
"I don't want to hear that!" 188

PART 4: Pashmul, July 8–10, 2006

Chapter Eleven
"A little surreal." 201

Chapter Twelve
"The man who wouldn't die." 218

PART 5: The White Schoolhouse, August 3, 2006

Chapter Thirteen
"You know what to do." 237

Chapter Fourteen
"Just like World War One." 261

Chapter Fifteen
"A very bad day." 282

Epilogue 288
Acknowledgements 296
Index 299

FOREWORD
BY J. L. GRANATSTEIN

I have not been to Afghanistan, and it's more than forty years since I served in the Canadian Army. The great merit of Chris Wattie's splendid book is that it puts me, the reader, into Kandahar with the soldiers of Charlie Company of the 1st Battalion, Princess Patricia's Canadian Light Infantry. We are on the ground with them, fighting with them, living with and talking to them, and the war suddenly becomes comprehensible to those of us at home. There has not been a Canadian book like this.

Part of the reason is Wattie himself. He's an air force brat, the son of an RCAF navigator who flew on Argus and Aurora patrol aircraft. He went to Royal Roads Military College for two years then dropped out and became a journalist after attending Carleton University. After working at a number of newspapers, he took a position with the *National Post* and became for many years the paper's military and defence specialist. That took him to Afghanistan twice, first in 2003 to Kabul and then in 2006 to Kandahar with Task Force Orion, made up of the 1 PPCLI battle group. And although he is in his forties (and although he joined up intending to do research on the present-day military), Wattie is also a happy army reservist, a junior officer-in-the-making in the Governor General's Horse Guards, an armoured regiment in Toronto.

So he knows the military, likes soldiering and soldiers, and it shows. Perhaps that moved his editors at the *National Post* to decide either that he was too sympathetic to the military or that he knew too much. In what must rank as one of the more foolish journalistic decisions of the present twilight era of the newspaper business, Wattie was switched to the police beat which, he says, "isn't much different when you come right down to it, except that Toronto has better plumbing" than Kandahar.

There doesn't seem to be any plumbing in Kandahar Province, and not much running water either, at least none that the men and women of Task Force Orion could find in 2006. The sere landscape broken up by age-old grapevines, marijuana fields, and acres of opium poppies; the squalor of near-subsistence living for a population of strikingly good-looking children, veiled women, and Afghan men looking rough, fit, and potentially dangerous—it certainly wasn't Edmonton, where 1 PPCLI were based.

Well-trained and superbly led by Lieutenant-Colonel Ian Hope, the battle-group commander, Task Force Orion found itself on the hot seat in the summer of 2006. The Taliban believed that the Canadians, new to Kandahar but a known quantity from their quasi-peacekeeping deployment in Kabul three years earlier, would be easy meat, just another weak NATO (North Atlantic Treaty Organization) nation whose politicians lacked the will to fight. The way to hit them, Taliban leaders decided, was to concentrate on the Canadians in the field and, they hoped and believed, seize Kandahar city and completely demoralize ISAF, the International Security Assistance Force.

As Wattie's book makes clear, this was a serious mistake for the fundamentalists. First, Task Force Orion was well armed, its LAV IIIS, the Canadian Forces' light armoured vehicle with a 25-mm chain gun, able to go almost anywhere and to bring devastating fire on any target. There was Canadian M777 howitzer artillery, capable of a near-pinpoint accuracy that would astonish old sweats who fought in Canada's previous wars. There was air support that could be whistled up in a hurry, dropping bombs on Taliban positions.

And there were the soldiers of 1 PPCLI. The men and women of the Princess Pats and their associated units were, except for the reservists who had trained and bonded with them, professional soldiers. Professionals. They had worked their way up in the army, many over two or more decades, and they had served in countries around the world on peacekeeping and peace-enforcement missions. They had trained rigorously in Canada and even more when they arrived in theatre. Service in the Former Yugoslavia had hardened some of them; others had been in Afghanistan in 2002 when a PPCLI battalion had served well with a United States division. They were tough, physically fit, disciplined but informal, and they understood their role, their tactics and weaponry, and the importance of what they were doing in Kandahar.

Not that most of the soldiers saw the conflict in the sophisticated manner of political scientists as a struggle between militant Islam and the West, occurring in a strategic location between old Soviet Russian republics and the Indian sub-continent. The officers and senior warrants might have understood this and read histories of long-past British and much more recent Russian experiences fighting in Afghanistan, but not the soldiers. As professionals, their task was to go where their government sent them and to do the job they had been given. They fought for their friends, their platoons and their companies, and their regiment, much as soldiers have always done. They fought to kill the enemy and to stay alive and, as Chris Wattie makes clear, they did both so well that they saved Kandahar.

The hero of this book, if there is a single hero in a Charlie Company replete with heroes, is Lieutenant-Colonel Hope. In his mid-forties with a quarter-century of service in the British and Canadian armies, Hope understood his role as Task Force commander, and to watch him (through Wattie's eyes) steering his manoeuvre sub-units around, bargaining for support, dealing with his superiors, and keeping his subordinate officers and warrants focused on their leadership tasks is to recognize yet again why commanding troops in the field can be simultaneously exhilarating and terrifying. Very few Canadian officers in the years since the Korean War—ended more than a half-century ago—have been required to deal with a skilled, determined enemy, and with Canadians killed in action. Hope did this and did it supremely well; so too did his officers and men and women.

Canadians should read this book and be proud, very proud, of the men and women who serve in their name. Chris Wattie has told their story in fine prose and with much understanding of why soldiers risk their todays for our tomorrows.

—J. L. Granatstein

INTRODUCTION

"The history of a battle is not unlike the history of a ball. Some individuals may recollect all the little events of which the great result is the battle won or lost, but no individual can recollect the order in which, or the exact moment at which, they occurred."
—Arthur Wellesley, Duke of Wellington

Wellington fought in an age when outcomes were decided in a single day, at most two, and when events could be viewed in their entirety by a general sitting on a horse atop a high-enough hill. Even so, the Iron Duke found it difficult to recount the story of a battle, even one witnessed largely with his own eyes. How, then, can we hope to comprehend a battle that stretched over nearly three months, involved dozens of separate firefights and ambushes, and stopped and started on at least three occasions?

Despite its intermittent and scattered nature, the fighting in Afghanistan's Panjwayi District in the summer of 2006 constituted one conclusive military action—the first battle fought by Canadian soldiers since the end of the Korean War more than fifty years earlier.

The Taliban certainly saw it that way. They had a definite goal: a high-profile attack or series of attacks on Kandahar City that would drive a wedge between the U.S. and the other NATO nations operating in Afghanistan. The Canadian battle group, named Task Force Orion by its remarkable commander, Lieutenant-Colonel Ian Hope, recognized the enemy's goal and set out to deny them that end.

Yet the Battle of Panjwayi went largely unrecognized, despite the presence of literally dozens of embedded journalists in Kandahar, several of whom were present at the firefights that made up the battle. Even many senior Canadian and U.S. generals did not realize what their troops were involved in until well after the fact. The only Canadians who did recognize what was happening on the ground in the orchards and villages of Panjwayi during that long, hot summer were the soldiers of Task Force Orion—the sergeants, corporals and captains who fought the Taliban at places like Bayanzi, Seyyedin, Pashmul, Nalgham and the White Schoolhouse.

This is a story about those Canadian soldiers, told as much as possible in their own words about their own experiences and what they saw and did. It is, in particular, the story of one company of Task Force Orion—the 148 officers and soldiers of Charlie Company, 1st Battalion, Princess Patricia's Canadian Light Infantry regiment. Throughout the entire period during which this battle was fought, between May 16 and August 3, 2006, Charlie Company was involved in every major action in the Panjwayi region. Its soldiers fought in every phase of the battle, suffering more casualties and winning more decorations for valour than any other unit within Task Force Orion.

This in no way diminishes the accomplishments of the soldiers of Alpha Company (the Red Devils), or of Bravo Company, who spent so many weeks and months hunting the Taliban in the Panjwayi, or of any of the engineers, armoured reconnaissance troopers, gunners, medics, military police or members of the dozens of other trades that made up the Canadian battle group. But the one constant in the story of the Battle of Panjwayi is the company of soldiers that came into contact with the Taliban so often that they earned the admiring nickname Contact Charlie.

To the many soldiers I spoke to for this book who appear only in passing, or not at all, I offer my thanks and sincere apologies: your absence from these pages is due entirely to the demands of space and the need to hone the story of the battle to a coherent narrative, not to the value of your stories or your experiences.

This book is for all the men and women of the Canadian Forces who served and continue to serve their country in Afghanistan, especially those who came home wounded or maimed or did not come home at all. Their stories deserve to be told.

—Chris Wattie

CONTACT
CHARLIE

PROLOGUE

"Where do these guys keep coming from?"

Panjwayi District, Kandahar, Afghanistan
August 3, 2006
1500 hours

Lieutenant-Colonel Ian Hope stepped out from the small patch of shade around his command post and into the molten Afghan sun, the soles of his dusty tan combat boots crunching loose stones and gravel underfoot. His blue eyes, darkened by the shade beneath the brim of his helmet, scanned the broad shallow wadi of the Arghandab River then swept north towards a low white building a few hundred metres away, still partly shrouded by the dust and smoke of four hours of battle.

All around him the armoured vehicles of his command were wheeling into defensive positions or idling in place, the powerful diesel engines of LAV III armoured troop carriers, Nyala patrol cars or the lighter G Wagon jeeps thrumming a rhythm he could feel through his boots. The snap of bullets occasionally crackled overhead, but Hope ignored them. The short, wiry career soldier pulled a thin cigar out of one of the dozens of pockets in his tactical vest and calmly lit up, pulling a long draw and staring with naked hatred at the whitewashed buildings in the distance. He hardly noticed the handful of Taliban mortar rounds that landed further down the wide, flat riverbed, sending clouds of fine powder dust high into the air. Hope was face

| 21

to face with the hardest decision of his life: what to do about that cluster of mud-walled buildings—the buildings his soldiers had been fighting and dying for over the past twelve hours.

Hope had spent the past three hours glued to the handset of one or the other of the four radios in his mobile command post—code-named "Niner Tac"—pleading with staff officers in distant operations centres for artillery or air support to help his beleaguered soldiers, calling up reinforcements, cursing the new satellite radio (which was working only intermittently), and nursing the short-range conventional radio sets, the famously finicky "Ticks" (or TCCCS, short for Tactical Command and Control Communication System). He had listened in frustration and anguish to the brief bursts of transmissions that were his clearest, almost his only, window into his troops' desperate battle with nearly two hundred Taliban fighters just over the rim of the wadi, a bare six hundred metres away.

Four soldiers were already dead and more than a dozen others wounded, some of them critically. Two of the Canadian battle group's massive LAVs—the heaviest firepower at Hope's immediate beck and call and a precious resource in a firefight like this—were smoking wrecks, already being hauled away by the hard-working crews of the Canadian brigade's combat recovery vehicles. The small tent he had just left, almost the only shade for a kilometre in any direction, was crowded with wounded soldiers, scarred and bleeding from Taliban bullets or shrapnel, or the concussion of bomb or grenade blasts. Many were in shock, staring at the dust-coated walls with glazed eyes. Others had fallen victim to the blast-furnace heat of the Afghan summer, which had climbed to 52°C and rendered some of his toughest infantrymen as weak as infants, unable to move or even lift their own arms without help. The fire support Hope so desperately needed for his pinned-down troops had been slow in coming and, for the first time since the Canadians had arrived in southern Afghanistan six months ago, inadequate to the task.

The Taliban had stubbornly remained in their foxholes and well-protected firing positions behind thick mud-brick walls, and had continued to pour fire onto the Canadians.

While Hope glared at the distant buildings and steadily reduced his cigar to a stub, a pair of LAVs roared up to the edge of his command post in a swirl of diesel fumes and hot, gritty dust, one dragging its armoured rear ramp behind it like a wounded wing. Both of the huge vehicles were peppered with the scars left by the rocket-propelled grenades (RPGs) and hundreds of bullets that had ricocheted off their thick green armour. Hope barely noticed the LAVs, rapt in concentration over his next move in the day-long battle, but a moment later the unmistakable bark of an irritated non-commissioned officer made him snap his head around.

"Hey! Can I get some fucking help here?"

Hope turned and blinked in surprise, taking in the scene before him. A sergeant was standing on the lowered ramp of the nearest LAV covered in blood and dirt, his face blackened by soot from firing the assault rifle that now dangled over one arm. He was struggling to drag the motionless figure of another soldier out of the rear compartment of the LAV, whose normally crowded but functional interior had been turned into a charnel house. Blood, sand and dirt were splashed all over the pale-green metal walls, while the two benches reserved for the seven infantrymen the LAV normally carried were littered with discarded rifles, piles of empty brass casings and discarded or shattered equipment. Bodies were slumped on the floor, some not moving. Hope leaped to help the sergeant gently lay out one body after another on the ground just outside his tent. When they finished, there were three motionless figures covered by tarps scrounged from the back of one of Hope's command vehicles. Inside the tent, more than a dozen wounded soldiers crowded into the scant relief its canvas offered from the searing heat.

Through the open flap, Hope could see that even the men who had brought in their comrades were suffering. Corporal Shawn Felix, a twenty-five-year-old from Calgary, stood like a statue staring blankly into the middle distance with what soldiers in the Second World War called the thousand-yard stare. Felix had not been wounded in the desperate fight for the buildings just beyond the wadi's edge, but the exhaustion written on his dirt- and blood-smeared face made it clear he was near the end of his endurance.

Hope reached up and put his hand gently on the young soldier's shoulder. "I'm going to get us out of this, Corporal," he said quietly, "but I need you with me if I'm going to do it. Fully with me."

Felix looked at his commander in astonishment, realizing where he was and with whom he was talking. His dark eyes came back into focus, he took a deep breath and nodded a reflexive "Yes sir!" then trudged out of the tent to rejoin his section, walking through the waves of heat like a man in a dream.

Hope saw a familiar stocky form walking towards him from the nearby LAVs. Sergeant Pat Tower was a veteran even by the Canadian Army's demanding standards, having served three tours in the Former Yugoslavia, including the 1993 battle for the Medak Pocket in Croatia. Casualties had elevated him to second-in-command of the platoon of about thirty soldiers of Charlie Company who had been fighting that day, immediately under his best friend Sergeant Vaughn Ingram. Tower reported to Hope that his platoon was back from the fight.

Hope frowned at him, puzzled that the platoon commander had not reported in person. "Where's Sergeant Ingram?" he asked.

Tower paused, then nodded down at the bodies laid out by the entrance to the command post. "Dead, sir," he said flatly. "That's him there."

With a start, Hope realized that one body was that of his most reliable sergeant, the seemingly indestructible Newfoundlander with whom he had served in the former Airborne Regiment so many years ago. Beside Ingram lay Private Kevin Dallaire and Corporal Bryce Keller, both killed in the fierce firefight just beyond the low ridge of gravel and dirt that marked the edge of the dry riverbed. Hope took a deep breath and ordered Tower to take stock of his equipment and ensure that nothing and no one had been left behind. Then he returned his gaze to the dozen or so buildings in the distance.

Another element of his command, the battle group's Bravo Company, was still locked in a vicious but much more successful fight with a large group of Taliban just a few kilometres to the north. And he now had three fresh platoons of reinforcements. More than 120 soldiers in a dozen of the all-important LAVs had just arrived from Kandahar, eager to finish off the fight that had begun hours before. Hope was itching to take this force into the fight and destroy the enemy that had hit his soldiers so hard in the morning and early afternoon. He finally had artillery support from the gunners of the Royal Canadian Horse Artillery, firing their lethally accurate M777 howitzers from a spot a few kilometres to the northeast and dropping 155-mm high-explosive rounds within yards of the targets called in by the infantry.

Just then, the ground was shaken by a huge blast from somewhere behind the Canadians' position. It was the biggest explosion Hope had ever seen, and he watched with a frown as the resulting column of smoke rose from the Panjwayi District Centre, less than a kilometre away. A suicide car bomber, his small Toyota Corolla packed with explosives, had attacked a column of reinforcements called up to help deal with the hornet's nest of Taliban Hope's troops had stumbled upon. Only the quick thinking of a young officer in the convoy had averted disaster. Lieutenant Doug Thorlakson had seen the car accelerating towards the line of Canadian vehicles driving towards the sound of the nearby fighting and opened up on it with his C6 medium machine gun, forcing the driver to prematurely set off his bomb.

Hope realized his command was in danger of becoming surrounded, and while his every instinct was screaming to attack the *dushman*—the Pashtun word for enemy that Hope had taken to using over the past two months—he was beginning to conclude that this day's fight was not worth the lives of any more of his soldiers.

As he tossed away the well-chewed butt of his cigar and lit another, Hope wondered, not for the first time in his six-month tour of Kandahar Province, "Where do these guys keep coming from? And why?"

PART 1

**Prelude to Battle
Winter 2005–2006**

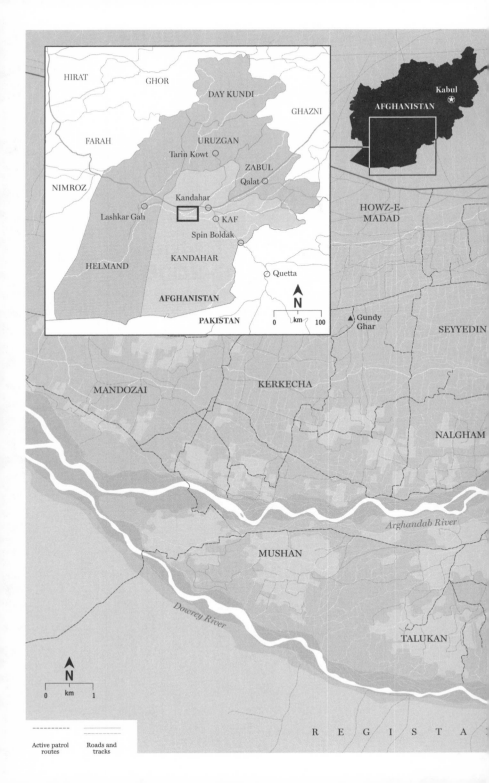

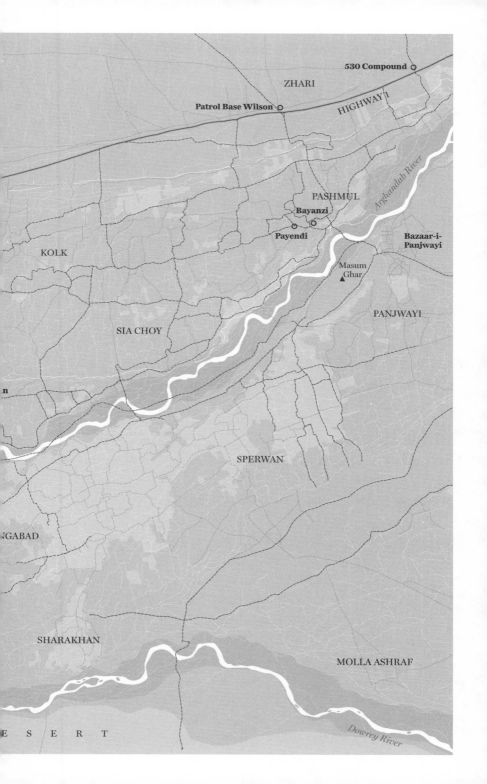

CHAPTER ONE

"No shortage of fighters."

Quetta, Pakistan
November–December 2005

Sometime in the late winter of 2005, a small group of Afghans made their way to a compound on the outskirts of the frontier town of Quetta in northwest Pakistan. They probably drove in a small convoy of two or three dusty Land Rovers—the vehicle of choice among the warlords, smugglers and strongmen who roam Quetta's maze of streets and high-walled compounds.

The men were Taliban and their convoy had come a long way on this particular cold winter day, driving for hours through Baluchistan's sparsely populated mountains and high plateaus, and speeding past the small towns and even smaller villages huddled together in the territory's handful of fertile valleys. The drivers would have chosen their way carefully from among the thousands of roads and tracks that criss-cross the vast and largely lawless border province, avoiding major towns and the rare signs of authority.

The Taliban tried to keep a relatively low profile in Baluchistan and most particularly in Quetta, the sprawling capital of the Pakistan province. It was an area they had openly dominated during their years in power in Afghanistan. Now, the nineteenth-century British garrison town served as the base of operations for the insurgency they were fighting just over the border, and while they had many allies and supporters in the city—including

Quetta's nominal government and many of the region's Pashtun tribal leaders—the hard-line Islamist militia that had run Afghanistan until 2001 did not want to draw too much attention to themselves. The Pakistani government occasionally swooped into Quetta to exert what little authority it had in the region by arresting militants—usually local Baluch separatist guerrillas, but sometimes Taliban leaders as well—and there was always the danger of a precision air strike by the hated and feared Americans.

Quetta has a long and colourful reputation as a haven for smugglers and guerrillas. It served as a home base for the *mujahedeen* during their guerrilla war against the Soviet occupation of Afghanistan in the 1980s, and the Taliban used it as a supply centre in the early 1990s, when they were extending their power from their base in the southern half of Afghanistan to eventually cover most of the country. The Taliban's sponsors and advisors in the Pakistani Inter-Service Intelligence—Pakistan's powerful spy agency—were based in and around Quetta as well, and after September 11, 2001, the city was a natural bolt-hole for Taliban leaders fleeing the U.S.–led coalition in Afghanistan that chased them out of power in a few weeks. The region is still thick with Afghan refugees crowded into camps first set up during the Red Army's long and brutal occupation, and the Taliban fit seamlessly into the mix of spies, drug dealers and gun runners that dominate the town.

The Pashtuns who dominate southern Afghanistan and make up almost the entire leadership of the Taliban have always regarded the international border with Pakistan as a fiction perpetrated by *ferrenghi* (foreigners) and for more than a century have used Baluchistan as a hideout. The territory's local government was dominated by Pakistan's powerful religious parties and from the very beginning of the Taliban's exile from power, the central government in Islamabad was less than enthusiastic in its pursuit of them. The few army or government officials turned a blind eye to the young men who filled Quetta's winding streets and bustling bazaars, eyes lined with kohl and dressed in well-worn black turbans and *khameez*—the baggy, pyjama-like garments common throughout central Asia. Their black-and-white garb, well known in Afghanistan as the unofficial uniform of the Taliban, could be seen in tea houses and *madrassas* (religious schools) throughout Quetta. Until a recent crackdown, the walls of the city had been lined with posters hailing Taliban martyrs. While Pakistan denies it, western intelligence officials have long known that the Taliban use Baluchistan as a headquarters, setting up safe havens for their fighters in dozens of heavily defended compounds in and around the city, recruiting youths from the local madrassas and organizing and supplying their campaigns in Afghanistan. Their insurgents can walk or drive across the porous 1,500-kilometre-long border at any one of dozens of mountain passes or desert tracks.

The line of Taliban vehicles roaring through Quetta on that winter day in 2005 had come down one such road. Although the drivers and gunmen had made the trip many times before, they were cautious, even when they reached the relative safety of Quetta's bustling, colourful streets.

Their leader, surrounded by bodyguards and lieutenants, was a tall, muscular man with a typical weather-beaten Pashtun face—a prominent hooked nose, broad features and a bushy dark beard under a loosely knotted turban. His black eyes, said by those who knew him to be his most striking feature, usually exuded intelligence, ferocity and charisma. But on this cold day in the high mountain city they were probably thoughtful, watching the passing mud-brick walls and buildings as the convoy splashed through pools of muddy water left by the winter rains.

The convoy was carrying Mullah Dadullah Akhund, one of the movement's key commanders, to a meeting of its leadership to discuss plans for the coming year's campaign against the U.S. and their allies in Afghanistan. The meeting would focus largely on the much-anticipated arrival of more than one thousand Canadian soldiers who were then training in western Canada to deploy to the restive Kandahar Province in southern Afghanistan, the heartland of the Taliban's ongoing insurgency.

Mullah Dadullah had come to Quetta with a plan that hinged on the Canadian battle group's move south. It was a daring proposal, completely in character for a commander who had in a few short years developed a reputation for audacity and ruthlessness even among the Taliban. Dadullah is believed to have hatched his plan during the previous year's fighting, when he is known to have been present in the region around Kabul, the Afghan capital, where more than one thousand Canadian soldiers had been stationed since 2003.

At the time, Canadian intelligence officers did not know about the Taliban leaders' council in Quetta, nor were they aware of Dadullah's interest in their battle group, which was to arrive in Kandahar the following February. But in the months after the summer offensive, they pieced together a picture of how the Taliban likely planned and organized its months-long series of attacks on NATO troops in the southern half of Afghanistan. Much of what they believe happened is surmise, based on past experience and information on other Taliban leaders and the group's decision-making processes.

The Canadian intelligence community had certainly heard of Mullah Dadullah in late 2005. He was about forty years old, although like many Afghans he looked older, aged by decades of hardship and fighting. And like most of the senior Taliban leadership he was missing a limb, in his case a leg lost to a land mine during the fighting that followed the retreat of the Soviets from Afghanistan and the eventual collapse in 1992 of their puppet government in Kabul. He was the Taliban's commander in the five southern provinces, including Kandahar, and a well-known—and greatly feared—figure throughout the country.

Even by Taliban standards Dadullah had a reputation for

brutality. While he was a front-line commander in northern Afghanistan in the late 1990s, fighting rebels against the Taliban's hard-line Islamist regime, he would make a point of casting the first stone at public executions of women convicted of prostitution. The charge was often a legal fiction, levelled against women the Taliban believed were supporting the rebels. He was also well known for personally presiding over public hangings, usually from atop a construction crane raised in the central square of a city or town for that specific purpose.

In 1999, Dadullah was removed from his post following a particularly bloody episode in the central Afghan province of Bamiyan, during which Dadullah's troops prosecuted a scorched earth policy that, according to the United Nations' Human Rights Watch, was intended "to render these areas uninhabitable." Ordered to put down a revolt by ethnic Hazzaras—a minority group much despised by the majority Pashtuns, and the Taliban in particular—Dadullah launched an attack and subsequent massacre that, according to some estimates, killed as many as four thousand people. Many of these were women and children or the elderly and infirm who were unable to flee the advancing Taliban and shelter in the hills.

The resulting international and internal outcry had forced Mullah Mohammed Omar—the one-eyed cleric from Kandahar Province who founded the Taliban movement and who remains their supreme leader—to strip Dadullah of his command. But within a few months he had reinstated the younger commander, in part because of the escalating civil war with the Northern Alliance (a mainly Tajik-based rebel group), but also because of his growing popularity among the Taliban's rank-and-file fighters.

Dadullah's star had been on the rise among Taliban commanders since the movement was ousted from power in 2001 by the Northern Alliance. The rebel group had been stubbornly clinging to about ten percent of the country until it gained the backing of U.S., British and allied (including Canadian) special forces commandos and airpower in the aftermath of the September 11 attacks on New York and Washington. Dadullah's dramatic escape from Northern Alliance commander General Abdul Rashid Dostum in December 2001, when the U.S.–allied warlord trapped him and several other senior Taliban leaders in the northern Kunduz Province, made him something of a legend. Dadullah rejected an offer to surrender, an offer other Taliban commanders and fighters in the area eventually accepted, and slipped past the Uzbek warlord's troops on horseback to make good his escape to Kandahar.

He was an early and vehement opponent of the foreign coalition forces that backed the government of Hamid Karzai— picked by the U.S. to lead a caretaker administration created to fill the power vacuum left by the abrupt departure of the Taliban—and one of the first to organize attacks against the U.S. and other troops that had swept the Taliban out of power. While most of the movement's leaders were on the run and lying low in the mountains of southern and eastern Afghanistan or just over the border in Pakistan's tribal areas, Dadullah was organizing small insurgency cells in the southern half of the country, rallying the remnants of the Taliban in their Pakistani hideouts and recruiting new soldiers for the cause among the masses of poor, unemployed but devout students in the madrassas of northwest Pakistan.

In the winter of 2005, he is thought to have been living at least part of the year in Quetta, although he was probably often absent on secret trips to southern Afghanistan. He is known to have kept a house in his home province of Uruzgan, just to the north of Kandahar, and another somewhere in Kandahar province, probably near the Pakistan border. He likely spent most of his time flitting from one safe house to another, trading on Pashtun tribal loyalties and fear of the Taliban to ensure his safety and allow him to travel with relative impunity, even through areas patrolled by U.S. and coalition forces. He had been reported killed or captured by Afghan or U.S. forces several times, adding to his mythic status in the Taliban ranks, and was known for "leading from the front," careless of his own personal safety.

But Dadullah's growing fame within the Taliban and beyond, as well as his aggressive and ruthless tactics, had brought him increasingly into conflict with Mullah Omar, who began to see the younger man as less of a protégé and more of a rival. Omar had been chosen to lead the Taliban not because of his charisma or military skills, but primarily because of his famous piety. His reclusive, almost bureaucratic style of leadership was in direct contrast to Dadullah's more flamboyant personality. Dadullah knew the value of the media and was the first major Taliban leader to give interviews to foreign journalists, including a number of appearances on al Jazeera television in which he boasted openly about Taliban successes against the foreign troops in southern Afghanistan.

As Dadullah's Land Rover, a gift from admiring tribesmen in the Pakistan border region, bounced down Quetta's dirt and gravel roads towards the meeting, his strained relationship with the elderly supreme leader was likely foremost in his mind. He was probably rehearsing the arguments he was about to make to the ten-member *rahbari shura*, or ruling council—of which he had been made a member in 2003—to convince them to adopt his plans for a spring and summer offensive in Kandahar. It was an offensive that, if Dadullah had his way, would be aimed straight at the soon-to-arrive Canadian troops.

Dadullah believed he saw a way to strike a blow against the hated foreigners, a blow that might force them out of Afghanistan and perhaps even return the Taliban to power. The one-legged mullah, arguably the Taliban's most talented military leader, was about to propose to his fellow commanders that they aim at nothing less than the capture of Kandahar.

Dadullah's convoy pulled into a compound somewhere on the outskirts of Quetta's busy suburban sprawl. It may have been one of several houses Omar used for his occasional trips to the movement's centre of operations—private homes provided by well-heeled Pakistani or expatriate Afghan supporters—or even a leftover safe house from the early 1990s, when Pakistan's intelligence service was funding and supporting the Taliban's rise to power. It was most certainly surrounded by high walls and at least one guard tower, and dozens of well-armed Taliban fighters would have stood watch as Dadullah's vehicles rolled through the steel and iron gates.

Nothing is known about what was said at the resulting shura, but the best indications of what it was like are from similar meetings described by Pakistani journalist and author Ahmed Rashid in his astonishing landmark book, *Taliban*. The shura would have been held in a large room, with rugs thrown over the concrete floor and well-stuffed cushions strewn around for the comfort of the leaders and their entourage of lieutenants, bodyguards and servants. Most, if not all, of the ten-member council would have been present, sitting cross-legged or reclining against the cushions in a loose circle around well-creased maps of Afghanistan unrolled on the floor. Befitting his status as supreme leader, Mullah Omar may have lounged on a low bed, surrounded by secretaries and guards at the head of the meeting while junior aides circulated with trays of cookies or cakes and the hot green tea sweetened with rock sugar present at every major Afghan social event. Dadullah and his fellow commanders would each have brought their own train of aides and bodyguards, partly to reinforce their status, but also for more practical reasons: the Taliban's leadership was not without its rivalries and internal tensions. Everyone who entered the meeting was likely searched before being allowed into Omar's presence, mainly for cellular or satellite phones, about which the leader was obsessively paranoid.

Like many Afghan shuras, most of this meeting probably consisted of long speeches punctuated by questions and back-and-forth debates over the plans for the coming year. Omar himself was known for keeping his own counsel, listening to all of his commanders and their deputies, nodding and fingering his thick greying beard before announcing his decision and issuing his orders. In all likelihood, these orders were written on the same scraps of paper on which he wrote out his instructions and rulings while he was running Afghanistan during the Taliban's years in power. He may even have kept the tin trunks from which Rashid describes him dishing out wads of Afghani notes or U.S. dollars to commanders and plaintiffs alike.

Dadullah, with his formidable reputation and forceful personality, would have taken centre stage from the beginning, seizing the chance to describe a plan he was convinced would set the Taliban on the road back to power. He probably got the first inklings of his scheme while travelling in and around Kabul the previous year, organizing the Taliban's campaign of suicide bombings that began slowly and tentatively in 2003 but which grew steadily.

He was an enthusiastic proponent of the tactic, noting the success of both insurgents in Iraq and various Palestinian groups in Israel. Although suicide bombing was virtually unheard of in Afghanistan, Dadullah quickly organized and equipped groups of bomb makers to assemble car bombs and suicide vests, rigged with high explosives scrounged mostly from the seemingly endless cache of arms that still litter the Afghan landscape, left behind by the former Soviet occupiers or the warlords who took over in their absence.

The first waves of Dadullah's suicide bombers were notorious for blowing themselves up long before getting anywhere near their target. Just before the first Canadians arrived in Kabul for the International Security Assistance Force (ISAF) mission in 2003, an enormous explosion tore through the largely abandoned King's palace just a few hundred metres from where engineers were constructing the Canadian camp, a well-fortified base later known as Camp Julien. A few men had been preparing a suicide bomb, probably for an attack on the Canadians as they arrived. Investigators were never able to determine positively whether there had been two or three would-be bombers: there was that little left.

But when "Dadullah's martyrs" did hit their targets, they proved a cheap, effective weapon against the better-armed and -trained western troops. In June 2003, a suicide bomber drove a taxi loaded with explosives into the side of a bus that was carrying German troops posted in Kabul to the airport for their flight home. Four soldiers, one Afghan civilian and the driver of the suicide car bomb were killed.

Kabul was Dadullah's first look at Canadian soldiers, who made up the bulk of an international contingent that was at the time confined to the area immediately around the capital. And although the Canadians' large, imposing LAV III armoured troop carriers had made a definite impression on the Afghans, the veteran Taliban commander detected a weakness.

Not long after the suicide attacks began, Canadian intelligence officers began hearing reports that senior Taliban leaders had reached some important conclusions about the Canadian troops patrolling the streets of Kabul. Time and again, the same phrase was turning up from Taliban sources in the military's ASIC compounds—the acronym for the All Source Intelligence Cell, a sort of central clearing centre for rumours, intercepted radio and satellite telephone conversations, spy-plane pictures and thousands of other forms of intelligence gathered by coalition troops in Afghanistan. The word among the Taliban according to the intercepted communications was: "Canadians are good fighters, but their politicians are weak."

The words may have originated with Dadullah himself, and they were certainly the genesis of his plan for the summer of 2006. It was an article of faith among the Taliban leadership that the West did not have the stomach for a long fight, particularly the Americans' European and other allies, including the

Canadians. The Taliban believed the first step in driving the hated Americans from Afghanistan was to separate them from their allies and Dadullah thought he saw a golden opportunity to do just that.

As Dadullah argued forcefully to the group of men clustered around the anonymous room in Quetta, the military coalition they were fighting was about to change. In August 2006, command of the western forces in Afghanistan was to shift from a U.S.–led operation—code-named Operation Enduring Freedom that had been in effect since the weeks after the September 11 attacks—to the NATO–led ISAF. The change would see thousands of British, Dutch and Canadian soldiers flying in to reinforce U.S. troops in the Taliban heartland of Kandahar and Helmand Provinces over the next summer. But for the first crucial months of the transition, in the spring and early summer, the Canadians would be the only non–U.S. soldiers on the ground.

And, Dadullah told the faces staring impassively at him from around the room, the Canadians were vulnerable. He, or one of his lieutenants, had read with interest the ongoing debate in the Canadian media about the Afghan mission and in particular the extraordinary public outpouring of grief that followed the first deaths of Canadian soldiers in the fall of 2003. He concluded that if the Taliban could cause enough deaths and injuries among the battle group due to arrive the following February, the Canadian public would raise an enormous outcry. If, in addition to the death and maiming of their troops at the very height of the bombing and ambush campaign, Canadians saw television images of the white Taliban flag flying over a prominent building in Kandahar—say, the heavily fortified compound of the provincial governor in the oldest section of the city—then they would clamour even more loudly for Ottawa to pull out their troops and the politicians would have to comply. In the aftermath of such an offensive, the Dutch, certainly, and perhaps even the British, would balk at sending their soldiers to

Kandahar. Deprived of their allies, the Americans would be isolated and distracted by their entanglement in Iraq, and would eventually be forced to withdraw as well.

Dadullah's strategy was optimistic, but basically sound. "These guys read: they're not dummies," one Canadian intelligence officer said after the fact. "Thinking they're a bunch of savages living in caves is wrong." Another, who served in Kabul during the early years of the Canadian mission, agrees: "They may be religious fanatics, but they're technologically savvy and they are NOT stupid."

Dadullah's plan, laid out on the map before the shura, was to surround and isolate the city of Kandahar, with a mounting campaign of suicide and roadside bomb attacks beginning in the spring and rising in a crescendo of violence towards August 19—the Afghan national Independence Day. The bombing attacks would demoralize the foreign soldiers and the Afghan police and military and keep them off balance, striking them in different districts at different times to distract their attention from Dadullah's real intentions. Meanwhile, Taliban fighters would begin filtering across the border into the southern provinces in small groups, riding in the cabs of the colourful Pakistani "jingle trucks"—the painted and heavily decorated transport trucks named for the jingle of the chains and medallions that hung in curtains from almost every surface—through the harsh Reg Desert south of Kandahar, making the uncomfortable two-day journey by donkey cart, camel back or on foot through the high mountain passes.

When the time was right, the Taliban fighters would pour into Kandahar and seize one or more government buildings—chosen more for their symbolic than their military value—and raise the movement's flag, white with the Arabic lettering of the *shahadah* (testament of faith) in black. It did not matter that the Taliban could not hope to hold their captured targets for long. Given the enormous weight of firepower at the command of the

U.S. and NATO soldiers in and around Kandahar, their eventual defeat was certain. All that mattered, Dadullah argued, was ensuring that international television cameras were there to record the event.

Although Dadullah was sure of the inevitable success of his scheme, he would have had difficulty convincing many of the rest of the Taliban leadership. First and foremost would have been Mullah Omar. Omar, counted among the most wanted men in the world after his long-time ally Osama bin Laden, was already wary of his charismatic military chief. And he was reportedly less than enamoured of Dadullah's "martyrdom operations," as the suicide bombings were euphemistically known, especially when they involved Afghan suicide bombers or caused deaths or injuries among Afghan civilians. Not only did Omar see suicide bombing as theologically troubling—the Koran specifically forbids suicide—he also feared they would create a backlash among ordinary Afghans.

There was also Mullah Akhtar Mohammad Osmani, a former Taliban foreign minister and "corps commander" in Kandahar and probably Dadullah's chief rival in the Taliban's inner circle. Osmani and Dadullah heartily disliked each other, in part because they both claimed leadership of Taliban forces in the southern region of Afghanistan, but also because of Osmani's close personal ties to Mullah Omar. The Taliban leader had taught in the same madrassa in Kandahar from which Omar founded the Taliban in the early 1990s, and Omar was reported to have named Osmani as his successor in 2001 as he fled Afghanistan just barely ahead of the advancing Americans and their allies. In return, Osmani is said to have personally guaranteed the safety of Omar—an important symbolic rise in his status within the movement.

But Dadullah also had supporters on the council, including Mullah Obaidullah Akhund, the deputy to the supreme leader and the defence minister when the Taliban had been in power.

Obaidullah, widely considered the overall military chief of Taliban forces, was from the Panjwayi District just west of Kandahar, and the plan intrigued him. Panjwayi, a fertile valley less than an hour's drive outside the city, was a rare oasis of green wedged between the red sand desert to the south of Kandahar and the dry moonscape of the Arghandab Mountains to the north. It had been a hotbed of resistance to the Soviet occupation and its network of deep irrigation ditches, grape fields and massive, thick-walled fruit-drying huts made it ideal for the Taliban's war of ambush and hit-and-run attacks. Moreover, Panjwayi was dotted with hundreds of towns, small villages and farmers' compounds, giving Taliban fighters almost limitless hiding places among the local population.

The shura likely took all day and into the chilly Quetta night, possibly lasting well into the next day. Almost everyone present would have been given the chance to speak and the tradition at such gatherings is for long speeches and even longer listings of problems, grievances and requirements. The ten leaders, and likely their many deputies, would have spoken of their accomplishments in fighting the "foreign invaders," the number of fighters under their command, and their need for ammunition, explosives or other supplies. Dozens of possible courses of action for the coming campaign season would have been explored at length and the pros and cons of Dadullah's plan would have been argued over for hours, the senior commanders occasionally stabbing their fingers at points on one of the well-creased maps for emphasis while Mullah Omar listened and nodded sagely.

Omar is known to have had some reservations about Dadullah's plan, particularly over his reliance on teams of suicide bombers to distract and frustrate the foreign troops during the build-up to the eventual attack on Kandahar. Prompted by Omar, the council agreed on a compromise: Dadullah could use his suicide bomb squads in the coming spring offensive, but only provided the suicide bombers were not Afghan. With no short-age of volunteers for martyrdom among the Pakistani graduates of madrassas along the Afghan border, Dadullah would have readily agreed.

In the end, Mullah Omar decided in favour of Dadullah's plan for the campaign, and the Taliban commanders began to depart the shura, sending out orders even as they were leaving the compound.

The Taliban commanders under Dadullah's nominal control operated largely independently, with wide discretion over when they attacked and how. Directly beneath him were fourteen sub-commanders, each responsible for a certain region or district and with a widely varying number of cells of fighters who answered to them. Each cell could be made up of twenty to one hundred fighters, including local recruits and those drawn from the madrassas. A small core of so-called "hard-core Taliban" would give the group backbone. As long as a cell commander got results, he was given a more or less free hand in his area. Dadullah or one of his lieutenants would provide new recruits, supplies and ammunition (particularly the electronic triggers and wiring necessary to make what the Western militaries called IEDs, or Improvised Explosive Devices), experts such as snipers or bomb-makers and the occasional broad order, shifting the cells into different areas or aiming them at specific targets.

The hard-core Taliban were experienced and determined fighters, many of whom were drawn from the ranks of "profes-sional jihadists," which could include Chechens, Arabs, Pak-istanis, Bosnians or fighters from almost anywhere in the Islamic world. They knew the tactics of ambush, and the importance of flanking attacks (hitting their enemies from as many sides as possible) and speedy movement on the battlefield. The recruits drawn from madrassas, both in Pakistan and Afghanistan, would fight as long as this cadre of veterans were alongside them, but most were painfully young, and without their leaders tended to melt away. They were used by the Taliban as cannon fodder, pure and simple. Local recruits were even less reliable—unemployed men drawn by the lure of cash, the call of the faith or often levies drafted by force or to fulfill an obligation for their local tribal elder. They tended to hide behind walls or other cover, fire all their ammunition at the first sign of a foreign soldier and then retreat as quickly as possible, more often than not tossing their AK-47 assault rifles into the handiest ditch as they did.

When the Taliban leaders dispersed after the shura, Dadullah was sent to begin raising a small army in the madrassas along the Pakistan-Afghan border. He spent the rest of the winter travelling from one school to the other, preaching jihad to hundreds of young students. Dadullah was reported as far afield as Karachi, touring madrassas run by local Taliban sympathizers and funded with Saudi or Persian Gulf oil money.

He was enthusiastically received. As early as December 2005, Dadullah issued a videotape to Afghan news agencies boasting that he had thousands of fighters and five hundred volunteers for suicide bomb attacks against the U.S. and its allies in Afghanistan. "We have no shortage of fighters," he told the Pajhwok Afghan News. "In fact, we have so many of them that it is difficult to accommodate and arm and equip them. Some of them have been waiting for a year or more for their turn to be sent to the battlefield."

Their turn would come within a few weeks, when Dadullah's recruits met the soldiers of Charlie Company, 1 PPCLI, in the Panjwayi.

CHAPTER TWO

"Kick the door in, throw in the grenade and 'Follow me, boys!'"

Edmonton, Alberta
2005

While Mullah Dadullah was laying out his plan for his fellow Taliban leaders in that small room in Quetta, Task Force Orion was coming together on a windswept patch of Alberta prairie, more than ten thousand kilometres away.

The nearly eight hundred soldiers who made up the core of Task Force Orion—the infantry, artillery, armoured troops and combat engineers of the battle group—began training almost a year before they boarded air force transports for the long journey to Afghanistan. The government, under then Prime Minister Paul Martin, had announced in the spring of 2005 that Canada was sending troops to southern Afghanistan. The 1st Battalion of Princess Patricia's Canadian Light Infantry, based in Edmonton, was next up in the army's rotation of units to go on overseas missions.

Lieutenant-Colonel Ian Hope had taken command of the battalion in September, 2004, and almost immediately began organizing it into the battle group that would eventually be sent to Kandahar. The battalion's three rifle companies, each composed of about 150 soldiers and one headquarters company, would become the core of the battle group. Once sent overseas, they would become known as a task force. Combat engineers, armoured reconnaissance troops, the gunners of the artillery, military police and dozens of other smaller units would be added on to the battalion as needed for the mission. Hope would not know for certain where his troops would be going for several months, but there had been talk in Ottawa about a beefed-up mission in the restive southern half of Afghanistan ever since General Rick Hillier had been appointed Chief of the Defence Staff, the top soldier in the Canadian Forces. Hope had a strong suspicion that his soldiers were bound for Kandahar.

Hope was not supposed to have taken command at all. Although he was an experienced soldier and highly regarded by his fellow officers, at forty-one, Hope was considered too old for a command position by an army intent on pushing younger officers up the ranks. Until a few months before he took command of the battalion, he was not on the list of lieutenant colonels eligible to command one of the country's nine infantry battalions. But in early 2004, he was sent to Afghanistan as a staff officer in the headquarters of the NATO–led International Security Assistance Force in Kabul. The ISAF commander at the time was Rick Hillier, then a lieutenant general, and Hope so impressed Hillier that he insisted the army put him back on the command list.

The son of an artillery warrant officer who had passed on to his son a love of reading and history, the short, wiry Hope was fond of saying he had joined the infantry "as soon as I was safely away from home." He enlisted in the army reserve's West Nova Scotia Regiment as a private and later advanced to lieutenant. Hope was an unusual combination of intellectual and man of action. He brought a small library with him to Afghanistan that included Homer and the Ancient Greek historian Thucydides as well as *The Bear Went Over the Mountain*, a collection of essays on Soviet tactics during their invasion of Afghanistan in 1979. He left the Canadian Army Reserve in 1982 to join the British

Army because, he admits—a touch sheepishly—"I wanted to get into the Falklands." Hope returned to Canada in 1983 and transferred from the part-time reserve force to the regular army. He became a platoon commander with the Princess Patricias and served in Germany, the Balkans and Africa, as well as a tour with the Canadian Airborne Regiment and as an exchange officer with the British Army's Parachute Regiment. An introverted, even shy man, Hope could be a demanding boss and his officers had to work long, hard hours to keep up with him. He rarely raised his voice and was sparing with praise, but his soldiers soon grew to respect him because of his insistence on leading from the front, spending as much time as he could with the forward troops.

Although there had been no official word, Hope expected that his troops would be bound for Afghanistan in 2006 and began preparing for a deployment within days of taking command. He faced the monumental task of organizing soldiers from dozens of different units and trades into one unified battle group. From the beginning he had to cope with a shortfall at the core of his force: one of the battalion's three rifle companies would not be deploying with the rest of the unit. Bravo Company of 1 PPCLI was already on tour in Afghanistan, acting as the Force Protection Company for the Canadian mission in the capital of Kabul, and would not be rested and reinforced for another overseas tour until well after Hope's scheduled departure in early 2006. To make up the difference, Hope had to "borrow" another Bravo Company, this one drawn from the 2nd Battalion of the Patricias, based in Shilo, Manitoba.

In addition, the battle group would include Hope's headquarters company, made up of a reconnaissance platoon and a sniper group; a troop of Coyote armoured surveillance vehicles from 12e Régiment Blindé du Canada, based in Valcartier, Quebec; and a platoon of military police. Hope also had to incorporate a battery of artillery from the 1st Regiment of the

Royal Canadian Horse Artillery, equipped with the newly purchased M777 155-mm howitzer; a squadron of military engineers from 1 Combat Engineer Regiment in Edmonton; a tactical Unmanned Aerial Vehicle (UAV) troop; a Health Services Support Company of sixty medics and support staff; and his own support group of maintenance, logistic and transport soldiers.

Also included in what Hope would eventually name Task Force Orion were elements of the Kandahar Provincial Reconstruction Team (PRT). This was a new concept for the Canadian Forces, mixing military and civilian representatives in an attempt to combine the protection of the army with the badly needed development and governmental aid provided by the Department of Foreign Affairs and International Trade (DFAIT), the Canadian International Development Agency (CIDA), the Royal Canadian Mounted Police (RCMP) and other police agencies, Corrections Canada, and the United States Agency for International Development (USAID). The roughly two hundred soldiers assigned to the reconstruction team would have their own base—a former canning factory on the outskirts of Kandahar City, a half hour's drive from the huge coalition base at Kandahar Airfield (KAF). The PRT represented the cutting edge of the Canadian government's new "3-D" approach to Afghanistan—based on defence, development and diplomacy. The team put civilian aid workers, government officials and police officers assigned to train their Afghan counterparts in among the soldiers protecting the camp and the Civil Military Co-operation (or CIMIC) officers who ran the army's small, underfunded and overstretched aid program.

Hope's challenge was to weld these diverse elements into a cohesive whole—one that would hold together under the harsh conditions in Afghanistan and the almost unimaginable stress of battle. And it became clear to him soon after his first trip to scout out the region in 2005 that his battle group was heading into combat. Task Force Bayonet, the U.S. Army battle group that the Canadians would be relieving in Kandahar, had been in almost constant contact with the Taliban over the preceding year and had been hit with IEDs and rocket and mortar on a daily basis. Hope knew his soldiers would be thrust into a maelstrom for which it was almost impossible to fully prepare. The key to holding them together would be their loyalty to each other.

Hope's task was made all the more complicated by the politics of the Afghan mission. In March, 2005, General Hillier gave the task force its marching orders: they were bound for southern Afghanistan under the U.S.–led Operation Enduring Freedom. It would be a difficult transition operation, with the Americans handing off control of the Afghan mission to their NATO allies partway through the PPCLI's six-month tour of duty. As part of this transition, Canadian Brigadier-General David Fraser would take command of the southern region—including the province of Kandahar for which the PPCLI battle group was responsible, and the four other southern provinces. Dangerous Helmand Province, the centre of the flourishing opium poppy trade, was to be home to British troops, while a Dutch battle group was to be based in Uruzgan Province to the north. Other coalition troops, including Americans, were scattered through the rest of the region. The Canadians were to become the "bridge" between the U.S. mission and the NATO operation, but for several critical weeks during the handover—between April and early August—Hope's battle group would be the largest, indeed almost the only, combat force in the southern region.

The shift from American to NATO command was an attempt to expand the Afghan mission beyond the U.S.–led war on terrorism. It would allow the U.S. to focus more attention on the growing insurgency in Iraq and give NATO the chance to prove its relevance for more than just defending Western Europe from the now-vanished Soviet threat. Canada was seen by both NATO and the Americans as the logical "transition team": they were trusted by the U.S. and by NATO nations such as France and Germany, who had become increasingly estranged from Washington over the Iraq war.

There was a tendency among the upper echelons of the American military to view NATO troops—including the Canadians—with a patronizing eye and even a faint degree of suspicion. Although Canadian and American soldiers and junior officers on the ground worked well together and—aside from the good-natured taunting that is customary among soldiers—developed a mutual respect, senior U.S. generals harboured more than a little condescension towards their Canadian and British colleagues. The U.S. Army had been fighting the Taliban since 2001, mostly on its own, and regarded NATO troops as inexperienced johnny-come-latelies. One American general visiting Charlie Company in a forward base early in the mission raised hackles by loudly questioning their fighting spirit. "You Canadians. Don't get me wrong, I love ya," he proclaimed to a group of PPCLI officers. "But you're always doin' this aid and reconstruction stuff. Ya got to get out and kill more of them Taliban!" The Canadians, who had been in an hours-long firefight with the Taliban the day before, bit their tongues and kept their expressions carefully neutral until the general hopped back in his helicopter and flew out of the base after a whirlwind, three-hour tour.

In the face of all this, Hope wanted his battle group to develop a distinct identity that would bring together soldiers from dozens of different units and trades. On the last night of his first reconnaissance trip to Kandahar, he stepped out of a briefing by his American counterpart into the warm Afghan night, lit a cigar and looked up into the brilliant star field of a moonless night. The constellation Orion dominated the sky and Hope smiled: he would name his battle group Task Force Orion. "Because Orion is the hunter," he told his soldiers when he gathered them together upon his return, "and that's what we're going to be doing: hunting down the enemy."

Hope wanted his task force to be flexible enough to deal with the many difficulties and hardships he knew southern Afghanistan would throw at them, so he organized the three companies at the heart of his battle group to be as self-contained as possible. The roughly one hundred and fifty foot soldiers in each company—"trigger pullers" as the infantrymen proudly called themselves—would be augmented by their own engineers, military police, artillery forward observation parties, CIMIC officers and others, essentially creating three miniature battle groups within the task force. Hope had seen the vast area that his battle group was to be responsible for, an area larger than the province of New Brunswick, and wanted his companies to be able to operate independently for long periods of time. Hope also emphasized flexibility within each company, training them to "plug and play," adding or subtracting different vehicles, equipment or troops to tailor their force to each mission they were given. "Don't be template about doctrine," Hope would tell his officers. "Do what works."

At the heart of Hope's plans for the battle group was the Light Armoured Vehicle (LAV)—the armoured vehicles that 1 PPCLI rode into battle. Built in London, Ontario, by General Dynamics Land Systems, the seventeen-tonne, eight-wheeled troop carrier was—and still is—the top of the line. The LAV, from the same family of armoured vehicles that the U.S. military knows as "Strykers," can carry soldiers safely up to the edge of a fight, disgorge them out the back and then support their attack with considerable firepower. Affectionately called "the car," each LAV carries up to seven soldiers in its troop compartment, in addition to its three-man crew of driver, gunner and commander. Its flat, box-shaped turret mounts two machine guns and a 25-mm Bushmaster chain gun, an automatic cannon that can fire up to two hundred one-inch-diameter shells a minute. Its computerized gunsights include the latest night-vision technology, able to penetrate the blackest darkness and reveal targets kilometres away as if it were a sunny afternoon. Because the LAV is wheeled, instead of tracked like a tank, it can travel at speeds of up to 100 kilometres per hour and go more than 400 kilometres without refuelling. Its sharply sloped sides and bottom are designed to make land mines, enemy bullets and cannon shells bounce off, and its engine and heavy-duty suspension are well protected behind hardened steel armour. The LAVs can absorb incredible amounts of enemy fire and take days of punishing conditions, and the Canadians pushed them to their limits and beyond in southern Afghanistan.

The textbook method for using the LAV in combat is to roll them up to within a safe distance of an area being attacked, dismount the infantry out the big armoured ramps that drop open in the back of the vehicle and fire over the heads of the soldiers as they run towards their objectives. The Americans used only lightly armoured vehicles in Afghanistan, in part because of the terrain, but also because of the demands of their war in Iraq, and Hope quickly realized that his seven-metre-long LAVs were the biggest, most imposing vehicles being used by any army in Afghanistan. That gave his battle group an enormous psychological edge over the Taliban, an advantage that was magnified by the LAV's deceptively quiet engine. In close country or urban areas it was often difficult to hear the huge vehicles until they were only a few metres away. If they were heard, it was hard to tell exactly where they were coming from. As well, the Taliban had no effective way of penetrating the LAV's armour, particularly after the vehicles were fitted with the extra protection of additional bolt-on armour plates. So Task Force Orion began training to use their huge vehicles differently, racing them up to within one hundred metres or less of their targets, then using their heavy firepower to pummel the enemy and cover the infantry dismounting out the back. The LAV became the extra man in the task force's attacks, a factor that was to prove decisive in the battles through the fields and compounds of the Panjwayi.

The man Ian Hope chose to lead Charlie Company was Major Bill Fletcher, a thirty-four-year-old graduate of the Royal Military College, Kingston, who had only just been promoted from captain. He had served as Hope's adjutant—the commanding officer's chief assistant and right-hand man—for the first few months of his command and had impressed Hope as an aggressive, no-nonsense leader. Like so many of the battle group's officers, Fletcher had grown up in the army, the son of a logistics officer with the Canadian Airborne Regiment whose earliest memories included squinting up into the sky to watch his dad parachuting out of a Hercules on an exercise with the rest of the regiment. "And I thought: 'That's pretty cool,'" he said. "So as soon as I was old enough, I joined the army."

With the broad shoulders and lean, muscular physique of a rugby flanker—a game he still occasionally played—Fletcher approached most military operations like a pit bull, tackling problems head-on. More often than not, this included personally leading his company on attacks during training exercises. There was one hitch in naming him as Charlie Company's Officer Commanding (oc): according to the army, Fletcher was technically unqualified. He had not taken the combat team-leader's course—a four-week series of lectures, tests and field exercises at the Canadian Forces Base in Gagetown, New Brunswick—that was the prerequisite for command of a company. "I was unqualified," he said later with a grin. "I still am."

Hope didn't care. He had a high opinion of Fletcher, although he was careful not to let the younger major know it, and had watched him command a company on exercise long enough to be confident he knew what he was doing. He told those who questioned his choice that he picked Fletcher over other more experienced officers because he was a "kick the door in, throw in the grenade and 'Follow me, boys' kind of leader." Which was, in Hope's estimation, exactly what Charlie Company needed.

Charlie had always been the quiet kid of the battalion, especially compared to the boisterous Alpha Company, which called itself the "Red Devils" after the nickname German troops in the First World War had given the PPCLI for their red shoulder patches. Alpha Company was louder and more visible, slapping the stylized cartoon devils of their company crests on their lockers and on every available surface of their barracks rooms, and Fletcher quickly realized his company was developing an inferiority complex. After a few days in command, he had heard enough. "Well to hell with Alpha Company: we're Charlie Company!" He ordered a company crest designed, featuring a snarling grizzly bear, and set about building up the character of his new command.

Fletcher knew that the key to success in leading Charlie into battle would be the non-commissioned officers (NCOs), particularly the sergeants and master corporals who led the infantry sections, the basic tactical unit of the company. In a mechanized infantry company, the bulk of the work is done by the eight to ten men mounted in each LAV, headed by a sergeant and a master corporal. The three sections in each of Charlie's three platoons did the "heavy lifting" in any operation, leading assaults on enemy compounds or forming the "fire base" to rain bullets and grenades down on the enemy while their comrades moved in to attack at close quarters. Each section included a pair of machine gunners hefting the C9 light machine guns that provided the majority of the section's firepower; two grenadiers, with grenade launchers attached to their C7 assault rifles that launched egg-shaped high-explosive grenades at enemy positions; and two riflemen.

Fletcher sat down with all of his sergeants soon after taking over Charlie and listened intently to their complaints and suggestions—everything from which weapons they carried to better ways of utilizing their vehicles. Fletcher was impressed by his crop of non-commissioned officers, soldiers with fifteen or more years' experience and multiple overseas missions under their belts.

The leadership style of Charlie's NCOs seemed to mesh with the company's quiet, no-nonsense character. Men like Sergeant Mike Denine—the thirty-five-year-old Newfoundlander who had wanted nothing more than to join the army "ever since I was a youngster"—set the tone for the younger privates and corporals who made up the bulk of the company's nearly 140 soldiers. Denine was a stocky bear of a man, whose gruff manner concealed a fierce loyalty and devotion to the young soldiers under his command. He was fond of playing the "good old boy from Newfoundland," his accent thickening whenever he told one of the seemingly endless stories in his repertoire. But this hid a keen intelligence and remarkable cool-headedness that made an immediate impression on Fletcher.

There was also a wealth of experience in Charlie's junior ranks, corporals and master corporals with almost as many years of service as the sergeants and senior NCOs. Soldiers like Master Corporal Matthew "Kiwi" Parsons, a thirty-year-old transplanted New Zealander, gave the company an enormous depth of experience. Kiwi had been in the Canadian Forces only since 1998, but had served five years in New Zealand's military before emigrating to join the Canadian army because, he said: "New Zealand never sent its army anywhere." Kiwi had a cheerful disdain for many of the military's more arcane rules and procedures and like almost all of the junior NCOs was not shy about expressing his opinions, usually bluntly and laced with profanity delivered in a faint New Zealand accent.

Fletcher also relied heavily on the handful of officers in the company, none more so than Captain Ryan Jurkowski, his second-in-command. Jurkowski also came from a military family: his father had been the air force general in command of the 1999 allied bombing campaign over Serbia and Kosovo. The short, cheerful career officer was one of the most senior captains in the entire battalion and admitted privately that his OC occasionally worried him. Fletcher was notorious for charging in at the head of attacks and more than once Jurkowski thought he would have to replace his commander because he was missing, wounded or worse.

Like the rest of the PPCLI battle group, Charlie Company was a surprisingly informal military unit. Most of the junior soldiers called each other by their first names, particularly in the field, or more often by the nicknames that, sooner or later, almost everyone attracted. The NCOs had almost all known each other and worked together for years, and while they always called their seniors and officers by their ranks, the emphasis was on "getting 'er done." Hope quickly became known as "The Boss," a sign of the growing respect with which the softly spoken colonel was regarded by his troops. The informality didn't mean that orders weren't followed or that discipline was lax, but Charlie was a far cry from the movie stereotype of an army unit. While it was accepted that a lapse in discipline or a serious mistake would get a soldier "jacked up" (army slang for getting chewed out or otherwise disciplined), Fletcher made it clear that he would not tolerate "beasting the troops"—shouting at or abusing the soldiers. At least one senior NCO found himself transferred out of the company for abusing and riding his soldiers mercilessly, a practice Fletcher knew could create a poisonous atmosphere in a unit and kill the morale he was trying to build before he took his company overseas.

In the first few months of training leading up to the mission, the battle group focused on the basics: working together in their sections and platoons, practising firing their weapons under the most realistic conditions possible. They also spent long hours working on their physical conditioning—a crucial factor in southern Afghanistan, with its brutal heat and risk of crippling dehydration and strength-sapping exhaustion.

Sergeant Vaughn Ingram, a former Canadian Airborne

Regiment commando, and one of the most senior sergeants in Charlie Company, made "PT"—or Physical Training—one of his pet causes. Although he was old enough to be the father of most of his young privates and corporals, and smoked incessantly, especially while he was in the field, Ingram took a fiendish delight in outlasting his juniors on what his men came to call his "death runs." Ingram would even join Hope when the commanding officer was out for a morning run, pushing him to run faster and farther with his characteristic grin. The two had met when both were much younger and serving in the now-disbanded Airborne and had developed a mutual respect for each other's abilities. Ingram had taught the colonel how to command a LAV and Hope trusted his knowledge and toughness implicitly.

When four RCMP officers were ambushed and killed by a heavily armed gunman in Mayerthorpe, Alberta, in March 2005, Hope had to interrupt his unit's training and provide a team of soldiers in an armoured vehicle to support the police. He chose Ingram to lead them without a moment's hesitation. Before the veteran sergeant left the Edmonton base for the short trip to the northern Alberta town, Hope jumped up onto Ingram's vehicle, leaned over and quietly told him that he trusted him to bring all his soldiers back alive. "If the situation deteriorates and men start to die, you take charge of the fight and win," Hope said quietly. Ingram looked up at his commander and simply nodded before driving away.

Ingram's best friend in the battle group, Sergeant Pat Tower, was one of the men in charge of the company's marksmanship training. The "gunfighter" program, as it was known, taught soldiers how to react and shoot under realistic conditions. Tower led the troops through dozens of live-fire ranges, where they fired real bullets instead of the blanks usually used on manoeuvres, to get them used to the feel of real bullets leaving their barrels. The quiet, bespectacled thirty-four-year-old set up practices where the soldiers would walk through an area and shoot at targets as they popped out from behind bushes, hills or buildings. Often "civilian" targets were mixed in among the ones showing the silhouette of a charging soldier, to teach the troops to look at their targets before snapping off shots. By the time they left for Afghanistan, the soldiers had taken part in more than four hundred live-fire exercises, including moving and firing with their LAVs on ranges in the vast expanses of Wainwright, Alberta, a short drive from the battalion's base in Edmonton.

The Afghan mission, which the army had code-named Operation Archer, was Sergeant Tower's fifth trip overseas. Although his tours in Bosnia and Croatia had been no picnic—in 1993 he had been part of the 2 PPCLI that fought a battle with Croatian security forces in the Medak Pocket—he sensed that southern Afghanistan was going to be different. Fletcher thought so too. He believed his company and the rest of the battle group was heading into something completely unlike the peacekeeping operations of the past two decades and did what he could to prepare the men for the shock of combat. With the help of Edmonton's paramedics, he arranged for some of his soldiers to ride along in the city's ambulances for a few nights to acclimatize them to the sights, sounds and smells of the badly injured. He invited a military search and rescue technician—a former infantryman—to lecture the troops on trauma care, and veterans of the Second World War to give blunt, no-holds-barred talks on what to expect in combat.

One guest in particular had a marked impact on the soldiers. Lieutenant-Colonel Dave Grossman, a U.S. Army veteran and an expert in battle stress, told the troops that the stress of combat was going to play tricks on their minds: some would get tunnel vision, seeing only a narrow area in front of them; others would go temporarily deaf to certain sound and hear others, such as gunfire, acutely. He warned them to expect time to slow down or speed up or both and that they might well lose control of their bladder and bowels. He told the troops that the important thing to remember was that these were normal physical reactions to combat, not the result of cowardice, and could be overcome by continuing to follow their training automatically. Fletcher was so impressed by the American officer's presentation he went out and bought his book, *On Combat*, which has since become almost required reading in the combat arms branch of the army. The talks made a sobering impression on the young soldiers who comprised the bulk of the battle group's ranks and Fletcher noticed that their "gung-ho" machismo dialed down a notch after Grossman's lectures.

Canadian Forces Base, Wainwright, Alberta
September 2005

By September, most of the pieces of Task Force Orion were in place and the battle group began training together for the deployment, a mere four months away. On the eve of their last major training exercise before they began final preparations for the long trip to southwest Asia, Hope called all of his soldiers together for a "smoker"—an evening party in a field near the battle group's temporary home, a clutch of tents in the Wainwright training base. All of the nearly nine hundred soldiers were drawn up in three ranks in a large bowl-shaped valley, barbecues were set up and cases of beer were stacked nearby (with a limit of two per soldier, according to Canadian Forces regulations). Hope climbed up to the top of a stack of wood that was set up for an enormous bonfire and announced what the army rumour mill had been predicting for months but had not yet been confirmed: "We're going to Kandahar!"

The soldiers all cheered, a rare thing for Canadian troops who pride themselves on being "quiet professionals." Hope jumped down from the stacked-up wood and the bonfire was lit. The soldiers' mood was aggressively upbeat: even among the experienced NCOs who had been on overseas missions before. It wasn't that the soldiers were bloodthirsty. But they had been training for years for just such a mission—for combat—without getting the chance to put their long hours and days of practice to use, and many were looking forward to the opportunity to show their mettle.

The next day, the task force began their final four-week exercise: the BTE, or Brigade Training Exercise. Although Charlie Company and the rest of the task force went into the four-week exercise on a high note, things quickly soured. The troops began joking that BTE stood for either "Broken Training Event" or "Badly Timed Event," as what was supposed to be their final opportunity to prepare for the dangerous mission devolved into a near farce. The training was supposed to be a "confirmatory" exercise, a demonstration for senior generals that all the battle group's soldiers, non-commissioned officers and commanders knew their jobs and had the skills to carry out the mission.

But instead of teaching the battle group what it needed to know, or allowing its soldiers to practise their skills at fighting mobile, hit-and-run insurgents like the Taliban, the troops grumbled that the exercise was using them as "training dummies"—props used to train the brigade headquarters staff that was to be flying into Afghanistan to take command of the southern region. Hope's officers were specifically told: "This is not about Afghanistan," leaving Fletcher and others wondering why not, when they were due to land in the heartland of the Taliban in a few weeks. Exercise planners used models based on Cold War war games, pitting NATO against the Russians in Europe, or replaying peacekeeping operations in the Former Yugoslavia. Several times during the exercise, one of the generals observing forced the task force to stop and repeat simulated attacks because they had not been carried out to his satisfaction, or according to the hopelessly outdated tactics.

In addition to the problems with the BTE, there was a severe shortage of night-vision goggles. When clipped onto soldiers' helmets and flipped down over their eyes, these scopes allowed them to see clearly even in the darkest conditions. There were only enough of the infrared and light-enhancement scopes to equip one of the three companies at a time, despite the fact that they were considered critical in tracking and defeating the Taliban when they were most active, in the pitch-black Afghan night. There was no training in combat first aid, especially in using the new blood-clotting bandages and powder specially purchased for the coming mission. Nor was there a chance for the soldiers to familiarize themselves with the other new kit available for this deployment—new U.S.-made satellite radios that would allow the battle group's far-flung companies to stay in contact with their headquarters even in the deepest of the Afghan mountain valleys—or the new Nyala patrol cars, specially built to survive blasts from land mines or roadside bombs.

The soldiers were denied permission to call in live artillery fire and had no opportunity at all to practise directing air support onto targets, both skills that Hope knew would be put to constant use in Afghanistan. One bright spot was the assignment of the artillery Forward Observation Officers (FOOs) to the battle group, the gunners' eyes and ears on the battlefield. One artillery LAV, with a FOO artillery technician, or FOO Tech, and complete crew was attached to each of Task Force Orion's front-line companies. Their job was to move forward with the infantry and accurately direct artillery fire and air strikes where the foot soldiers needed them most. Captain Nichola Goddard was attached to Charlie and made an immediate impression on Fletcher and the other officers in the company. Even before she arrived at Wainwright to join the company, Goddard was peppering Jurkowski with e-mails and files detailing what the artillery could do for Charlie, especially with the new M777 long-range howitzers they would be using for the first time ever in Kandahar.

But the shortcomings outweighed even Goddard's professional enthusiasm. Pat Tower observed sourly that the first time he got to try on his new protective vest—the latest generation of body armour with specially designed chest and back plates that could stop high-calibre rifle bullets—was on the flight into Kandahar.

The soldiers' complaints about some of their equipment were dismissed or ignored, including questions about their hand grenades, which had a reputation for not exploding, and tactical vests that only carried a fraction of the ammunition needed in a lengthy firefight.

Two days after the long, wet, cold and frustrating exercise, Hope took twenty of his key officers and NCOs on one last reconnaissance trip to Kandahar. After ten days of meetings with their American and Afghan counterparts, and accompanying U.S. patrols through the vast area that they were taking over, the Canadians were concerned.

"We're going into an intense shooting match," Hope thought during the long flight home. "And we're not ready for this: what are we going to do?"

He huddled with the senior leaders that he had taken on his reconnaissance trip soon after they landed back in Canada, and they all agreed.

"I think the only option we have is to deploy early," Hope said finally. "We're going to have to train in theatre."

In early November 2005, less than three months before Task Force Orion was scheduled to begin flying into southern Afghanistan, Hope went to Lieutenant-General Marc Caron, the head of the army, and General Rick Hillier, the chief of defence staff, to formally request permission to send his soldiers into Afghanistan two weeks earlier than planned. He outlined the shortcomings in their training, how he planned to make up for them with two extra weeks of "on-the-job training" in Kandahar and—for the clincher—invoked regimental history. In 1951, Lieutenant-Colonel "Big" Jim Stone led the PPCLI as the first Canadian contingent to the Korean War. When he arrived in Korea, he insisted that his soldiers not be sent to the front lines until he felt they were ready, ignoring demands and pleas from senior officers for several weeks before accepting his first combat mission. Hope argued that he would do no less for his soldiers.

Hillier and Caron agreed and in early January 2006, the first soldiers of Task Force Orion began landing in Kandahar, four weeks ahead of schedule.

"Nobody believed we were getting into anything as serious as we got into," Hope said later. "Including me."

PART 2

Bayanzi
May 16–17, 2006

BAYANZI MAY 17, 0400 - 1200 hrs

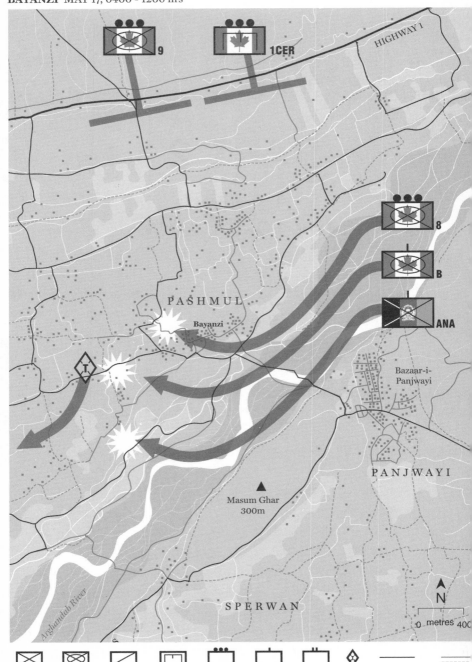

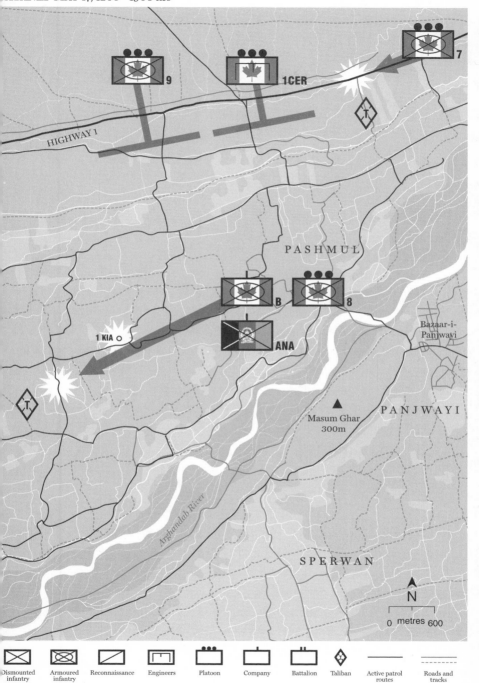

HIGHWAY 1

PASHMUL

9

1CER

7

B

8

ANA

1 KIA

Masum Ghar
300m

PANJWAYI

Bazaar-i-
Panjwayi

Arghandab River

SPERWAN

N

0   metres   600

Dismounted infantry
Armoured infantry
Reconnaissance
Engineers
Platoon
Company
Battalion
Taliban
Active patrol routes
Roads and tracks

CHAPTER THREE

"The Taliban are coming."

Panjwayi District
May 14, 2006

In the dull pre-dawn light of an Afghan spring morning, Lieutenant-Colonel Ian Hope led a small convoy of vehicles out of the main coalition base at Kandahar Airfield (KAF), and rumbled north along the cracked asphalt of the heavily travelled Highway Four into the still-sleeping Kandahar City. The three LAVs and three other vehicles that made up Niner Tac (the military call sign of Hope's mobile headquarters) included his command LAV and two more of the large armoured vehicles carrying his artillery and combat engineering officers; an electronic warfare vehicle; a Bison armoured vehicle converted to a command post; and a Nyala anti-mine patrol car. In the semi-darkness they sped past the check points set up along the highways. Hope was not eager to spend any more time than necessary on this dangerous stretch of road: Highway Four running between KAF and the city was a choke point—the only road that linked the vast airfield base and the capitol—and it had been the site of several suicide bomb attacks, roadside bombings and ambushes over the three months that Task Force Orion had been operating in Kandahar Province.

The battle group had spent a difficult winter in southern Afghanistan for the first half of its seven-month tour. The initial plan had focused attention on the mountains to the north and west of Kandahar City—a rugged, isolated and thinly populated area that the Taliban had used as a transit area during the five years since they'd been chased from power. The Canadian military's planners believed the region would be the focus of the insurgents' activities. Each of the battle group's three companies had been assigned an area of responsibility. Alpha Company was given the mountainous region to the north, an area almost the size of New Brunswick, while Bravo Company, in its more lightly armoured but nimbler G Wagons, was to cover Kandahar City and the area immediately around it, including the Panjwayi region. Both would operate out of the Provincial Reconstruction Team (PRT) camp on the outskirts of the city. Charlie was assigned to an area around Spin Boldak, a city on the border with Pakistan about half an hour's drive to the southeast of Kandahar and a centre for the Taliban's cross-border activities.

Almost as soon as the first soldiers of Task Force Orion arrived on the ground, however, events forced those plans to change. On January 15, a suicide car bomb detonated next to a Canadian G Wagon carrying diplomat Glyn Berry, killing the sixty-year-old head of the Canadian reconstruction team's foreign-affairs section and wounding three soldiers in the vehicle with him. In the wake of the attack, officials at the Department of Foreign Affairs (DFAID) and the Canadian International Development Agency (CIDA) had suspended their funding and participation in the reconstruction team pending a full review of the program. The PRT was supposed to have been the centrepiece of the Canadian mission in Afghanistan, the embodiment of the government's "3-D" approach that combined diplomacy, development and defence. But the death of Berry, a career diplomat who was popular with the soldiers, caused near panic in the Ottawa headquarters of CIDA and DFAIT. It took months before either department would resume its work with the military-led team and during that time, two of the "Ds" all but ceased to operate in Kandahar Province. For most of their tour the battle group got virtually no Canadian diplomatic or aid assistance, areas Hope knew were critical to defeating the Taliban over the long run. As far as the rest of the Canadian government was concerned, Task Force Orion was on its own in southern Afghanistan.

Charlie Company, meanwhile, was experiencing a different set of problems. The unit was left without an area to patrol when the promised departure of French soldiers occupying their base in Spin Boldak was delayed several times. While that freed up Charlie to act as Hope's "fire brigade"—a force he could rush from one hot spot to the next to stamp out flare-ups of Taliban activity—it also left Fletcher and many of his troops feeling frustrated. Ryan Jurkowski took to calling his company "the battle group's homeless." In late March, the company was sent to shore up a U.S. special forces base in a remote part of Helmand Province that was surrounded by Taliban, and subjected to nightly attacks. At dawn on March 31, forty LAVs and other vehicles from Charlie, along with Hope's Niner Tac and artillery and headquarters vehicles, rolled into the besieged U.S. base like the proverbial cavalry, bringing fresh supplies and reinforcing the American troops and their Afghan Army allies. Charlie spent more than a month in Helmand, patrolling through Taliban-dominated areas and fighting the occasional skirmishes to pacify the region in preparation for the arrival of British troops.

The charge into Helmand cost Charlie its first loss. Private Rob Costall, twenty-two, was killed in a furious nighttime battle with the Taliban on March 28 at Forward Operating Base Wolf, the American special forces base. One American soldier died and three other Canadians were wounded in the battle—a Taliban assault on the small, isolated fire base. A joint U.S. and Canadian investigation later determined that Costall had been killed by fire from an American machine gun behind him, but his death sobered the soldiers of Task Force Orion. He was the twelfth Canadian to die in Afghanistan and the first to be killed in combat. He would not be the last.

Meanwhile, Alpha Company was roaming the mountains and deep ravines of the Arghandab and Showali-Kot Districts, north of Kandahar City, successfully cutting off what had been a main transit route for the Taliban. Until the arrival of the Canadians, large groups of "Timmy"—the derisive nickname the soldiers had given the Taliban—were able to move around the district's rugged terrain more or less openly, cajoling or intimidating the impoverished villagers into supporting them either by feeding and sheltering their fighters or by "volunteering" their young men. The Canadians established patrol and fire bases at key points in the region, forcing the Taliban to keep a low profile and demonstrating that their powerful LAVs could go almost anywhere in the province at will. The Taliban quickly learned to fear the armoured vehicles, which they called *bala* (Pashtu for "monster"). They were wary of its rapid-fire 25-mm cannons, as well as the range and accuracy of the Canadian artillery, which, they discovered to their chagrin, was capable of raining down high explosive and shrapnel on them within minutes of their attacks or ambushes.

In response, the Taliban resorted to ambushes and roadside bombs which injured many soldiers and left the Canadians increasingly frustrated at their inability to find their attackers and strike back. In Kandahar City, Bravo Company had to contend with a growing threat from suicide bombers and a disturbing rise in attacks in the Panjwayi region. At first, the attacks were directed primarily against Afghan Army and police vehicles and bases, but eventually Canadian convoys were targeted as well. In mid-April, the soldiers of Bravo fought several fierce skirmishes with the Taliban and by early May Hope had decided to do something about the increasingly restive region.

That decision had led him to the early morning drive into Kandahar and beyond. It was a recce (military short-hand for a reconnaissance mission), a look at the ground over which he planned to send his soldiers in the next few days. His six vehicles roared along the long curve that led into the city, past the distinctive gates the troops had nicknamed "the Golden Arches" for their resemblance to the sign outside a Macdonald's, and raced through Kandahar's nearly empty streets at a brisk pace. Turning west to follow the grey ribbon of Highway One into the Panjwayi District, Hope's LAV led the others up a steep rise and into a gap in the long, sharp ridge of volcanic rock that rose to the west of Kandahar City like the edges of a half-buried prehistoric knife. As the convoy crested the top of the treeless grey ridge, Hope could see the first glimmers of daylight outlining the green orchards and muddy brown and grey walls of the Panjwayi region. The eight-wheeled LAV geared down its powerful diesel engine for the sharp turn into what the Canadian soldiers were already calling The Panj.

Hope was familiar with the area. Over the past few weeks, Bravo Company had been running into increasing numbers of Taliban fighters in the Panjwayi's tightly packed labyrinth of footpaths, roads and orchards. Ambushes on coalition military vehicles had become commonplace, especially along Highway One. The only paved, all-weather road in the area, this dangerous stretch of asphalt ran along the northern border of the district, connecting Kandahar to Helmand Province to the west.

The Panjwayi itself is a lush oasis in the dust and dirt that dominates the rest of Kandahar Province. Less than half an hour's drive from the capital, the district is a wedge of green hammered into the fault line between the red-brown sands of the Reg Desert to the south and the forbidding black of the Arghandab Mountains that rise abruptly to the north. The area, which could fit comfortably into the boundaries of the city of Toronto, was a green crescent—a lopsided smile reaching from the outskirts of Kandahar City to the border with Helmand Province to the west. At its widest, the Panjwayi it is less than fifty kilometres across, and it narrows to a kilometre-wide point at the western end, where the Dowrey, Tarnak and Arghandab Rivers join. Historically, the area was one administrative district, the next level of government below the provinces (much like a Canadian rural municipality). Not long before the first Canadians arrived in Kandahar, however, it was split in two: Zhari District, the area north of the Arghandab River, and Panjwayi District, to the south. With unforgiving desert dunes on one side and a tangle of mountains, deep valleys and boulder fields to the other, it is little wonder that almost every prominent local tribe has settled in the Panjwayi over the centuries. The area is thick with the Afghan equivalent of suburban sprawl, a maze of dry riverbeds, deep irrigation ditches and mud-brick walls enclosing fields, farms and villages of low, mainly single-story buildings. Those villages that Hope could see from his perch atop the LAV's armoured turret seemed to go on forever, stretching away into the early morning mist in an interconnected knot of compounds and walled-in fields. Each village was linked to the next by walls, dirt tracks and roads, and was more often than not tied to its neighbours through complex tribal and family links.

A typical Panjwayi village enclosed a dozen or more family compounds—called *qalas*—a handful of low structures ringed by two-metre-high mud and brick walls (often topped at the corners by guard towers) that was home to an extended family. The larger villages contained as many as one hundred walled enclosures huddled along the "main street," often a narrow, winding track of hard-packed dirt or gravel framed by high sand-coloured walls broken by the occasional iron or steel gate. A bewildering number of alleys led off each road, most of them footpaths barely wide enough for one man. Criss-crossing the entire region was an irregular network of canals and ditches, impassable for the Canadian vehicles except in places where culverts or bridges stood. Often, these were little more than mud piled atop a framework of sticks and rocks.

Most of the Panjwayi's villages looked as if they had not changed since the Bronze Age. In many, the only sign of the modern world was a battered loudspeaker tied haphazardly to a pole atop the roof of the local mosque, used to issue the five-times daily call to prayer. Otherwise, the mosques looked much like any other building in the village, mud brick and plastered walls and thatched roofs coated with sun-dried mud. The only new buildings were the schools and clinics built by U.S. reconstruction teams, many of which were abandoned, burned out or vandalized: a sure sign of the Taliban's continued presence.

The region's narrow dirt roads wound through large orchards and fields of grain, opium poppies, marijuana plants, melons and grapes. The marijuana, in particular, grew incredibly high, turning each field into a virtual jungle. Panjwayi was once known as the fruit basket of Afghanistan, its orchards watered by a widespread and well-maintained system of canals and ditches. But when the Soviets invaded and began their long, bloody war with the mujahedeen, the area became a battleground. It offered a nearly perfect hideout for the local rebels, who used its ditches and orchards both for refuge and to mount attacks on the Russians.

The grape orchards were the region's most striking feature: acres of leafy vines planted in neat rows atop metre-high walls of mud. Because wood is scarce in southern Afghanistan, farmers propped up their vines by building up low walls of sun-baked mud and clay at their roots. Most orchards were planted around a squat, rectangular grape-drying hut—a hulking structure with walls of mud and stone more than a metre thick, used to hang the harvested crop of grapes and dry it into raisins. Each hut was perforated by dozens of narrow slits that allowed air to circulate. To Hope's eye, they looked exactly like concrete machine-gun nests.

In many places, Panjwayi's roads were almost completely covered by overhanging tree branches, the most annoying to the Canadians being the mulberry. When brushed by passing vehicles, the trees thick boughs would deposit hundreds of red, teardrop-shaped pieces of fruit into the open hatches, leaving crews and equipment covered in dull, brownish red stains that looked uncomfortably like dried blood.

As his line of vehicles slowed and turned off Highway One, Hope scanned the undergrowth along the dirt road closely for signs of the enemy. Just days earlier—while he had been away on the three weeks of mid-deployment leave to which every soldier was entitled—Niner Tac had been ambushed not far from where they were now heading, and intelligence officers later confirmed Hope's suspicion that he was being personally targeted by the enemy. He had already lost one member of his crew—Master Corporal Mike Loewen, wounded in a suicide bomb attack on Hope's command LAV near Kandahar City on March 4—so he began to take extra precautions. While on the move, Hope changed his routes without notice, veering onto different roads apparently at random and constantly shuffling the order in which his six vehicles drove. When driving at night, one vehicle would keep its headlights on for the first portion of the journey, switching with another midway through—a tactic that made it difficult to distinguish one LAV from another. Hope's favourite trick was to darken the lights on all the vehicles but the second from the front, confronting oncoming traffic with the frightening silhouette of a towering LAV bearing down on them.

Despite the danger, Hope was secretly pleased when he learned that the Taliban wanted to take him out. Clearly, his presence was being felt. Hope understood the macho nature of Pashtun culture, one that viewed conflict as a highly personal matter, and went out of his way to taunt the Taliban whenever he could. Hope was in no way looking to gratify his ego. Instead, he wanted to make an impression on the villagers in the remote rural areas where the task force operated. During one trip through the Arghandab Mountains, he taught a crowd of the cheerful children that swarmed around Niner Tac whenever it stopped near their village how to say his name, encouraging them to chant it until he was certain they would remember. "We're telling the Taliban: 'we're here, we're staying and there's nothing you can do about it,'" he told his troops afterward. There was another reason for Hope to spread his name around the villages in the Canadian area of operations. After every name-chanting session, the battle-group commander would instruct the Afghan translators who monitored Taliban cell-phone and walkie-talkie transmissions to listen for his name over the airwaves. It was an effective way to keep track of the villages into which the Taliban had spread their tentacles.

From the height of the crew-commander position, on the right-hand side of the LAV's flat, boxy turret, Hope and his crew could often see over the imposing walls of the region's compounds. Women were rarely seen outside their family homes. If they did venture out, it was only when veiled or covered head-to-toe by the all-concealing burkha, and always in the company of their husbands or another male relative. But from the three-metre height of the LAV, the Canadian soldiers occasionally got a glimpse into the lives of ordinary Afghan women. Some quickly went inside when the vehicles rumbled past, but others stopped and stared, obviously unafraid of the odd-looking foreigners with their helmets and body armour ("Starship Trooper gear" as some soldiers called it). A few even smiled and waved, provided there were no men present. Such rare sights were often the sub-ject of ribald jokes among the overwhelmingly young and hor-monally charged male soldiers, but the brief encounters always left Hope feeling sad, like watching a caged tiger in a zoo.

But on this spring day, Hope wasn't looking over walls. Instead, he was scanning the ground around him with the eye of an experienced soldier, trying to judge how it would affect his plans for operations in the area. What he saw was troubling. The Panjwayi was nearly perfect terrain for the Taliban, tailor made for hit-and-run tactics. The shaded roads and deep irrigation ditches allowed them to move from one end of the district to the other without being seen by the coalition's aircraft, helicopters or UAVs—unmanned spy planes launched from KAF that could circle for hours overhead taking detailed pictures of any movement below.

Hope also knew the Taliban had increased their presence in the region over the past few weeks, although American intelligence officers within Operation Enduring Freedom insisted that there were only two or three cells—a total of 50 to 100 fighters in the entire district. But the U.S. intelligence officers were in the central headquarters at Bagram, north of Kabul, and more than 500 kilometres from Panjwayi. The Canadians were up-close-and-personal. For the past month, Major Nick Grimshaw's Bravo Company had been engaged in almost daily contacts with the enemy. Just two weeks before, Major Tod Strickland—Hope's second-in-command—had taken Niner Tac on a probe into the region, looking for signs of Taliban activity. As his vehicles manoeuvred along the dry bed of the Arghandab River, the lead LAV got bogged down in a large patch of soft sand. The Taliban quickly pounced. Within minutes, the north bank of the riverbed erupted in gunfire. Only the quick action of Regimental Sergeant-Major Randy Northrup and Master Corporal Jason Froude—who ignored the incoming fire and leaped onto the back of the stuck LAV to organize a tow cable—saved the Canadians from disaster.

Now, Hope was planning a major operation to sweep through the unsettled district. His recce mission was to identify routes in and out of the Panjwayi's maze of roads and tracks, and possible "hot spots" where there were signs of a Taliban presence. Such places were all potential targets for the Canadian battle group to cordon off, surround, and sweep clear with their infantry. Niner Tac rolled through the area all morning, while Hope took careful notes in his dog-eared field message notepad and marked up his already well-worn map of the district.

Finally the convoy slowed, then turned down yet another side road leading up to the old hilltop fort at Gundy Ghar—known as "The Nipple" to the troops. The crumbling walls of the Iron Age site overlooked most of the western end of the Panjwayi, sitting atop a small flat-topped hill that erupted abruptly out of the otherwise flat landscape. A perfect place to wait and watch. A perfect place for a meeting.

Hope was headed for a sit-down with a man who was to become one of the Canadians' most important allies in the coming battles, Captain Massoud of the Afghan National Police (ANP). Like most of his soldiers, and almost all Afghans, Hope had mixed feelings about the ANP. Villagers had a great deal of respect for the soldiers of the Afghan National Army (ANA), tough, well-disciplined troops who were trained by American, European and Canadian soldiers. They were well equipped and—by Afghan standards—well behaved. But there was only a handful of such troops in the Panjwayi for most of the summer of 2006, the rest called away to fight in other parts of the country. That left the Canadians with the ANP as the only "Afghan face" of their operations.

Most would rather have done without. The police force was national in name only and most of its constables were poorly paid (when paid at all), notoriously corrupt and badly equipped. Almost every Canadian patrol that encountered local ANP officers, particularly in the smaller rural outposts, was besieged by pleas for ammunition for their AK-47s. Usually, three or four policemen would share one magazine of ammunition, often because the supply of bullets or the funds to purchase them had been "diverted" by corrupt officials in Kandahar or Kabul. The Canadian reconstruction team, which included two RCMP officers, was working to improve the force's training and equipment, but their efforts had been slow to bear fruit. The ANP varied wildly in quality, from tough and loyal fighters to uniformed thugs whose only qualifications were kinship to a local leader. They were notorious for preying upon villagers for bribes, especially those from different tribes than their own. Some ANP could fight and many were almost suicidally brave, but the Canadians quickly learned they were useful for manning roadblocks and highway checkpoints and little else.

Massoud was the exception. Hope had met him almost a year earlier, during his first scouting trip to Kandahar. The short, wiry police captain was the head of the Afghan force's Unit 005, a quick-reaction team organized more along military than police lines. An ethnic Tajik, from the northern half of Afghanistan, Massoud had fought the Taliban for more than twelve years, first with the Northern Alliance rebellion in the late 1990s and then after September 11, 2001, with the U.S.–led coalition and the Karzai government. He had impressed Hope immediately as tough, intelligent, capable and passionate in his hatred of the Taliban.

Massoud's English was almost flawless, and he was always asking his western counterparts for the definition and correct pronunciation of new words. He wrote down his orders and instructions, a rare thing in Afghanistan's orally based culture, and was eager to learn from his coalition allies. The American commander who had been responsible for the area before Hope had recommended Massoud as a reliable ally and the police captain soon became the unofficial Afghan liaison in the Canadian task-force headquarters. In his blue-grey uniform and the black U.S. special forces baseball cap he habitually wore instead of his uniform hat, he soon became a fixture at Hope's command post.

Massoud greeted Hope and his crew as soon as they climbed out of their vehicles, striding down from the trenches that ringed the top of the small hill. He had been occupying the ancient ruined fort for several days with his men, all veterans of the Northern Alliance's long rebellion against the Taliban and all personally loyal to Massoud. They had set up heavy machine guns and generators atop the fort, which provided the power for security floodlights that lit up the slopes below them at night—a useful way to prevent Taliban infiltrators from sneaking up on their position. The lights also helped them to keep an eye on a school just to the south, one of the only new structures in the village and one that had been built under a U.S. reconstruction program. That alone made it a target for the Taliban. The Afghan policemen had been clashing with Taliban fighters almost daily, and although he was visibly tired, Massoud offered Hope and his Niner Tac crew hospitality, brewing up the inevitable Afghan tea while they sat cross-legged in one of the few pockets of shade.

Over glasses of tea and a few pleasantries, Massoud filled Hope in on his men's activities. They had been fighting frequently and had met with some success, including killing a senior Taliban commander and capturing several minor commanders. Massoud told the Canadian colonel that the Taliban had begun moving into the region in force, although he was still uncertain of their exact strength, and were trying to establish a large, permanent base in the Panjwayi. They had at first hidden among villagers in the southern half of the region, where many of their leaders had relatives, but local elders would not allow large Taliban groups to stay permanently for fear of attracting the unwanted attention of the ANA or coalition forces. So, now, the Taliban were looking to the northern half of the region where there was no single dominant tribe and the families and towns were smaller. This made it easier for them to move into the area and prey on locals who were too few to resist, strong-arming supplies, shelter and support from villages closer to Highway One and thus to Kandahar itself.

The Taliban usually laid low during the daylight hours, travelling in small, unarmed groups to conduct negotiations with local leaders. After dark, however, they retrieved their hidden weapons and openly intimidated villagers while also mounting ambushes and attacks. They had set up supply routes and secret caches of weapons, ammunition and other supplies, and had even established rudimentary medical clinics for their wounded.

One of the first things the Taliban had done when they began flooding into the Panjwayi in April was to attack the local ANP, killing a dozen or more in ambushes or attacks on police stations. Massoud and his men had been sent in two weeks earlier to reinforce the small local contingent of Afghan police by the governor of Kandahar himself and had been skirmishing with the enemy regularly. But now they were in a standoff. Massoud controlled Highway One and protected the school south of the Gundy Ghar feature, while the Taliban roamed more or less freely through the labyrinth of villages and towns in the heart of the district, between the highway and the Arghandab River.

Eventually Massoud came to the point. "The Taliban are coming to attack Kandahar," he told Hope. "They want to capture the city."

Massoud knew that night letters, or *shabnamas*—anonymous notes left at the doors of village elders or others—had been circulating in Kandahar and the Panjwayi for weeks, calling for the populace to rise up against the Afghan government and their western allies, and warning that the Taliban would soon return. The mujahedeen had used night letters to communicate with the people in the 1980s, and Mullah Omar favoured them as a way of spreading the Taliban's word and cowing opponents. Massoud did not think these particular letters were idle boasts. His men had seen a dramatic increase in the number of Taliban in the district—mostly young men who slipped into the area amid the hundreds of unemployed who travelled to the Panjwayi each spring to help with the summer harvest of opium poppies and marijuana.

Once in the Panjwayi, the Taliban fighters could live off the land, sheltered and fed by local sympathizers or villagers who supported them out of fear. There was always plenty of food available locally and the bustling markets of Kandahar City were only a short drive away. Even in villages that did not particularly welcome the young men from Pakistan or the mountains, there were too few fighting-age men to challenge the heavily armed Taliban cells.

But Hope was skeptical. He knew from the reports of his own soldiers that Taliban numbers had been rising, but he believed this was due to the local poppy and marijuana harvest, crops upon which the Taliban relied for much of their funding. And while it was true that rumours had been flying around Kandahar City's bazaars and tea houses that the Taliban was going to retake the city, there were always rumours. Hope put down the talk of a Taliban offensive to enemy propaganda.

Still, he was intrigued by Massoud's certainty, and the Afghan policeman's instincts had to be respected. The energetic and efficient Massoud had set up a network of informants in the Panjwayi through the simple expedient of handing out new cellular phones as gifts in hundreds of the region's villages, with the added incentive of cash rewards for information about Taliban movements. His informants had yielded reliable and often valuable information to coalition forces in the past.

Hope was also concerned by the recent change in the Taliban's tactics: the fighters that Task Force Orion had been running up against in the last few weeks were not playing the usual game of hit and run. These insurgents were standing up and fighting in broad daylight.

When the Canadian task force had arrived in Kandahar in January, there were at most two hundred Taliban fighters scattered across the entire province. By May, their numbers had doubled in Panjwayi alone. While many of these hard-core Taliban were Afghans, including some veterans of the guerrilla war against the Soviets, their ranks included Pakistanis, Chechens, Arabs, or Kashmiri insurgents. They were organized into cells of five fighters, one responsible for a rocket-propelled grenade launcher (the Taliban's all-purpose heavy weapon, used against armoured vehicles, buildings, helicopters and even clusters of troops); a machine gunner, armed with a Soviet-made PKM medium machine gun; two riflemen, with their AK-47 assault rifles; and a commander. That number was small enough to travel without drawing undue attention—squeezing into a single car or onto a few motorcycles—or to blend in with the area's civilians. When the Taliban were planning an attack or an ambush, three or four cells would combine, meeting at a predetermined spot to uncover hidden weapons and move into their ambush positions, using cellular phones or cheap, hand-held walkie-talkies to communicate. When their mission was important enough, or if their commander had sufficient influence within the Taliban, they would also use 82-mm mortars or light, recoilless anti-tank rifles. When they needed to make roadside bombs, there was an almost unlimited supply of material, usually old Soviet artillery shells with the fuses carefully removed and wired to a jury-rigged detonator such as a cell phone or garage opener.

The hard-core Taliban fighters were tough, experienced and determined, but they made up only a small minority of the insurgents' fighting strength. Most of their numbers in the Panjwayi were either farmers drafted by threat or intimidation, or young graduates of the madrassas. While they obediently followed the lead of the seasoned fighters, these men were inexperienced, had terrible aim and often left the fight after the first exchange of fire.

For the first two months of their tour in Kandahar, the Taliban had largely kept its distance from the Canadians, using roadside bombs, remotely launched rockets or quick, hit-and-run ambushes to attack them. In April, however, that began to change. The battle group's convoys began to be hit by well-planned attacks, and the Taliban fighters would not simply fire a barrage of bullets before retreating. Instead, they would direct a flood of fire down on their target, using the walls, orchards and ditches of the Panjwayi to keep the Canadians from closing with them. They would retreat only when they sensed an air strike or artillery was about to be called down on their positions. Then, they would fall back in good order in the direction they believed the Canadians were heading and wait patiently for the convoy to come under their guns once more.

Hope listened with growing unease to Massoud's summary of the situation. He had already started to plan a large-scale sweep through the most troublesome parts of the Panjwayi, and Massoud's information confirmed the need for a coalition show of strength in the district. Before he climbed back into the turret of his LAV, Hope promised Massoud that the Canadians would be back in force within a few days and invited him to join his command post as the Afghan police liaison for the operation.

Two days later, on May 16, Hope launched his sweep: Operation Bravo Guardian—the opening shots in what would prove to be a two-month struggle with the Taliban. And Charlie Company was to be the tip of the sword.

CHAPTER FOUR

"An unattractive target."

Kandahar Airfield
May 16, 2006

Captain Marty Dupuis was never supposed to be LAV captain of Charlie Company—the third in command and the officer who controlled the LAVs when the rest of the company dismounted to fight on foot—let alone be left in command for the first full-scale battle of the deployment. The affable dark-haired francophone from Ajax, Ontario, had been slotted into the company at the last minute after his predecessor had been posted to another job in KAF, "a stroke of luck," he was fond of saying, that saved him from the boredom of a staff job at headquarters or worse, back at the regiment's home base in Edmonton.

The twenty-seven-year-old was just four years out of Royal Military College in Kingston, Ontario, when he landed in Afghanistan on his first overseas deployment, and was only temporarily in command when orders came down for Charlie Company to "kit up" and prepare for action. Major Bill Fletcher had just left on his mid-deployment leave and his second-in-command, Captain Ryan Jurkowski, was still en route back from his own leave. When he got his orders to move, Dupuis swallowed hard and began issuing instructions to move two of his three platoons out of KAF. He sent Number 8 Platoon, including Sergeant Mike Denine, to hook up with Bravo Company and get the details of the mission while he prepared Number 9 Platoon to leave with him and a troop of engineers, moving directly from the air base to the Panjwayi area. Charlie's third platoon, Number 7, would remain in KAF as the quick-reaction force, ready to move up at a moment's notice.

Charlie was the clean-up hitter for Operation Bravo Guardian, Lieutenant-Colonel Hope's plan to clear out a suspected nest of Taliban in a cluster of villages at Nalgham, in the heart of the Panjwayi area. Bravo Company, equipped with only the lightly armoured G Wagon jeeps, was to sweep through the collection of small villages from the south, accompanied by Charlie's 8 Platoon to add heavy punch to their advance. The LAVs and troops with Dupuis were to wait to the north of the triangular clutch of villages, ready to block the Taliban's retreat and hopefully catch them in the open as they fled Bravo Company's attack.

It was a good plan, Dupuis thought, as he stood atop the turret of his car and began lining up the LAVs and engineers in KAF's vehicle-marshalling area in the pre-dawn darkness. He wondered fleetingly if the action would last more than a few seconds.

By early evening, Sergeant Mike Denine and the rest of 8 Platoon were already on Highway Four. They were headed into Kandahar City to link up with Bravo Company in the relative safety of the Canadian PRT camp, where they would spend the night receiving detailed orders for the following day's sweep through the suspect village. Captain Dupuis had given him only a few minutes to get his section of ten soldiers kitted up and crammed into the back of their LAV to take their place in the 8 Platoon column. The first he had heard about the coming mission was a hurried "You got orders coming down real quick" from his platoon warrant officer, Ron Gallant. "We're going to go out and tee up with B Coy at this grid and then from there we're going to go and start doing stuff: initiate contact or fuckin' sweep, I dunno."

"Where're we going?" Denine had shouted after the warrant's retreating back, already pulling on his bulky body armour, helmet and the harness of straps and pockets that held all of his ammunition, grenades and other equipment. His rifle, even in the well-protected Kandahar base, was within arm's reach.

"The Panj," the warrant shouted back. "Someplace called . . . Nalgham?"

Denine shook his head. The burly Newfoundlander couldn't keep track of the names of the villages in which he'd patrolled and fought for the past three months, let alone pronounce most of them. But he remembered each corner, wall and street he and his section had passed through and knew the routes in and out of every village with barely a glance at his map. He shrugged: he and his soldiers would find out soon enough where they were heading. Denine shouted orders and encouragement to his privates and corporals to get their equipment together and get moving.

They needed little prompting, he noted with approval. All had prepared their equipment, meticulously cleaned their weapons and loaded up the LAVs two days earlier when they'd returned to the KAF base after three days of sweeps through the Panjwayi. What was supposed to be a week's rest—with hot meals, showers and the unaccustomed luxury of bunk beds in the BATS (short for Big-Ass Tents)—had been cut to less than forty-eight hours.

Last week's swing through the area had resulted in what the troops called "soft contacts"—occasional potshots with rifles or RPGs, almost all wildly inaccurate. But he suspected this time would be different, if only because 8 Platoon would be attached to the more lightly equipped Bravo Company. The smaller, thin-skinned G Wagon jeeps that Bravo Company drove were vulnerable to Taliban ambush, especially their RPGs, so platoons from Charlie, with their heavily armoured LAVs, would often accompany them as a sort of mobile shield. "Every time we're out with them we know we're getting into it," Denine told himself glumly.

It was a pitch-black night, overcast and moonless, and the air was still heavy with the heat of the day as the troops rolled out of Kandahar City and down Highway One to collect their ANP allies at the edge of the Panjwayi District. The Canadians moved in two convoys: Bravo Company, with Charlie's 8 Platoon in the lead, headed into Panjwayi then swung south to hit the suspect area from below, while Dupuis followed behind with almost a dozen LAVs to form a three-kilometre blocking line north of the villages.

Both groups had to drive straight past Ambush Alley, a stretch of Highway One where the grape fields ran right up to edge of the busy road, giving Taliban ambushers plenty of cover to lie in wait for a passing coalition convoy. Afghan police and army convoys were regularly hit along this stretch of road and the attackers had seemed to grow bolder recently, not even shying away from launching attacks on the feared LAVs moving down the highway by night. The gunners and crew commanders of Charlie's vehicles kept their turrets moving, gears whining as they rotated back and forth to watch every wall and rooftop for signs of trouble. Although the darkness outside was complete, the undulating mounds of the grape orchards and the walls and buildings crawling past were clearly visible in the eerie green glow of the LAVs' night-vision gunsights and to the soldiers standing up in the rear hatches, meticulously scanning their own areas of responsibility.

Marty Dupuis looked back at the long, barely visible line of vehicles snaking down the highway and marvelled. "Man, we're right spread out." To Dupuis' frustration, the convoy moved at a crawl, slowed by the darkness and dozens of minor problems with the vehicles. "Every road move in Afghanistan is the road move from hell," he grumbled to himself. "Especially at night. We're moving at what? Like five kilometres per hour? It takes forever."

Dupuis sat down on his seat inside the turret with a thump. He had just begun to copy down orders coming in over his radio when another LAV commander interrupted: "Sir, you've got to see this," he said into Dupuis' headset.

The young captain stood up and looked out of the turret. Hundreds of civilians lined the highway, pouring out of side roads and footpaths and patiently walking east, away from the Panjwayi. "They're just coming out like crazy," he told his driver, watching the seemingly endless procession of women, children, old people, and a handful of adult men. They struggled by on foot, pushing carts or riding bicycles, occasionally sitting astride a ramshackle motorcycle that chugged along the cracked and pitted tarmac on the edge of the highway.

At first, Dupuis had his soldiers stop the refugees and ask what they were running from. Not all of the civilians were eager to talk with the foreign soldiers, but those who did said they were running from the Taliban, who had taken over their villages and ordered them to leave. When the Canadians tried to get information about where exactly the insurgents were hiding, they ran into a cultural wall of misunderstanding. Maps were a completely foreign concept to most Afghans, who would give directions based on local landmarks and place names that changed according to who was giving the directions. Even those villagers who wanted to help the Canadians were able to give only the haziest notion of the Taliban's location.

Two kilometres to the south, Mike Denine was watching a similar parade from his perch in the rear hatch of his LAV. He shook his head grimly as the civilians streamed past the line of Canadian vehicles. It was the first time he'd seen such an exodus, and although he didn't know precisely what it meant, he was certain it wasn't a good sign.

"What the fuck is that?" Corporal Kory Ozerkevich—"Oz" to the men and women of C Company—spoke from the rear hatch beside Denine, shouting to be heard over the engine noise.

"Just keep an eye on 'em," Denine answered as the refugees trudged past the LAVs' armoured flanks, visible in irregular flashes as each vehicle rolled past then moved on. "They're moving out of the town, so there might be something going on."

The line of Canadian vehicles eventually reached its turnoff point. As planned, Denine's LAVs veered south towards the wide, relatively flat sand and gravel wadi of the Arghandab River, the dried-out bed of a river that filled only during rainy season, and even then only in one year out of five. The wadi meandered straight down the heart of the Panjwayi, providing the Canadians with an expressway—a high-speed route to get the lumbering LAVs within striking distance of their targets without risking the twists and turns of the district's narrow roads and dubious trails. Charlie's LAVs, with their heavier armour and bigger guns, moved up into the lead as the column bounced down the rough trail of dirt and rocks towards the villages at Nalgham, the lighter jeeps of B Company falling into line behind them as the eastern sky began changing from midnight black to deep blue.

Meanwhile, Marty Dupuis took 9 Platoon and the engineers farther down Highway One. His goal was to time his arrival so that he would be able to set up a blocking position at about the same time the others were ready to begin sweeping through the villages. But before either convoy got very far along their respective routes, fresh orders came down from call sign Zero—task force commander Lieutenant-Colonel Ian Hope.

Hope had led his Niner Tac ahead of the main Canadian force back to the ruins atop the hill at Gundy Ghar. With him were a troop of gunners from the Royal Canadian Horse Artillery and two of their new M777 howitzers, high-calibre artillery pieces capable of hurling a high-explosive shell more than thirty kilometres and dropping it within a few metres of its target. After greeting Captain Massoud and his small band of Afghan police, Hope stationed his LAVs around the edges of the hilltop in position to cover the assault on the villages just visible in the growing light. From the top of Gundy Ghar, Niner Tac could bring the rapid-fire cannon of its LAVs down on anyone moving in or out of the huddle of small, interconnected compounds, while the artillery's 155-mm howitzers could drop their deadly rounds wherever the attacking companies called for them.

Nichola Goddard, the Forward Observation Officer attached to Charlie Company, roamed more or less independently, looking for the best spot from which to direct the artillery's volleys of fire. Using the sophisticated computers and targeting systems in the back of her armoured vehicle, Goddard could call down a fire mission within minutes, directing the barrage with pinpoint accuracy onto a specific building or even smaller target and showering it with hundreds of kilograms of high explosives and steel shell fragments. Goddard was one of only a handful of women in the overwhelmingly male battle group but was a popular officer, as much for her skill at calling in fire from the faraway guns as her toothy grin and apparently boundless enthusiasm for her dangerous work. Nich, as she was known to her fellow officers, and her FOO crew were often in the most exposed positions on the battlefield, constantly positioning and repositioning their LAV to get the best view of possible targets and "walk" artillery rounds onto enemy positions as quickly as possible.

While Hope watched the distant vehicles crawl towards their objective in the still-dim pre-dawn light, Massoud walked up to the side of his LAV and looked out over the green fields and sand-coloured buildings far below. His eyes strained to penetrate the darkness beneath his customary special forces baseball cap. "You'll be fighting within thirty minutes—guaranteed," he said quietly, looking up at the Canadian colonel. "You'll see."

Massoud's cell phone buzzed. After a brief conversation in Pashtu, the bearded Afghan police captain turned to Hope. "They've moved," he said simply. One of his informants had told him that while a large group of Taliban had indeed spent the night in a schoolhouse in Nalgham, they had left before dawn and were now hiding in a mosque in the village of Bayanzi, several kilometres to the east of where the Canadian battle group was now headed. Hope picked up his radio handset.

The Canadians were just beginning to move into position for their sweep through the first village when Hope called an abrupt halt to the manoeuvring. "Stop. Right where you are," the colonel's voice came over the radio, unmistakable despite the hiss of the background static. "New orders."

Dupuis was still on Highway One, far north of B Company and Mike Denine's 8 Platoon when he heard the new orders. As quickly as Hope's instructions came in over one channel, Dupuis relayed them to his LAV crew commanders on the other.

In the back of his own LAV, Mike Denine heard the radio chatter in the turret behind him as he stood in the rear of the troop carrier, clutching the edges of the square air sentry hatch as they bounded along the undulating gravel of the dry riverbed. Dawn had already lit up the Arghandab wadi and the glare of the sun was beginning to heat the air like a furnace. Denine took off his sunglasses, wiped a thin veil of sweat and grit off his face, and shrugged off the change in destination. "I get paid either way," he told himself as the convoy reversed course and headed for its new objective: the village of Bayanzi.

Located across the mostly dried-out Arghandab River from the Panjwayi District Centre, Bayanzi was one of the largest communities in the area. Denine's LAV moved into the lead as they approached the village of Bayanzi. The driver swung its blunt, massive nose to the north, climbed out of the wadi with a roar of acceleration and headed towards the distant collection of walls and buildings. The Canadians approached from the east and south, with Charlie's LAVs leading the way out of the sun-baked wadi to take up their position on the far left flank of the attack. As the troops swung into a line to sweep through the spread-out tangle of compounds, the soldiers of Bravo Company jumped out of their jeeps and jogged ahead to seek the cover of a wall, a tree or just a low mound of dirt to await the word to begin the advance.

Charlie's lone platoon had the farthest to go to reach its objective, so the drivers gunned their engines to get into position for the sweep through the village. Standing in the rear hatch, half in and half out of the LAV, Denine hung on desperately as his car made a hard turn and led the three other vehicles into a long alley leading into the village—a bumpy dirt road lined by a patchwork of walls of varying heights on either side, barely wide enough to let them pass. Denine's LAV had just entered the narrow choke point when it lurched to a halt and the sergeant heard the whine of the turret's motors as the gunner and crew commander took aim at something up ahead.

The popping of gunfire sounded behind him and Denine turned to see Corporal Ozerkevich leaning out over the edge of his hatch. He was aiming his rifle around the LAV's wide turret and firing steadily.

"Oz, what the fuck are you doin'?" Denine asked brusquely. "What are you shooting at?"

Oz paused long enough to turn his head and shout back: "There's fuckin' guys coming out all over the place. They got weapons."

Denine heard the first snap of a bullet passing by, a sound like a bullwhip cracking beside his ear, and watched curiously for a split second as the canvas strap holding a box of rations onto the side of the LAV's turret parted just inches away from his eyes.

"All right, good enough," he said through gritted teeth, suddenly angry. "You wanna go, we'll go."

Denine leaned out over his side of the LAV and immediately caught sight of a Taliban gunman peering past the corner of the crumbling wall at the end of the alley. He calmly put three bullets into the turbaned man, who was close enough that Denine could watch his face contort as the rounds struck his body. The Taliban fighter fell limply into dust and out of sight, his AK-47 clattering onto the ground.

All at once, a storm of machine-gun and RPG fire rained down on the exposed LAV, bullets ricocheting off the angled front armour or singing over the Canadians' heads. "Here we go, boys!" Denine shouted down to the five soldiers still inside the carrier, raising his C7 again and squinting through the rifle's sights to snap off shots at the blossoms of fire from the Taliban's muzzles. He emptied a magazine, dropped it into the troop compartment at his feet and reloaded, leaning out again to continue firing at muzzle flashes or brief glimpses of silhouettes. Denine saw the flash of a grenade launch right in front of his LAV and followed the projectile as it accelerated straight towards him. The grenade whooshed past, missing the equipment strapped to the side of the vehicle by inches before hitting a mound of dirt behind them and tumbling end over end into a field. "Holy fuck!" he whispered to himself.

As he automatically fired and reloaded, Denine thought idly that the pre-deployment training lectures had been wrong: "Time doesn't slow down; it fucking stops." He knew his section was in a precarious position. The irregular walls on either side of the alley prevented the platoon's other LAVs from moving up to help out and made it pointless to lower the back ramp and let out the soldiers inside to join the fight. The laneway was too narrow even for one man to move up beside the LAV and return the Taliban's fire. The car could not move to either side and the prospect of backing up the LAV blind was not an attractive option, particularly with RPGs coming at them in clouds. The huge vehicle could easily become stuck, making it a sitting duck for the Taliban gunners.

Denine was dimly aware of Oz standing in the other rear hatch, firing grenades at the ambushers ahead. Corporal Ozerkevich was one of the two grenadiers in Denine's section, his rifle fitted with a special launcher under its barrel, a foot-long tube that fired egg-sized M203 fragmentation grenades. Suddenly, Denine realized that something was wrong: he and Oz were the only ones firing.

Bellowing to be heard over the explosions and gunfire, Denine told Sergeant Gerry Moores in the turret just ahead of him to start firing the LAV's cannon at their attackers. "Get the fuckin' gun goin'! Get 'em on the target and start fucking getting them," he shouted.

The 25-mm chain gun fired once before Denine heard gunner Jeff Trowsdale shout: "Misfire!" The gun had jammed.

"Great, here we go!" Denine said grimly, leaning out to snap off more shots.

The turret crew tried their backup weapon, a 7.62-mm medium machine gun mounted to fire along the same axis as the main gun. After a brief burst, it too stopped. "Stoppage!" Trowsdale cried from inside the turret.

"Aw fuck, that's great! Just great!" Denine swore as the flood of Taliban fire increased.

"Get that gun goin' and get it goin' now!" he shouted. "This is not a good spot to have all our weapons go down."

While Oz and Denine emptied their magazines at the enemy, the two men in the turret worked feverishly to get their big guns working, pounding at their mechanisms in a desperate attempt to clear them, but both were hopelessly jammed.

Denine fired steadily at the Taliban in front of him, only vaguely aware of his soldiers inside the LAV reloading magazines and handing ammunition up to him and Oz—the only ones in position to fire. The much-younger privates were laughing and cheering, which almost made the burly sergeant smile. "Pretty slick there, boys," he said as a private in the crowded compartment at his feet calmly passed up a fresh magazine full of ammunition.

While bullets cracked past or thumped dully into the LAV's armour, Denine tried to concentrate on the dim silhouettes and flashes of movement he could just make out through the dust and smoke. Shouting to be heard over the fire of his own rifle and the occasional roar of an RPG launch, Denine alternated giving orders to Oz with more swearing at the turret crew working on the broken weapons. "Get your ass goin'!" he shouted at Moores and Trowsdale. "Get your act in gear! Trowsdale, start making it happen!"

But the gunners' heaving and hammering on the action of the 25-mm cannon was having no effect. Finally, the brawny sergeant decided he had to do something himself. "Enough of this." Denine dropped an empty magazine at his feet, pulled a fully loaded one out of one of his pouches and slid it smoothly into the rifle.

"Oz, stop! Don't shoot, I'm gonna hop up and get the pintle-mount [light machine gun] goin'—we gotta get something goin'. Something more than two rifles, for fuck's sake."

Mounted on a post in front of the crew commander's hatch, on the highest point of the turret, was a C9 light machine gun. It was a smaller and less powerful weapon than the LAV's other main armaments, but Denine reasoned that it at least might be working. Looming like a linebacker in his armoured vest and helmet, he clambered out of the hatch and onto the top of the turret he had been using for cover. Denine was now the highest—and most visible—thing on the car. He sat on his backside and grabbed the machine gun's stock, his legs sprawled in front of him on either side of the crew commander's hatch. With bullets and RPGs whizzing past, he looked down between his legs to see Gerry Moores staring back up at him in disbelief from inside the turret.

"Just get that gun going," Denine growled as he cocked the machine gun in front of him: "This thing had better be working or somebody's going to get a very long talking-to out behind the woodshed after we're done all this."

Denine pulled the trigger of the machine gun and held it down, but instead of the customary burst of gunfire, he was rewarded with a single "bang." One shot.

"Fuck!" He cocked the weapon and fired again. Another single shot, then nothing.

A Taliban bullet whipped past Denine's ear, close enough that he felt the heat of its passage. He turned his head to shout at Oz, who had resumed firing from the left-hand air sentry hatch: "Get me some oil!"

Within seconds, Oz tossed a small plastic bottle of gun oil to Denine. He caught the bottle deftly, calmly opened up the machine gun's breech and hosed down the bolt and moving parts with oil as if he were cleaning it back home in Edmonton. He re-cocked the weapon, said a brief prayer, then pulled the trigger. A burst of fire erupted from the machine gun's barrel and Denine began playing bullets up and down the shallow ditch ahead where he could see the Taliban gunmen had taken shelter.

"Just keep the ammunition coming!" he shouted over one shoulder at Oz.

Denine was amazed at the speed with which the Taliban fighters were reloading their rocket-propelled grenade launchers. "Speedy little fuckers," he murmured as he aimed the machine gun like a garden hose and watched it kick up clouds of dust wherever he sprayed his bursts of fire. A rocket-propelled grenade skimmed past his head, close enough to singe his hair.

"Holy shit!" he shouted, thinking: "If one of these hits the turret and goes off, I'm cooked."

Denine caught a hint of motion to one side and swung his sights over, firing a salvo just as a Taliban gunner stood up behind a low mud wall with his launcher at his shoulder, ready to fire. The sergeant emptied half of a two-hundred-round box of ammunition into the man, virtually cutting him in two before he could fire his armour-piercing grenade at the trapped LAV.

After several more minutes of firing bursts of 5.56-mm bullets at enemy muzzle flashes, the Taliban's fire gradually died away as they retreated into the maze of walls and buildings behind them. Denine levered himself stiffly to his knees and crawled back off the exposed turret onto the flat deck of the LAV behind him. "Guess I made myself an unattractive target," he said, lowering himself into the relative safety of the air sentry hatch.

A few minutes later, the call came for Charlie's LAVs to pull back to another position, and a second after that, Moores cleared the main gun. One of the thin pieces of metal used to link the 25-mm shells into a continuous belt for the rapid-fire cannon had gotten caught in the weapon's working parts, rendering it useless.

When Moores reported the gun was ready for action, Denine just laughed. "Gerry, you're killing me," he said wearily. "Just drive straight back to where we were and don't worry about what we run over."

CHAPTER FIVE

"My Sunray's down."

Bayanzi
May 17
1200 hrs

While Denine had been fighting his private battle with the Taliban ambushers, Bravo Company and the rest of Charlie's 8 Platoon had been engaged in a series of fierce firefights all along the line of their advance into the village. The decision had been made to call in the artillery to pound the buildings and other well-protected positions farther inside the village to which the Taliban had retreated. Because FOO Nich Goddard was on the opposite end of the stretched-out Canadian line, far to the south, one of the Bravo Company vehicles called in the coordinates of a target building full of Taliban, more than two hundred metres in front of Denine and his section, still catching their breath after the firefight in the alley. Watching from his air hatch, the veteran sergeant saw the first burst of orange from a howitzer shell land a scant seventy metres in front of his LAV: "Very goddamn close for a high explosive round." He quickly dropped down into the safety of the troop compartment and listened to shrapnel pinging off the armour all around him. "You bastards!" he shouted at the distant Bravo Company troops. "Don't tell me you don't know how to call in a grid reference!"

The close call was due to a breakdown in the battle group's high-tech navigation computer and orders quickly came in over the radio to prepare to clear the village "the old-fashioned way"—on foot, one house at a time. By now the sun was at its highest point in the sky and the temperature was climbing towards 50°C. While adrenaline and danger had rendered Denine oblivious to the growing heat during his desperate fight with the Taliban, he realized now that his sand-coloured camouflage uniform was soaked through with sweat under his body armour and he was feeling light-headed and lethargic: the first symptoms of heat exhaustion.

But there was no time to deal with that. With the LAVs now out of immediate danger, Denine had work to do. He and his soldiers had used up hundreds of bullets and grenades fighting off the ambush and they needed to restock their supplies before they launched their sweep through the village on foot. He sighed and stepped out the back ramp, telling the soldiers still packed inside to sit tight. "Stay here: stay with the car," he ordered. "I'm going to run over there and tee up some ammo, get re-bombed and bring it back."

He'd gone only a few feet when he noticed he was being followed by Private Calvin Berube, one of the youngest soldiers in his section. "Sarge, you always told us never to move around by ourselves," the private told him earnestly, "so I'm going with you."

"Oh, for fuck's sake," Denine replied, taking a deep breath. "It's good that you're listening to what I've been saying, but there's times when you can just do it quicker yourself."

The young private's expression grew stubborn and Denine realized it would be faster to avoid an argument. "Oh, c'mon then, let's go."

Denine and his escort jogged from one vehicle to another, looking for ammunition. No one had any to spare. "How do we come out here, knowing we're gonna be gettin' into shit like this and we don't have any extra ammo ready?" he wondered to himself.

A few minutes later, he found Ron Gallant, his platoon warrant officer, who had rifle ammunition for him, but no grenades to replace the dozen that Oz had lobbed at their attackers. By the time he reached the vehicle of his platoon commander, Captain Jon Snyder, Denine was dripping in sweat. "Jonny, you got any extra M203 [grenade] rounds?" he asked, squinting up at the young officer sitting in the turret of his LAV.

"No, and you better get back to your car: we got orders coming down in a minute," Snyder replied.

Denine swore and headed back to his car. On his way he met a LAV from Charlie Company's 7 Platoon, which had been called up from Kandahar when the firefight turned into a major engagement. They were able to hand him several replacement grenades. "Thank God for Charlie, or we'd be fucked," he said, tucking the bandolier of grenades under one arm and trotting the rest of the way.

Denine and his section barely had time to reload before the order came to dismount from their vehicles and begin the laborious process of clearing the village on foot. Exhausted and overheated, Denine led his section into the tangle of alleys and footpaths, stopping outside each building or compound and going through the room-clearing procedures they had rehearsed hundreds of times back in Canada. The stocky sergeant stopped just short of every door and barked, "Doorway: Stack!" His soldiers lined up outside the door or opening, backs against the wall and packed close together like football players in a huddle. When Denine gave the signal, the soldiers piled through the door in a rush and fanned out to cover the entire interior, their rifles at the ready, muzzles scanning from side to side seeking any threat. Each soldier would shout "Clear left!" or "Clear right!" as they determined that their area of responsibility was safe. Once they had all reported in, Denine would call: "Room clear!" The same steps would be repeated for any other rooms inside the building before moving on to the next.

Clearing every building, walled enclosure and hut in the village was an exhausting task in the crushing heat. Every time the soldiers bundled through a doorway, their adrenaline was pump-ing, anticipating a room full of the enemy on the other side. But they found little evidence of the Taliban who had been firing at them just an hour earlier. When they reached the scene of their brief but fierce firefight with the rocket-propelled grenade team that had ambushed their LAV, Denine found bloodstains in the dust, shiny brass bullet casings scattered everywhere and a pair of abandoned sandals. The Taliban gunman he had shot at the opening of the firefight was nowhere to be found. The only sign that he had been there, firing at Denine and his section from behind the corner of the wall, was a small pillow he had kneeled on and a pair of scuff marks in the hard dirt of the foot-path beyond. "Drag marks," Denine said, pointing out to his soldiers the trail in the dirt where the Taliban had clearly dragged away their dead and wounded.

In the hour the Canadians had spent rearming and regroup-ing, the Taliban had swept the battlefield clean. Almost. Denine and the other soldiers found small black chunks of hashish amid the empty casings indicating where gunmen had been firing, drugs dropped by the Taliban fighters in their haste to escape the advancing Canadian troops. "They all carried dope on 'em," Denine said later. "They were smoking up before every fight."

The bulk of the Taliban cell had slipped away to the north, using ditches, grape orchards and covered pathways to hide from the Canadians. But the village was not completely deserted. Although the civilian occupants were long gone, the soldiers clearing steadily through Bayanzi's complex web of walls and buildings found small groups of Taliban hiding in obscure cor-ners. Many had thrown away or hidden their weapons and all surrendered without a fight.

Denine's section found one small group of men, unarmed and squatting together in the corner of a small walled com-pound, glaring at the Canadians as they piled into the tiny court-yard with their weapons bristling. One of his privates suggested they shoot them, just to be on the safe side: the men had clearly been part of the Taliban force that was occupying the village. "We can't just light 'em up for being in the wrong place at the wrong time," Denine said. "But keep an eye on them."

At the other end of the village, seven Taliban fighters were captured by Master Corporal Mike Burdge, a combat engineer attached to the battle group. Burdge and a small group of Afghan soldiers came around a corner and were abruptly face-to-face with the Taliban fire team, their assault rifles and machine guns laid aside while they rested and prepared a simple meal. They threw up their hands immediately and were taken prisoner without a shot being fired. The Canadians handed them over to the ANA, who sent them to the rear of the advance under guard.

The setting sun was lighting up the clouds of fine Afghan dust that still hung in the air by the time Denine and the rest of Charlie Company made it back to the relative comfort and safety of their LAVs. They had been fighting for nine hours and many were completely exhausted by the effort of working in the searing heat. They plodded back to the cars, sucking on the drinking tubes connected to water packs on their backs. The heat had warmed the water to bath temperature, making it unpleasant to swallow. Still, it was better than nothing. Many, including Denine, were so dehydrated that they had to pause during the march back to retch up the water almost as fast as they had gulped it down.

The soldiers collapsed into the backs of their cars, sprawling on the two long benches inside the troop compartment and switching the small, overworked fans onto high in an attempt to get some relief from the heat. They had been back for only a handful of minutes when they heard the muted roar of a rocket-propelled grenade racing overhead and the popping sound of gunfire coming from the north. The Taliban that had slipped away from Bayanzi had run into a platoon of B Company, and a firefight had erupted at a compound just northwest of the main village.

"Holy fuck, here we go again," Denine said wearily.

Marty Dupuis had spent the long, hot day in a blocking position outside of the village with Charlie's 9 Platoon and a troop of the battle group's combat engineers, lying in wait for the fleeing Taliban. He had anxiously followed the nearly two-hour firefight over the radio, hoping for the best for his soldiers embroiled in the action just to the south of his position.

Eventually the firing died away and Captain Jay Adair, the acting commander of Bravo Company, called in to say the Taliban were fleeing the village ahead of the Canadian attack, pushing off to the west and north. Dupuis quickly ordered his long, strung-out line of LAVs to take up "hasty" blocking positions to seal off the enemy's retreat. The Taliban, however, saw the Canadian vehicles moving through the open fields north of the town and veered away to the west, taking cover in a cluster of buildings just outside the village.

Dupuis' vehicle, positioned with LAVs from the combat engineers attached to Charlie, began receiving potshots from scattered Taliban riflemen. Despite the failing light, one shot did manage to hit a vehicle of his blocking force, shredding one of its eight tires, but otherwise there was little damage. Dupuis shrugged it off as "nothing fancy."

But soon after sunset, with the last daylight fading from the battlefield, the retreating Taliban came into contact with B Company's soldiers just north of Bayanzi. Nich Goddard's FOO team had been racing back and forth along the battle lines all day, her quiet voice an almost constant presence on the radio as she directed artillery fire and air strikes onto Taliban positions. As Bravo Company and Charlie's 8 Platoon had advanced steadily through the village, Goddard's LAV had moved with them, shifting positions constantly to get the best vantage point from which to call the shots for the distant guns. From his position north of the highway, Dupuis could barely make out Goddard's FOO LAV, two kilometres away and advancing with the lead platoon of Bravo Company, perilously close to the enemy. He looked away for a moment and when he looked back, the distant firing line of vehicles was shrouded in dust and wheeling and scrambling to move rapidly out of their positions. "What happened?" he asked his crew.

Neither his gunner nor driver could tell, but a few seconds later a distraught voice came over the airwaves: "My Sunray's down! My Sunray's down!" "Sunray" was the radio code-word for the commander of a crew, and the commander of the FOO crew was Nich Goddard.

Dupuis' line of LAVs was now being targeted by harassing fire from the Taliban in the compounds below, rounds zipping around or overhead. While the firefight continued, the soldiers from Bravo Company who were nearest Goddard's stricken artillery LAV tried to read out a list of "zap numbers." A four-digit code number was assigned to every member of the Canadian contingent, so named because they were designed to be read out over the airwaves to identify soldiers who got "zapped," meaning killed or wounded. But the list of numbers the radio operator had been given were written in badly smudged pencil and Dupuis, scribbling down the numbers he heard over the radio, knew they weren't right. "That doesn't match," he said. "That number's not anyone's."

He felt a brief rush of guilty relief, thinking that perhaps Goddard hadn't been the one hit. But a few seconds later, it became obvious that it had to be the popular artillery captain. Dupuis sighed and got on the radio. "I don't know if this helps but we verified the zap number of that call sign [Nich Goddard] before we deployed," he told the frustrated radio operator with B Company. He slowly and clearly read out Goddard's string of numbers and held his breath, hoping against hope that it had not been Goddard who he had seen drop from sight when the grenade hit.

After a long silence, the reply came over the radio net: "Yeah, that's her."

A few kilometres away, Hope was listening to the exchange over the radio with a hollow feeling in his gut. Even before the correct zap number had been read, he knew that Goddard was dead. For several minutes he had not heard her calm, collected voice over the air, distinctive not just because it was the only female voice on the battle group's radio net but because of her steady, unflappable coolness. For Hope, the absence of that voice rang out louder than any of the explosions and gunfire he could hear in the background of most of the transmissions that night.

Mike Denine also heard the anguished cry of Goddard's technician after she was hit. "You could hear it in his voice, the poor bastard. He was almost crying."

He and the rest of Charlie could see the flashes of fire from the Taliban gunmen hiding in a line of trees and brush more than five hundred metres or more away—extreme distance for their rifles, but well within range of the LAV's big chain guns and machine guns. They immediately began firing at the hidden gunmen, the rapid-fire thumping of the guns and the chatter of the machine guns echoing off the nearby walls and buildings.

Denine was certain the popular artillery officer was dead. While other units were urging the distraught FOO tech to "Get out of there," Denine calmly continued directing his LAV's fire onto the trees and ditches where the Taliban were still shooting at a pinned-down platoon from B Company. The platoon finally extricated itself from the Taliban killing zone and within minutes a barrage of artillery shells began to thump into the tree line where the enemy ambushers were taking cover, lighting up the night with a series of earth-shaking explosions. A pair of heavy, precision-guided bombs followed, tracking from a U.S. Air Force bomber high overhead to land directly on a compound behind the tree line where more Taliban had been spotted.

Denine watched the light show from a safe distance, taking a breather with the soldiers in his section after the long, hot day's fighting. He felt no sympathy for the Taliban fighters caught in the centre of the fierce storm of fire and steel. "You guys want to fuck around with us, well, here you go," he said coldly.

Back in his position north of the village, Dupuis had been forced to temporarily put aside his grief at Goddard's death and focus on the still-raging firefight. He had called up Charlie's 7 Platoon in Kandahar and ordered them to join the fight and bring in badly needed ammunition and water to resupply 8 Platoon and B Company after their long battle in the village below. As the reinforcements raced towards the Panjwayi along Highway One, they were ambushed within sight of Dupuis and his blocking force.

The ambushed LAVs immediately opened up on their attackers with machine guns and rapid bursts from the 25-mm cannons, which quickly silenced the Taliban's fire. Dupuis listened anxiously to the radio chatter from the brief but ferocious firefight, crew commanders directing their gunners onto targets and excitedly warning each other of incoming fire. "They're taking a shitload of fire—an insane amount of fire," he said, twisting around in his commander's hatch to watch the play of machine-gun tracers and rocket-propelled grenades launched from the Taliban ambushers, and the LAV's high-explosive shells.

Master Corporal Matt "Kiwi" Parsons was in command of one of Dupuis' long line of LAVs deployed along the bare hillside to the north of the highway, and had a perfect spot from which to watch the ambush. His first thought on seeing the Taliban tracers arching towards the Canadian vehicles, occasionally ricocheting skyward off the LAVs' armour like a fireworks display, was that the fight looked like a video game. "Hey wow!" he blurted out. "That looks pretty cool."

According to all the army training manuals, the standard

procedure for a convoy being ambushed was to get the vehicles off the "X" (the target area of the ambush) as quickly as possible. But the Canadians eventually learned that such ambushes were one of their few opportunities to pin down the Taliban and bring their vastly superior firepower to bear. Their standard operating procedure was quickly adapted: now, the ambushed vehicles stopped in their tracks, swivelled their turrets to face the attack and poured cannon and machine-gun fire down on the ambushers. This tactic proved highly effective.

After one early ambush along Highway One, the LAVs poured so many high-explosive shells into the orchard where the Taliban were hiding that when soldiers eventually dismounted to sweep through the area, they returned to report that they weren't sure how many enemy fighters there had been. "All that's left is meat," said one private.

Still, contact was contact, and Dupuis held his breath during the short, sharp firefight, avoiding talking on his radio while the fight was going on. After the fire died away, however, he quickly called for a report. To his relief, the platoon warrant officer reported only minor damage to their vehicles. The warrant was in the midst of listing the details of the damage when he suddenly stopped. "Holy shit!" he blurted out. A second ambush group had hit them from the opposite side of the highway, firing a barrage of rocket-propelled grenades at the stopped LAVs. The Canadian gunners calmly swivelled their turrets and began firing at the new threat.

Dupuis watched the second ambush with growing anger. He had been worried that one of the vehicles in the convoy would become a "mobility kill"—unable to move because of battle damage. That would have meant diving into the fight with his blocking force to get the crew of the stricken vehicle out of harm's way and an hours-long operation to recover the immobilized LAV. But watching the Taliban hit his soldiers again enraged Dupuis and he called up Parsons and his other crew commanders and told them to prepare to sweep through the ambush site. "I just lost a good friend and now those bastards are ambushing my troops," he thought. "Time to kick some ass."

But before he could charge down to hit the Taliban ambushers, Hope called in on the radio and told him to stand down: there was no air support available and it was nearly night. And by then the brief fight was over—the Taliban had either fled or were killed—and the line of Charlie LAVs below Dupuis resumed their trip down the highway, linking up with Dupuis' blocking force to take up defensive positions on the bare ground north of the ribbon of pavement for the night. The only injury was a private who broke his ankle jumping off the back of his vehicle after the platoon joined up with Dupuis.

Bravo Company and its attached platoon from Charlie had pulled back to a building on the southern edge of Bayanzi. It had become a prominent landmark in the region—a long, low and relatively new building painted with a coat of whitewash, which they immediately nicknamed the White Schoolhouse. The Taliban had looted the school of all its furniture and painted Pashtun slogans on the walls, warning villagers to keep their children away or face death. When the exhausted soldiers arrived at the schoolhouse they were met by a small detachment of troops from the ANA. The Afghan soldiers were guarding thirty-two Taliban prisoners captured in and around the village during the day-long fight. Denine eyed the prisoners curiously. Like almost every Afghan he'd seen they were all rail thin, but the Taliban fighters seemed for the most part painfully young, younger even than the soldiers in his own section.

One of the prisoners had a cell phone hidden in a pocket of his dark grey khameez—an item which had somehow been missed when he was searched. He was eventually caught with the phone to one ear, talking softly to some of the Taliban who had escaped the Canadian onslaught. An ANA soldier ripped the phone out of his hand before the prisoner could hang up and listened for a moment, then laughed at what he heard on the other end of the line and shouted into the phone in Pashtun. One of the translators explained that there was a Taliban commander on the other end of the line, threatening to come back into the village, attack them immediately and wipe them all out. The Afghan soldier had told him: "Come on down. Come on, and we'll be ready for you."

When the conversation was translated for them, the Canadians chuckled at the Afghan soldier's bravado, but Denine wasn't taking any chances. The platoon put their LAVs in a defensive square, their guns and night-vision sights pointed outwards in a "ring of steel."

Denine stretched out beside his LAV to catch some badly needed sleep and watched the headlights from dozens of civilian trucks shuttle back and forth on nearby Highway One all night, many of them likely carrying away Taliban wounded or dead. There was talk of calling in a U.S. Apache attack helicopter to strafe the trucks with its deadly arsenal of automatic cannons and missiles, but it was impossible to confirm whether the vehicles were convoying Taliban out of the battlefield or carrying civilians fleeing the fighting. "You know what they're doing, but you can't prove it," the sergeant said in frustration to one of the other Charlie Company NCOs.

Denine and the rest of the exhausted Canadians continued to watch as the enemy was being carried beyond their reach.

Bayanzi
May 18
0430 hrs

At first light, Captain Jon Snyder sent Denine and his section ahead on foot to search the compound that had been battered by bombs and Canadian artillery the night before, looking for any sign of the Taliban fighters that had defended it. The troops had just arrived and were carefully scanning the doorways and rooftops of the small buildings inside when a small car came chugging into sight. The driver took one look at the Canadians, jammed on the brakes, and threw the car into reverse, trying to back his dilapidated vehicle through the narrow lane from whence he had come.

Despite their heavy body armour and gear, the Canadians gave chase on foot and managed to catch the white Toyota as it became stuck negotiating a sharp corner. Denine was in hot pursuit when his foot came down awkwardly on a rock. He felt something snap, his ankle rolled, and he crashed heavily to the ground as daggers of pain shot up his leg. When his troops ran back to help, Denine looked up and snarled: "Don't stand there lookin' at me," he said, waving at the small car now wedged up against a mud-brick wall. "Go get him!"

While his soldiers took the driver prisoner, Denine hobbled back to his LAV helped by one of his young privates. After the area was cleared and confirmed to be free of Taliban, weapons and booby traps, the sergeant called his eight soldiers to the back of the vehicle. He stood in front of them, wincing and holding on to the side of the LAV for support.

"Look at this," he said, pointing at his swollen ankle. "I can't dismount with you guys, so I'll have to stay up in the LAV. If anyone's got any heartache with that, let me know now."

His corporals and privates looked at each other for a second. The idea of going into a mission without Denine, who had been their sergeant for the long months of pre-deployment training and, for some members, even longer, was unthinkable. Finally, Oz piped up: "Fuck no, Mike."

The platoon medic was called in. After taking off Denine's sand-coloured combat boot and examining the injured joint, he shook his head. "That's broken, man. We're not going to be able to keep you here. We're sending you home," the medic said.

"Not fucking likely," Denine said through clenched teeth. "I'm staying."

Marty Dupuis and the bulk of Charlie's LAVs spent most of the day racing up and down Highway One or one of the handful of easily passable main roads within the heart of the Panjwayi, searching for the hiding place where the Taliban they had fought so hard the day before had gone to ground. Captain Massoud's network of cell-phone informants was working overtime but the Taliban seemed to be both everywhere and nowhere. Reports flooded in of sightings, possible hiding places and suspected weapons caches all over The Panj. Dupuis and his LAVs were sent from one site to the next, sometimes getting diverted before they even reached one suspected Taliban hiding spot to check out another. Either the Taliban were moving very quickly, or there were a lot more of them in the Panjwayi than the Canadians had suspected.

"It's a shit show—a complete fucking shit show," Dupuis grumbled, scribbling down the coordinates of the latest target and hurriedly looking for the village on the map.

After a tiring and fruitless day of searching for the elusive Taliban, Charlie and the rest of the battle group were finally ordered back to KAF just before darkness fell. As the weary, dust-coated soldiers drove through the darkened streets of Kandahar, Afghans rushed out of their shops and houses to line the side of the road and watch the long Canadian convoy roll past. Dupuis smiled as the crowds waved, cheered and gave the thumbs-up to the soldiers. When the vehicles slowed because of traffic or to negotiate a turn, some of the Kandaharis even tossed oval loaves of their flat Afghan bread up to the troops, who caught them and grinned back at the cheering crowd.

Mike Denine rode back to KAF in a Bison armoured ambulance, lying on a stretcher as the medics delivered him straight to the Canadian field hospital. The military doctor made a brief examination of Denine's badly swollen ankle and shook his head. The sergeant's tour of duty in Afghanistan was over: he was off to the U.S. military hospital in Landstuhl, Germany, where all seriously wounded or injured soldiers were sent.

Denine got up from his hospital bed and defiantly hobbled around it once, forcing himself to keep his expression stoic (although he admitted later he was "screamin' like a little kid inside"). "Sir, there you go—it's not broken," the brawny sergeant told the doctor. "If it was broken, I couldn't stand on it."

The doctor reluctantly agreed to wrap Denine's ankle in athletic tape and let him go, but insisted that he be restricted to bed rest for the next seven days. It was only after his return to Canada that Denine learned he had torn several ligaments and tendons in the ankle and a more extensive X-ray discovered several hairline fractures.

As he limped out of the field hospital, wincing every time his injured foot met the rough crushed gravel that had been laid down to minimize the ever-present Afghan dust, all Denine could feel was relief. "I was petrified of gettin' sent back while the guys were still there," he says. "I mean, who would they get to take over? What if one of them got hurt?"

Denine eventually made his way back to the BATs, where the rest of Charlie Company had collapsed in their bunks. In the distance, he could see lights and hear music by the Canex compound, the military general store located near the centre of the huge base. The area was a hub of the recreation facilities for the forty nations represented in the coalition fighting in southern Afghanistan. Most of the soldiers working in KAF were American or British, but there was a sizeable Dutch contingent, a Romanian battalion and a number of French, German and Australian soldiers, among others. When Denine asked Ron Gallant what all the commotion was, Gallant told him it was the CanCon show—a morale-boosting music and variety concert put on by the Canadian Forces for most overseas tours.

"If your guys want to go up there and watch the show they can," the warrant officer said. "And if you want you can have two beers, but you gotta buy them yourselves."

KAF, as well as the much smaller PRT camp in Kandahar City, were officially dry bases: no alcohol was allowed. This restriction was the cause of much griping among the rank-and-file members of the Canadian task force, so the chance for a cold beer and a relaxed atmosphere would normally have been welcome. But after three days of fighting in the brutal heat of the Afghan summer and the loss of Nich Goddard, neither Denine nor most other members of the battle group felt like celebrating. Particularly if they had to pay for their two beers. "Fuck that!" Denine said succinctly and stomped off to find his bunk in the rows of beds inside the cavernous white BAT.

Camp Mirage, United Arab Emirates
May 18

Bill Fletcher had barely landed in Camp Mirage, on his way to a three-week vacation with his wife, when he got the news that something bad had happened to his company back in Kandahar.

Camp Mirage is the main staging base for the Canadian mission in Afghanistan, the transit point for all supplies, equipment and soldiers destined for Kandahar, and is so named because officially the Canadian government will not acknowledge its existence. The camp is located at one end of the airport in Dubai, in the United Arab Emirates in the southern end of the Persian Gulf, and Canada was allowed to lease the facility only on condition that it not reveal which country it was using to support its troops in Afghanistan. The Emirates were sensitive about the potential domestic fallout from being seen to support what amounted to a war on fellow Muslims. Still, the camp's existence was not much of a secret: cab drivers in Dubai, one of the most westernized and cosmopolitan of Arab cities, will cheerfully drive anyone who asks to its front gates.

Fletcher checked in with the base's operations centre, accompanied by Major Nick Grimshaw, the commander of Bravo Company who was also heading out on leave, and was told that there had been a fatality. "There's been one female KIA [killed in action] from call sign Three [Charlie Company]," the duty officer told him. "That's all we know."

For Fletcher that was enough. Before flying out of Kandahar, he had seen the platoon off on its way into the Panjwayi and he knew there had been only two females in its ranks: a medic and Nich Goddard. He knew immediately that it was Nich and the news hit hard. He gathered the dozen or so troops from Kandahar who were in Mirage on their way to or returning from leave and broke the news. Then he went looking for Ryan Jurkowski, who was returning from two weeks with his family in Australia and New Zealand.

Jurkowski had already heard. He had landed just before Fletcher and was told by a warrant officer from Charlie who had been in camp on his way out. The news left him numb with shock. Jurkowski had worked closely with Goddard, more than almost anyone else in Charlie except her own FOO crew, and he spent the rest of the night brooding about her death. The two had spent four months living and working together in the most stressful and intense environments imaginable and had become friends, talking about getting together with their spouses after they returned from Afghanistan. Jurkowski agonized over the "what ifs." During missions, Goddard had almost always set up her observation points close to him and his company headquarters

LAV, and he argued with himself for hours that if he had been in Bayanzi during the firefight in which she was killed he might have been able to protect her isolated FOO vehicle.

Fletcher too was struggling to cope with Goddard's death. He was particularly upset about the unfortunate timing that had his flight to Thailand leaving in the morning, before Goddard's body would return from Kandahar on the first leg of its long journey home. As Charlie's OC, Fletcher felt a deep obligation to his soldiers, both in life and death, and it troubled him greatly that he would miss Goddard's last trip home. By the time he met up with Jurkowski, both men were visibly upset.

At around 10 a.m. the next morning, the soldiers in camp assembled on the tarmac to see off Goddard's flag-draped coffin. The handful of soldiers from Charlie and from Goddard's own unit, the 1st Regiment, Royal Canadian Horse Artillery, were in front of the long ranks of troops that lined the path into the back of the waiting military transport plane. Jurkowski was irritated at the ceremony, which was longer and more involved than the brief but emotional farewells when the bodies of fallen soldiers left KAF. He felt it was being stretched out for the sake of the people in Camp Mirage, which was little more than a transit point in and out of Afghanistan. "All she needed was a salute from her brothers and sisters in arms," he thought. "Her closest brothers and sisters in arms have already bid her farewell and those who matter most will greet her in Canada."

As the flag-draped coffin passed, Jurkowski and the rest of the soldiers from Task Force Orion brought their arms up in unison, saluting Goddard one last time as she passed. They held the salute until the jet taxied down the tarmac, took off and disappeared into the haze over the Persian Gulf.

CHAPTER SIX

"Be careful what you ask for."

One day after the firefight at Bayanzi, the largest and most intense engagement of the mission to date, Ian Hope got word of a change in plans. The Canadians were ordered out of the Panjwayi by the commanders of Operation Enduring Freedom. The U.S. generals that led the operation were in Bagram, an old Soviet air base north of Kabul that had been converted into a huge American facility that dwarfed even KAF. The generals declared the Panjwayi a temporary special forces operation area—out of bounds to any coalition military units but the commandos of the U.S. Delta Force, the British Special Air Service, Canada's Joint Task Force 2 or their allied units. Special forces teams were planning a "hit" on an HVT—military jargon for high-value target; likely a senior Taliban or al Qaeda leader—who was believed to be hiding in or around a village in the southern end of the district.

The restriction irked the Canadians, none more so than Hope, who was itching to get back into the Panjwayi to find out exactly what the Taliban was up to. But he knew the restriction made sense. Special forces operate in small, mobile teams, often without recognizable uniforms, so there was a strong possibility that a regular army unit could blunder into one of their teams and mistake them for the enemy.

To most of the soldiers, the enforced absence from Panjwayi meant a few precious days of rest in the relative comfort of KAF and the chance to repair any damage to their vehicles and weapons. Despite the dozens of potentially deadly RPGs launched at them, including several that had ricocheted off the sloped armour, the LAVs were all still roadworthy. Even call sign Golf One Three, the forward-observation LAV in which Nich Goddard had been killed, required only relatively minor repairs. After spending more than four weeks living out of the backs of their vehicles or in the rough-and-ready forward bases in Helmand Province in April, most of the troops were more than happy to sleep in their bunks instead of on a patch of rocky ground behind their vehicles. More than a few were also looking forward to a hamburger or pizza from the fast-food franchises at the board-walk, a recreational complex just five minutes' walk from the BATs (including a Burger King, Pizza Hut and eventually, thanks to the large Canadian presence on the base, a Tim Hortons).

But not everyone was happy to be out of the fight, however temporarily. Three days after the battle at Bayanzi, Kiwi Parsons pulled his LAV into a small grove on the banks of the Arghandab for a meeting between Hope's Niner Tac and the officers and senior NCOs of Charlie. He pivoted his vehicle into its proper position in the defensive rectangle that the company had formed, their weapons facing outwards to defend against any threat from beyond the copse of trees. Kiwi had just hopped down from his turret to scrounge for cigarettes or a cup of coffee when he caught sight of Chief Warrant Officer Randy Northrup, the regimental sergeant-major. Kiwi lengthened his stride to catch up. The regimental sergeant-major was the senior non-commissioned officer in the battle group and an imposing figure in any regiment, responsible for the discipline and deportment of the soldiers but also acting as their representative to the commanding officer. And Kiwi had something on his mind.

He was in an irritable mood. Despite all the action Charlie had seen during the past few days, Parson's platoon had been spectators through most of it and he was angry that his boys had been denied the chance to put their years of training into practice.

"Sir, this is bullshit," he said when he finally caught up to Northrup. "Every other platoon in this company has been in a firefight but 9. When're we going to get a chance to get in the shit?"

Northrup listened carefully to Kiwi's complaints: his platoon was always getting the unglamorous work of being the blocking force, or routine patrols or roadblocks. Meanwhile, 7 Platoon had been sent by helicopter to fight in Helmand Province in April, and 8 Platoon had been sent into Bayanzi for the fighting two days earlier. When the list of grievances had wound down, Northrup smiled and slapped Parsons on the back. "Kiwi," he said calmly, "be careful what you ask for."

**Kandahar Airfield
May 24**

The special forces raids in the Panjwayi yielded few results—certainly not the top Taliban leaders the Americans had hoped to catch—and one week after the desperate fight at Bayanzi, Charlie Company was back in The Panj.

The American battle group the Canadians replaced had spent little time in the Panjwayi, so not much was known about the area. Hope's plan was for his own battle group to begin patrolling the villages and tracks scattered throughout the district, keeping their eyes out for signs of the enemy and making contact with the *maliks*, the head men of each of the hundreds of villages in the area. Officially, the Panjwayi was Bravo Company's area, but Hope wanted Charlie there to add some muscle to the operation. The officers called this type of work "developing the battle space": learning as much as possible about the ground on which they were fighting, including sizing up the locals to determine whether they were Taliban sympathizers, supporters of the current government or simple dirt farmers caught in the middle. The soldiers knew they were being sized up as well, not just by the Taliban lookouts they assumed were present in almost every village they entered, but also by the inhabitants. The Canadian Forces' credo for dealing with the resident population of any area where they operated was "firm, fair and friendly," but in Afghanistan the emphasis was on the first of the "Three Fs." The commanders of the task force knew that Afghans respected strength, and the Canadians did not want to be taken for patsies. The soldiers were told repeatedly how important it was to look like they meant business. "Present a strong, tough front and you'll be respected," they were told during the training leading up to the mission, "and the bad guys just might take one look at you and think twice about trying something."

And they were on the lookout for those bad guys—for signs that the Taliban had been in a certain village, for likely daytime hiding spots and for the paths the enemy travelled when they emerged after nightfall. One of the first patrols after Charlie returned to the Panjwayi was a battle-damage assessment (BDA) in Bayanzi. Their goal was to examine the scene of the fight, which occurred almost a week earlier, for evidence of what the Taliban had been doing there and just possibly for some clues to what they would do next. But when the Canadians returned, it was as if the day-long firefight had never happened. All signs of the Taliban who had swarmed in and around the clutch of low buildings along the village's twisting main road had vanished, save for a few fresh bullet holes in some of the walls. Only a handful of villagers were still living there, mostly old men and very young boys and all claimed ignorance of the Taliban's whereabouts.

Captain Ryan Jurkowski, Charlie's second-in-command, had finally made it back from Camp Mirage, barely in time to catch up with his soldiers. He jogged out of the back ramp of the Hercules transport plane that had flown him from the United

Arab Emirates almost as soon as it rolled to a stop in front of a dilapidated sheet-metal hangar that dated back to before the Taliban ran Afghanistan. He trotted almost the length of the base, his duffel bag bumping against his back the entire way, but when he finally reached the BATs he found them empty. "This is junk," he growled to the empty rows of bunks lining the arena-sized tent. "Where's my fucking company?"

He quickly grabbed his body armour, rifle and "go kit"—the rucksack carrying all of the gear a soldier might need in the field—and started hunting around the compound for a ride. Jurkowski eventually found a troop of gunners, members of the 1st Royal Canadian Horse Artillery Regiment that was attached to the battle group, that were headed out towards Panjwayi with their big 155-mm howitzers in tow. The guns were meant to provide long-distance fire support to the infantry of Charlie and Bravo Companies should they need it, but to Jurkowski they were a heaven-sent way of catching up with his troops. He asked to join up with their convoy, threw his bags into the back of his LAV and climbed up into the turret, reaching for the radio headset dangling from the roof so he could listen to the radio chatter during the short drive. The normally cheerful and outgoing captain was in a glum mood, and not only because he'd missed rejoining his company. Like Kiwi Parsons, he felt left out and more than a little annoyed that he had been absent when Charlie had seen its first major combat. Jurkowski had been in what he drily called "sticky situations" while on tours of duty before and didn't crave combat. But being away from Charlie when it was fighting in the Panjwayi felt to him like leaving his family to fend for itself. "All my soldiers have been in firefights but me," he muttered to himself. "This sucks."

The two days in Camp Mirage and the farewell ceremony for Nich Goddard had also taken their toll. Jurkowski knew he shouldn't dwell on it, but admitted later that he'd had "two very shitty days" after bidding a final farewell to Goddard. For the rest of the tour, for Jurkowski and every other soldier in Charlie, the absence of the cheerful and aggressively professional artillery officer was a constant cloud.

As the artillery troop drove out of KAF and turned onto the highway leading into the city, Jurkowski winced at the waves of heat cooking his face. When the line of dusty green vehicles reached the crowded streets of Kandahar his nose was assailed by the smell of the city's bazaars, the smoke from thousands of cooking fires, and the ever-present reek of open sewers. They were almost through the city when another Canadian convoy appeared around a corner, heading towards them and going in the opposite direction. Despite the goggles and khaki scarves the LAV crews wore—protection from Kandahar's swirling clouds of fine, powdery dust—Jurkowski recognized familiar forms and grinned at the passing vehicles.

Charlie was headed for the provincial governor's palace, a walled and heavily defended oasis of green in the dusty brown city, for a briefing before returning to Panjwayi. Jurkowski reached Marty Dupuis by radio, told him to slow down and ordered his own driver to do a U-turn. He radioed his thanks to the gunners for letting him join their convoy before racing after the rest of the company with a sigh of relief. He was back with Charlie.

After an hour-long briefing with Hope, ANA, ANP, and government officials the next day, Jurkowski had led Charlie back to KAF for a night's rest before returning to the Panjwayi. Their destination was an Afghan Army post on the eastern edge of the Panjwayi, just off Highway One. It was called the 530 Compound—little more than four mud and brick walls with coils of concertina barbed wire along the outside and sandbag-reinforced guard towers at each corner. There was a row of low buildings along one wall, but most were taken up with what the soldiers immediately declared "the worst shitter in Afghanistan," complete with a stench so powerful that the building was avoided even during the hottest parts of the day, when shade was at a premium. A simple metal pipe with a pump handle sitting in the middle of the hard-packed dirt ground served as the compound's water supply, but the Canadians stuck to the bottled water delivered daily by the boxload from Kandahar. Essentially, the 530 Compound was little more than a fortified parking lot for LAVs, as well as the pickups and small trucks used by the ANA. But for Charlie, it would be home for most of the next three weeks.

For almost the first time since they had arrived in southern Afghanistan, all three of Charlie's platoons were together, patrolling and sweeping through the areas where Captain Massoud's cell-phone network told them the Taliban were active. When Canadian patrols rolled into an Afghan village, they were usually met by an elder, or group of elders representing a village council. Often, the soldiers would be invited to a shady area for an impromptu shura. They would sit cross-legged and listen to the local farmers complain about the Afghan government or the security situation and ask subtly (or sometimes not so subtly) for western aid money. The men sat according to their status in the village: the closer a man sat to the head elder or elders, the higher his status or that of his clan. Where shuras were not held, the Canadians would talk with the elders as they walked through the village on their patrol.

But in most of the villages, no one other than the elders seemed eager to talk. The soldiers walked warily in a drawn-out single file of sand-coloured helmets and body armour, through villages that were largely deserted. Especially disconcerting was the absence of children, hordes of whom would have normally gathered at the novel spectacle of the foreign soldiers walking through their streets. In open country, the patrolling troops spaced themselves out widely to avoid creating a group that would tempt a Taliban fighter to attack several of them with one grenade or a burst of machine-gun fire. In the close confines of a village or compound, however, they tightened up to within a metre or less, everyone in the patrol watching their own designated arc of responsibility—a ninety-degree slice of terrain in front of them and off to one side or the other—so that there were eyes looking constantly in almost every direction. In some places, the patrols would cross a road or a ditch and suddenly find themselves in ghost towns, building after building and compound after compound entirely emptied of inhabitants. The day that Charlie had rolled back into the Panjwayi, they passed another mass exodus of villagers streaming out of the region, some in beaten-up cars packed to overflowing with people, others in wooden carts drawn by mournful-looking donkeys, and many more on foot. All had packed what furniture and belongings they could atop their transport.

The largely empty villages told the soldiers that the Taliban were in the area, but for the time being, at least, they were mostly keeping their distance. There were occasional brushes with the enemy, sometimes a "soft contact" such as a long-distance potshot or a fleeting glimpse of a suspicious group of men in the distance. In one sweep through four villages at the eastern edge of the region, Charlie surprised a Taliban cell and drove them into a platoon of Bravo Company that was blocking their retreat. The result was a short, sharp firefight that ended when the Taliban fled, once again taking away their dead and wounded so it was impossible to tell how badly they had been hit. Later that same day, several soldiers from Bravo Company and Reconnaissance Platoon (Recce Platoon) were ambushed, and only managed to escape by blowing holes in the high walls that had trapped them in the enemy's "kill zone"—areas to be swept by fire from rifles, grenades and machine guns when the ambush was triggered. The next day, Charlie and Bravo Companies chased the Taliban west to the village of Siah Choy and pinned down the small remnants of the cell in a grape-drying hut just outside the village, using the lethally accurate M777 howitzers of the artillery and strikes from U.S. Apache attack helicopters to trap the enemy, until eleven dispirited Taliban finally surrendered.

From intercepted cell-phone and walkie-talkie chatter, the Canadians knew the Taliban were disconcerted by Hope's tactic of driving the huge, intimidating LAVs right up to the edge of the fight and firing long bursts of deadly automatic cannon fire at close range, before disgorging infantrymen to clear out the centre of the village complexes. The speed and long reach of the ungainly-looking Canadian vehicles had also alarmed the Taliban leaders: intercepted enemy conversations had turned up a new Pashtun phrase for the tall, armoured LAVs. The enemy had begun calling them "the green monsters that shit white people," to the annoyance of Charlie's many non-Caucasian soldiers.

The patrols and sweeps through dozens of tiny villages and clumps of walls and huts made for long, gruelling and dangerous work for the soldiers, who sometimes had to march several kilometres in blistering heat only to find themselves in a firefight at the end. Charlie and Bravo Companies took turns, one acting as the blocking force to seal off the Taliban's escape routes while the other manoeuvred into position to attack and pin them down with rifle, machine-gun, LAV and artillery fire. The soldiers quickly learned that it was difficult to prevent the Taliban from melting into the landscape: many fighters would simply hide their weapons, pick up a hoe or shovel and just walk away, hiding among the farmers and labourers. Others could slink away, using the region's deep ditches and overgrown orchards and fields to cover their escape.

After four days of this, Hope called an "O group," or orders group, to discuss the lessons they had learned to date and to lay out his plans for the next few weeks. He picked a small patch of forested land on the edge of the Arghandab wadi and called in all of the officers and senior NCOs. Mike Denine, confined to

The officers and men of Charlie Company, 1st Battalion, Princess Patricia's Canadian Light Infantry, at their base in Spin Boldak on August 10, 2006. The Afghan and Canadian flags in the background are at half-mast for the four who died at the White Schoolhouse on August 3.

The soldiers of 9 Platoon pose in a field of opium poppies in Helmand Province. The battle group spent almost as much time in Helmand, the centre of Afghanistan's lucrative heroin-exporting industry, as they did in Kandahar, the province for which the Canadians were purportedly responsible.

Lieutenant-Colonel Ian Hope during one of his frequent news conferences Kandahar Airfield (KAF). Hope was well aware of his battle group's high profile in the Canadian media and of the importance of the dozens of embedded reporters that followed his soldiers' operations, but was often frustrated by the facile level of some the coverage. At least one reporter was barred from covering the battle group after repeatedly misquoting Hope's soldiers and distorting the outcome of their operations in the Panjwayi.

Hope and General Rick Hillier, the Chief of Defence Staff, hold an impromptu shura with a village elder in the Panjwayi region. One officer confided later that the only time he feared he would lose control of his soldiers was during Hillier's visit. He was convinced the troops were going to mob the popular general to shake his hand.

ppe enjoys his morning coffee atop his command LAV after a night leaguer (defensive sition) in Helmand Province. The task force commander made a point of being the st member of his crew to get up in the morning and of making the coffee for his men.

ajor Bill Fletcher, the commander of Charlie Company, holds a shura with village eld- in Helmand Province. The Canadians stopped to talk with locals whenever possible, effort that helped put a human face on the mission.

Master Corporal Matt "Kiwi" Parsons (left) takes a break on the rear ramp of his LAV with his driver Corporal Ben Weir. Parsons is wearing a New Zealand army camoufla smock, which he admits to wearing only when his superiors were out of sight.

Company Sergeant-Major Stevens, Major Bill Fletcher and Corporal Keith Mooney (le to right) during pre-deployment training at Canadian Forces Base Wainwright, Alberta

ptain Ryan Jurkowski, Charlie
mpany's second-in-command,
Panjwayi during a "rolling
len"—when the LAVs and
er vehicles of the company
uld replenish their fuel, food,
munition and the all-important
nking water in the field.

rgeant Vaughn Ingram (right) and Master Corporal Tom Cole rehydrate during a lull
operations. Heat caused almost as much trouble as the Taliban and the soldiers rou-
ely gulped down several litres of warm bottled water a day.

Ingram (left) and Corporal Chris Reid beside a LAV damaged during a Taliban ambush. Both men were killed on August 3 at the White Schoolhouse.

Her Excellency the Right Honourable Michaëlle Jean, Governor General and Commander-in-Chief of Canada, presents the medal of Military Valour decorations to Sergeant Michael Denine. PHOTO COURTESY OF COMBAT CAMERA

The fighting at Seyyedin, June 12. This photo was taken along the wall facing the grape-drying hut where a cell of Taliban took refuge against the Canadian attack. The LAV in the background belongs to Captain Marty Dupuis.

he soldiers of 9 Platoon were exhausted and filthy following the day-long action at yyedin. After clearing the position, the men immediately sought out the nearest patch shade, stripped off their heavy, smothering body armour, and gulped down bottles of ater. Bottom, left to right: Private Calvert, Corporal Rachynski, Sergeant Pat Tower, d Private Rustenburg after the fight.

Sergeant Pat Tower on patrol through one of the Panjwayi's winding streets.

Captain Jon Hamilton (left) and Sergeant Willy MacDonald of Reconnaissance Platoon share a smoke during a break in patrolling in the Panjwayi.

The Arghandab Mountains at dawn. From some spots in the lush grapefields of the Panjwayi, it was possible to see the grey and black mountains to the north and the red sands of the Registan desert to the south.

Charlie Company "hootch" at a forward base in Helmand Province. The Canadian soldiers became experts at improvising shelter from the blistering Afghan sun. Note the furniture, cobbled together from scrap wood, in the rear.

Captain Massoud of the Afghan National Police. He and his band of police officers, most of them ethnic Hazzaras or Tajiks from the north, were fighting the Taliban in the Panjwayi before the Canadians arrived in January of 2006, and his network of informants provided invaluable information to the Canadian battle group.

PHOTO COURTESY OF DR. SEAN MALONEY

A pair of Afghan National Army soldiers accompanying a Canadian sweep through Taliban territory in the Panjwayi. Although the Afghan troops had a lackadaisical approach to weapons safety that sometimes appalled their Canadian allies, their often reckless bravery impressed the soldiers of Task Force Orion. PHOTO BY ETHAN BARON

…zaar-i-Panjwayi—the Panjwayi District Centre.

…onvoy approaches a Forward Operating Base in Panjwayi District. The furrows in … background are mud banks supporting grape vines.

A platoon of Charlie Company leaves its base on Highway One on a sunset counter-ambush patrol.

Recce Platoon on patrol in the Panjwayi. Sergeant Willy MacDonald (foreground) an Captain Jon Hamilton (right) were partnered throughout the summer of 2006, living and fighting together for most of the battle group's six-month tour.

mplex urban terrain. The narrow, winding roads in the Panjwayi made life difficult
the Canadians, particularly the drivers of Charlie Company's LAVs, who had to
eeze 17-tonne armoured vehicles through roads designed for carts or small cars.

iew of the dense grape orchards and walled fields of the Panjwayi. In the foreground
two of the grape-drying huts that the enemy often used for shelter. Even the 25-mm
nons of the LAVs had difficulty penetrating their thick mud-brick walls, which could
nore than a metre wide. In the distance is the sand and gravel wadi of the Arghandab
er. The wadi meandered through the entire length of the Panjwayi and was used as a
;hway" by both the Canadian troops and the Taliban. PHOTO COURTESY OF COMBAT CAMERA

The 530 Compound. This Afghan National Army compound was little more than four walls, a handful of mud-walled buildings and what the soldiers called "the worst shitter in Afghanistan."

A Canadian patrol prepares to step off from its base on Highway One. Presence patro designed to show the local inhabitants that the Canadians could go where they want when they wanted to, were an important part of the task force's strategy in the Panjwa

Ramp Ceremony for Captain Nichola Goddard, the first Canadian female combat
ier to be killed in action since the Second World War. PHOTO COURTESY OF COMBAT CAMERA

Ramp Ceremony for the four soldiers killed in the August 3 battle at the White
olhouse. Almost all of Charlie Company travelled from their base in Spin Boldak
id farewell to their comrades.

PHOTO BY ETHAN BARON

the turret of his LAV by his swollen ankle, marvelled at the scenery as they drove into the tiny patch of greenery, a spit of land that would be surrounded by water on three sides during the river's brief period of flooding in the early spring, but which was now a rocky promontory overlooking the dry riverbed. Denine blinked at the pine trees and scruffy grass and shook his head in astonishment. "Looks like a provincial campground doesn't it, boys?" he said, bellowing over the vehicle's engine noise. "All it needs is a few RVs."

Niner Tac had arrived at the site first and Hope was smoking one of his thin cigars when the leaders of the two companies pulled in. The men exchanged glances when they saw their short wiry commander, normally a non-smoker, puffing on his cheroot. "We're in for some fun now," one sergeant said softly, with a smile. The troops had learned something during their training exercises in Canada—when their commanding officer was smoking, he was thinking. And the more he smoked, the hotter the action ahead was likely to be.

When everyone had gathered around his map, Hope got down to business. Their sweeps through the region had confirmed his suspicions that the Taliban were gathering in the Panjwayi in force. There were perhaps half a dozen villages where the enemy was sheltering, stockpiling weapons and ammunition and setting up command posts and rudimentary first-aid stations. The most problematic was the small grouping of villages known collectively as Pashmul, about a dozen small-to medium-sized communities in the eastern end of the Panjwayi that formed a sort of island within the district. The villages of Pashmul were ideal for the Taliban: close to both the Panjwayi District Centre—the main town in the area and the site of most of the Afghan government and police facilities—and to Highway One and the broad wadi of the Arghandab River, both of which led straight into Kandahar. Because Pashmul's dense maze of orchards, walls and tracks was too small for the LAVs to penetrate, the soldiers would have to root the Taliban out of each small cluster of walls and single-storey buildings by foot, an approach that would separate them from the firepower and protection of the LAVs. Bravo Company, under their second-in-command, Captain Jay Adair, was ordered to disrupt the Taliban in and around Pashmul and the Panjwayi District Centre. Then Hope turned to Jurkowski. "Ryan," he said, "I want you to stop the ambushes on Highway One."

For the past month or more, a group of Taliban, perhaps fifty all told, had been specializing in ambushes. All along a ten-kilometre stretch of the highway where the grape orchards of the Panjwayi lapped right up to the shoulders of the road, they had found places to attack Afghan police and army vehicles, coalition supply convoys and even the feared LAVs. The ambushes had begun in early May with sporadic strikes, mainly on police vehicles, but they were growing bolder.

The Taliban planned their attacks with patience and care, studying their chosen ground for days before an ambush. They memorized the location of every ditch and covered path leading in and out of the area, every place where they could lie in hiding until springing the trap, and every likely place to plant roadside bombs. Whenever possible, they used these devices to disable one of the vehicles in a convoy and trap the rest behind it, creating easy targets for their machine guns or rocket-propelled grenades. They would even aim their weapons in advance, planting sticks in the ground in front of a ditch or atop a wall by day so that all their RPG gunner had to do in the inky-black Afghan night was line up his launching tube with the tops of the sticks, a crude but effective trick. Some Taliban cells had night-vision equipment and even laser range finders, purchased in Iran or Pakistan, but they were the exceptions. They would set up several lookouts along the highway before an ambush, carrying cell phones or walkie-talkies to warn of the approach of a coalition convoy and of oncoming civilian traffic. The Taliban were careful never to ambush locals, which would have jeopardized their refuges in the nearby villages of the Panjwayi.

When they were ready, and when their lookouts had confirmed the approach of a target, the ambushers quietly and quickly moved into their predetermined positions. As the target vehicles reached exactly the right place, the cell leader would give the signal. His fighters would rise out of their hiding places and begin firing wildly, pouring machine-gun fire and RPGs onto the convoy for several minutes. Although usually inaccurately, the Taliban seemed to hope that by throwing a cloud of lead and high explosives at their target they would be able to wound or kill someone inside the vehicles. After a few minutes, or if they sensed that coalition artillery or air strikes were on their way in, the enemy would evaporate, racing away down one of the deep irrigation ditches that criss-crossed the Panjwayi to safety. Often, the Taliban would pull back to a second ambush site farther up the highway and wait patiently for the convoy to resume its trip, ready to strike again.

After Hope's briefing ended, Jurkowski sat in the cramped turret of his command LAV as it rumbled back to the 530 Compound and drew up a plan. The Boss had given the young captain a free hand, trusting him to get the job done any way he could, and Jurkowski did not want to disappoint him. He spent hours working on a plan that would turn the tables on the Taliban—a plan that would stop the attacks by ambushing the ambushers. The next day he gathered all three platoons of Charlie together in the dusty compound and laid out his scheme. "We want to totally disrupt the enemy's operations in this area. We want to stop these attacks and totally dominate the area," he told the assembled soldiers. "We want to own this battle space."

The plan was sound. While one platoon patrolled the villages and farm fields by day, talking to villagers and learning what they could of Pashmul's intricate maze of roads and pathways, a second platoon would hunt by night, slipping through the orchards to find and kill the Taliban's ambush cell. Charlie's third platoon would be the "flying squad," ready to race to the aid of either the day or night platoon should they find themselves in trouble. Each platoon would rotate through the jobs, to ensure that all got some rest and everyone got a crack at each assignment.

Although the nighttime counter-ambush patrols were quickly deemed the "fun" job, Jurkowski emphasized that the daytime patrols were just as important. "We need to understand the enemy to defeat him," he told the soldiers. "You have to understand this place and the best way to do that is to keep walking it, keep walking it, and keep walking it; by day and night."

The day patrols would have to contend with the moisture-sucking summer heat, scouring past ambush sites for clues to how the Taliban was setting their traps. Footprints or blood trails could tell the soldiers which path the ambushers took to get into position, while empty bullet casings, scorch marks from RPG launches or discarded water bottles indicated from where they had fired. Bubble gum wrappers quickly became a reliable sign that the Taliban had been watching the highway, even if there had been no ambush the night before. Local farmers couldn't afford chewing gum, but the much younger Taliban fighters, especially the volunteers from Pakistan's madrassas, could. The patrolling soldiers also learned to look for flattened patches of weeds or dirt, signs that the Taliban's lookouts had been in a "bed down" position, waiting to signal the ambushers that a target was on its way.

Despite Jurkowski's emphasis on the day patrols, Kiwi Parsons was delighted when he learned that his 9 Platoon would be the first on night shift, leaving the compound that very evening. The soldiers would have their body armour and the tactical vests that carried all their ammunition and equipment, their weapons and the all-important night-vision goggles. Night ambush patrols are supposed to leave in secret, helmets replaced by soft "floppy hats," and the soldiers' faces smeared with streaks of camouflage paint. But in Pashmul, that wasn't realistic: there were too many farmers and villagers in the area and the Canadians were bound to be noticed by someone, no matter how stealthy they were. So Jurkowski came up with a different idea: the patrols would walk down the main roads of the village, making a point of waving to the locals or talking to them until the last light from the sun was finally fading. Then, on a pre-arranged signal, the patrol would simply vanish into an orchard, a deep irrigation ditch or one of the forest-high fields of marijuana.

"So you go out looking like a normal presence patrol. If you come across locals, go up and say: 'Hi buddy! How's it going?' and all that," Jurkowski explained to the soldiers crowded around him in a corner of the 530 Compound. "They're going to be watching you, but at some point, you disappear into a grape field and they don't know where you are."

When the patrols were picked up the next morning, he would make as much of a production as possible out of their extraction, stopping traffic on the highway while the soldiers got back into their vehicles and ensuring that everyone in Pashmul knew they had been out there all night, not only unafraid of the Taliban but actively hunting them. "We want to let the locals and the enemy know that we own this ground: no one's going to fuck with us," Jurkowski added.

While the soldiers kitted up for their first night patrol, pulling on their gear and checking weapons in the lengthening shadows of the late evening, Kiwi and the other LAV crew commanders huddled to discuss ways of teasing the Taliban into setting up an ambush. The Canadians were looking for "triggers"—clues to what would prompt the enemy into setting up an ambush, which the dismounted infantry could then thwart by attacking them on the ground. They decided to try simply driving up and down

Ambush Alley at different times and in different formations after dismounting the soldiers inside, using one LAV far out in front as a stalking horse or driving the platoon's three vehicles very slowly down the darkened highway. They even considered faking a vehicle breakdown to lure the ambushers out into the open, a ploy they used more than once in the week ahead.

Parsons and the rest of 9 Platoon's LAVs rolled out of the 530 Compound just after dark, half an hour after platoon leader Captain Craig Alcock and the bulk of the soldiers had left the dusty compound on foot, in the single file of patrol formation. That left the three-man LAV crews free to roar out of the walled base's narrow gates to start trying to lure the Taliban ambushers out of hiding. Kiwi Parsons and his crew spent the rest of the evening "bombing around," as he gleefully put it, racing up and down Highway One and some of the more passable dirt roads just off the main route, trying as hard as they could to look like a tempting target. Every half hour or so, the three LAVs would stop on a piece of high ground, take up defensive positions and quietly watch for signs of activity in the cluttered grape orchards and fields to their south, using the long-range thermal sites in their turrets to penetrate the blackness for kilometres in all directions. But they saw nothing out of the ordinary and concluded that the Taliban had not taken the bait. "Right bait, wrong pond," one LAV gunner groused, voicing the disappointment of the entire platoon.

Meanwhile, Sergeant Pat Tower had been leading the platoon's dismounted soldiers on a slow, methodical sweep through the dense terrain south of the highway, picking their way slowly, quietly and carefully over walls and ditches and around farmers huts and the inevitable grape-drying huts. The platoon wove in and out of fields, along deep irrigation ditches and through jumbles of compounds and half-collapsed walls, carefully watching and listening to everything within two hundred metres of the highway. But they didn't sight anything more hostile than a handful of stray dogs, although Tower was surprised at the number of people who were up and about so late. "Jesus, there's no good time to be doing this, is there?" he whispered to Alcock as the patrol waited silently for another pair of farmers to walk past them in the blackness. Finally the heat—even with the sun down, temperatures remained over 30°C—and the soldiers' exhaustion led Alcock to call it a night. He radioed the LAVs to come and pick them up on the highway. The patrol was supposed to have returned to base on foot, but were so close to the road at the end that Alcock decided to load them onto the vehicles instead.

Kiwi Parsons rolled up to the shoulder and lowered his rear ramp for the tired and disappointed soldiers to board. "We know they're out there," one private said tiredly as he sagged onto the bench in the LAV's troop compartment. "We just couldn't fucking find them."

It was a tight squeeze to fit all the soldiers on board; only three of the platoon's LAVs had been sent out as the "bait" for the Taliban ambushers instead of the usual four. But the troops crammed themselves into the back of the LAVs, which raised their armoured rear ramps and veered back onto the pavement to begin rolling westward, headed for a small, ramshackle gas station where they planned to turn around and head back to their temporary home in the Afghan Army compound. Kiwi's car was bringing up the rear, just behind the artillery LAV Golf One Three, with Master Corporal Tony Perry's LAV in the lead.

The convoy had barely gotten back onto the highway when the ambush hit. Kiwi heard firing and then the snap of bullets overhead. Through his headphones came the voice of Tony Perry, so calm he sounded slightly bored: "Ambush left." Kiwi's driver was Corporal Chris Reid—one of the older soldiers in the platoon and widely considered the steadiest of Charlie's troops. Parsons breathed a quick thanks: he knew Reid wouldn't be flustered by the sudden eruption of fire and he ordered him to stop and pivot so the LAV was facing the ambushers. His gunner, Private Glen Van Mol, began swivelling the joystick that controlled his turret, swinging it back and forth in search of a target. He did not have to look very far: the field ahead of him was sparkling like a light show in the eerie green glow of the night-vision gunsight, lit up by muzzle flashes from Taliban machine guns and brighter flares from RPGs launching towards the LAVs. The enemy had chosen their ambush site well, a small field sheltered on either side by a large building and criss-crossed by low walls and deep ditches, which offered good protection from the Canadians' return fire. And they had waited until Charlie's LAVs were almost on top of them before they opened fire. "Fuck, they're close," Kiwi said to himself as he tried to bring his sites to bear on the ambushers, less than fifty metres away.

He shouted out the range and target to Van Mol, and the LAV's 25-mm main gun began thumping high-explosive shells at the Taliban's positions—a deep ditch running parallel to the highway and a series of shallower ditches and low walls just behind it. He could feel his vehicle rocking from the impact as the exploding grenades hit the road and pavement all around.

Kiwi ignored the blasts and scanned his night-vision screen for targets, firing at anything in his sites. After just five shots, the 25-mm chain gun jammed. As he had done in training a thousand times before, he switched to the coaxial machine gun, hosing down the area with 7.62-mm bullets while Van Mol tried to clear the stoppage in the bigger cannon.

"Get that fucking gun going!" Kiwi shouted at him.

"I'm trying to get the fucking gun going," Van Mol screamed back. "It's fucking jammed."

"Just get the fucking thing going!"

"Fuck you!"

"No, fuck you!"

The two swore at each other almost absent-mindedly, Van

Mol continuing to hammer away at the bolt of the jammed cannon and Kiwi's eyes never leaving the eight-inch-square screen of his gunsight, the crosshairs in pale green against the black and darker green display of the night-vision scope. He could make out two figures far to the rear of the rest of the ambushers, their body heat giving off a greenish-white glow in the gunsight's night vision. He swivelled the turret a few inches over to aim at the pair, who were standing behind a low wall watching the ambush from what they thought was a safe distance, and fired a long machine-gun burst that kicked up dirt and dust all around them. Both figures disappeared quickly, at least one falling backwards as if struck.

Pat Tower was in the back of the lead LAV when he heard the gunfire and explosions outside and looked over to the soldier next to him, Corporal Paul Rachynski, who was standing up in the rear air sentry hatch. All Tower could see of him was the dim outline of his baggy, sand-patterned camouflaged trousers, but he could hear him firing quickly and steadily back at the Taliban ambushers. Every few seconds he would thumb the release lever on the side of his rifle and an empty magazine would clatter down into the darkened troop compartment.

Tower could see tracer rounds zipping overhead through the open hatch above him and hear the explosions and the rattle of bullets bouncing off the LAV's armour. Then he felt something warm and wet spreading over the bench, coming from Rachynski's legs. "Hey, Rachynski!" he shouted, afraid that one of his soldiers was hurt and bleeding badly. "Are you hit?"

The corporal squatted down, patting down his stomach and legs with his hands. "No, I'm good!" he answered.

"Then what's all this? Blood?"

Rachynski stood again and looked around, then started laughing, despite the bullets whipping past. "It's water, just water," he shouted, still laughing as he took aim with his rifle and continued firing.

A Taliban bullet had struck a box of bottled water strapped to the back of the LAV, perforating the bottles and sending a gush of liquid—still warm from the heat of the day—down Rachynski's leg.

As quickly as the fight had begun, it was over. The Taliban abruptly stopped firing and disappeared, even from the LAVs' high-tech night scopes. It was only when the radio calls for a medical evacuation came in that Kiwi realized one of the cars in front of him had been hit.

530 Compound
May 30
0300 hrs

Ryan Jurkowski had been curled up on the ground outside his command LAV in the 530 Compound for a rare chance at uninterrupted sleep when he was awoken by the sounds of gunfire. The 9 Platoon LAVs had been ambushed about two kilometres from the base and the rising tide of small-arms and RPG fire carried clearly over the still night air, waking him instantly.

"Contact! Stand to! Get everyone in their vehicles!" he shouted, scrambling to his feet.

In a matter of seconds, the small compound was transformed into a hornet's nest of activity. Soldiers who had been sleeping a few moments earlier stumbled into defensive positions around the compound's walls and towers, their weapons at the ready, and LAV engines coughed into life, prepared to launch a rescue mission if necessary. Jurkowski strode over to the LAV where Marty Dupuis was manning the command post and fumbled the headset from the bank of radios in the back of the vehicle, pulling them over his ears just in time to hear the first reports of a LAV taking a critical hit from an RPG.

The radio call came from Sergeant Dave Redford, whose

ill-fated artillery LAV (the same vehicle in which Nichola Goddard had been killed) had taken another rocket-propelled
grenade hit during the confusion of the brief ambush. He listed
four casualties—two with serious injuries and two other "Priority Four" wounded. Jurkowski grimaced. Priority Four usually meant walking wounded, but it was also used to indicate
soldiers who were low priority because they were beyond help,
or VSA (Vital Signs Absent).

Redford rattled off the "zap numbers" of the wounded, and
Jurkowski felt the bottom of his stomach drop out. The artillery
LAV had been carrying Captain Craig Alcock and Sergeant
Vaughn Ingram, the senior sergeant in the platoon, and Alcock's
identity number was one of the Priority Four wounded.
Jurkowski and Alcock had become close friends over the past
year, and while they were at the regiment's home base in Edmonton they and their wives would socialize on most weekends,
having dinner or barbecues at each other's homes. Jurkowski
cleared his throat, trying not to let his anxiety show as he
radioed back. "Please confirm that none of the Pri 4s are VSA."

Most of Charlie's senior members had by now gathered
around the back of Dupuis' command LAV, lit only by the red
glow of its tactical light, and they held their collective breath
during the agonizing pause that followed. When the reply came
a few minutes later, it was in the unmistakable drawl of Craig
Alcock: "Ain't no VSAs here," he said. "The helo's inbound. I'm
jumping on the helicopter. Talk to you later."

Jurkowski, who prided himself on never showing emotion
"win, lose or draw" while in command, cracked a grin.

Jurkowski and the rest of Charlie got the full story a little
later. In the compartment of the patrol's second LAV—on their
way back to the 530 Compound after their unsuccessful hunt
for the Taliban—Ingram and Alcock had thought they could
relax, at least a little. The veteran sergeant was standing up in
the air sentry hatch just before the ambush was sprung, watching

the darkened landscape roll by. He had ducked back into the crew compartment to ask one of the soldiers inside for a cigarette just as the ambushers hit the convoy.

The Taliban gunner who launched the grenade made what Ingram later called "a one in a thousand" shot: the projectile found a tiny seam in the LAV's add-on armour, the thick plates of hardened steel bolted onto the exterior of the vehicle specifically to protect it against weapons like armour-piercing grenades. Fortunately, the grenade that punched through that tiny crack in the LAV's defences—a gap less than an inch wide—did not explode. Instead, it passed through the troop compartment in a fraction of a second and out the other side, spraying small shards of metal as it went and peppering the faces and arms of the soldiers inside.

Ingram heard the pop of the Taliban's AK-47s and RPK machine guns, followed by the roar of several rocket-propelled grenades. "I saw a big flash inside the vehicle," he said after the ambush, which became one of his favourite war stories. "That's when I felt the side of my face tore up and my shoulder, and that's when we went down." Although bleeding profusely, most of the troops were only slightly wounded. The soldier who had been standing in the second rear hatch next to Ingram, however, had been hit by a larger fragment that split his hand almost in half.

The grenade passed within inches of Alcock's head, so close that he began shouting: "My ears are on fire! My ears are on fire!" The platoon's medic, who was in the back of the same vehicle, had escaped unscathed but was so unnerved by the close call and the ensuing pandemonium that he fumbled the morphine injector and accidentally injected himself. With the medic rendered nearly unconscious, Alcock, Vaughn and signaller Tim Nolan gave each other first aid while the crew in the turret fought off the ambush.

Ingram had had a particularly narrow escape: the rocket-propelled grenade that found a chink in the LAV's armour had passed through the space where his head had been a moment earlier. If he hadn't ducked down to get a cigarette, it would almost certainly have killed him. "Smokin' saved my life, boys!" a bloodied but cheerful Ingram told everyone in Charlie after he was released from the Kandahar field hospital.

With both Alcock and Ingram wounded, Pat Tower took over as platoon commander. He ordered the LAVs to continue west down the highway to the nearby gas station. Once there, they could check over the vehicles to ensure there was no serious damage.

Meanwhile, at the rear of the convoy, Kiwi Parsons had his own problems. Although he and his LAV were almost untouched by the storm of Taliban fire, when the shooting stopped and the convoy carried on down the highway he found himself all alone on the ambush site. "I can't see shit, Kiwi," Reid said over the intercom.

Reid was driving with the headlights off, and the clouds of powdery dust kicked up by the fighting had turned the highway into a virtual fog bank, almost impenetrable even with night-vision equipment. Kiwi swore. "Shit, I screwed up," he said heatedly. "I'm going to get jacked up for sure."

As his vehicle rolled onwards at a crawl, Reid worried about drifting from the pavement and getting stuck in the soft earth just off the shoulder of the road. "This is not a good place to get stuck," he kept telling Kiwi over the intercom. Eventually, Kiwi managed to raise the rest of the platoon on the radio and caught up with them at the gas station just a kilometre up the road.

After a brief consultation, Tower decided to continue a few kilometres west along the highway to an empty field where the gunners of the Royal Canadian Horse Artillery had set up a fortified gun position for the night—a safer bet than running back through Ambush Alley to the 530 Compound. Medical evacuation helicopters were told to meet the platoon at the artillery site and fly the wounded soldiers out from there.

The platoon climbed back into their vehicles and roared out onto the highway again, speeding westward. Seconds later, about one hundred metres down the road, a burst of tracers once again reached out for the Canadian convoy and the flares of rocket-propelled grenades signalled the launch of more of the deadly projectiles. The other half of the Taliban's ambush cell had been lying in wait farther up the highway, in the dense cover of the orchards and farm buildings on the south of the road.

Perry called out: "Contact left!" not quite as coolly this time and Kiwi thought to himself: "Jesus, these guys just don't quit."

The LAVs swung their turrets to face the ambush and for the second time that night began to hammer away at their attackers. Van Mol had given up on clearing the main armament in a burst of profanity and was firing the coaxial machine gun, which was lined up parallel to the big 25-mm cannon and fired at exactly the same target in the LAV's gunsights. Then it too stopped, jammed like the cannon. Now only the two soldiers standing in the rear hatches, half in and half out of the vehicle's troop compartment, were firing back at the ambushers.

"Hell with it," Parsons said abruptly and stood up from his seat to use the smaller machine gun mounted on the top of the turret just in front of his still-open hatch.

The instant he popped out of the hatch a Taliban tracer round snapped past his head and an RPG exploded on the road just a few metres away. But Kiwi hardly noticed. He was thinking of the advice he'd been given by another LAV crew commander who had been ambushed a week earlier and had had to use the pintle-mounted gun: "Don't shoot off the goddamn antenna!" So intent was he on not shooting through the LAV's tall, whip-like radio aerials that Kiwi barely noticed the ongoing enemy fire. He only got the chance to fire off a few bursts before the second ambush ended, even more quickly than the first. After less than a minute of furious firing, the Taliban had retreated, dragging their wounded and dead with them. By the time the drivers, exhausted from the adrenaline boost of combat and the physical effort of muscling their cars up and down the highway all night, pulled into the artillery position, the U.S. Black Hawk medical evacuation helicopters were already there, waiting to fly the wounded back to KAF for treatment. The soldiers tumbled out of the vehicles, shed their bulky equipment and laid out on the ground behind their cars or in some cases inside the LAVs. They were asleep within minutes.

Not quite ready for sleep, Reid, a lanky thirty-four-year-old from Truro, Nova Scotia, walked up to Tower after climbing out of his driver's compartment in the front of Kiwi's LAV, shaking his head in disbelief. "Man, you wouldn't believe the explosion under your LAV," Reid said. "Fuckin' huge."

Tower frowned. "What explosion?"

"Two RPGs hit right under your front end," he said in his Maritime drawl. "A great big blast."

Tower shrugged. In all the excitement of the ambushes he hadn't even noticed.

Kiwi climbed down from his turret and looked in disbelief at the prostrate figures sprawled all around his LAV. "How the hell can you guys sleep?" he asked. "I'm totally wired—there's no way I can sleep."

The only answer he got was a few gentle snores. The soldiers of Charlie Company were getting used to combat.

A day after the ambush, Kiwi Parsons ran into Regimental Sergeant-Major Randy Northrup again. He was tired after long days and nights of patrolling, and the hours spent riding atop the turret of his LAV had covered him in a coating of fine, gritty Afghan dust. The sergeant-major looked him up and down and reminded him with a smile of his earlier complaint. "Remember what I said Kiwi? Still want to see more action?"

Kiwi just laughed.

CHAPTER SEVEN

"Spread the word, motherfucker."

South of Highway One
May 30

At first light the next day, a patrol went out to the ambush site to conduct a battle-damage assessment. They found blood pooled on the ground, discarded blood-soaked bandages and a handful of sandals and other articles of clothing, but no bodies. Once again, the Taliban had cleaned up after themselves. Ryan Jurkowski accompanied the patrol and ordered pictures taken of the entire scene. By counting the different blood trails and drag marks leading away from the ditch, walls and huts where the ambushers had been hiding, he estimated that Charlie had killed or wounded more than a dozen Taliban. The ambush cell was thought to be about twenty to twenty-five strong, meaning that Charlie had taken out half of their strength in a fifteen-minute firefight.

"They hit us, but we laid the slippers to them in the end," Jurkowski said with grim satisfaction.

The assessment patrol noticed something else: Pat Tower and the foot patrol had come agonizingly close to taking the ambushers by surprise. The dismounted members of 9 Platoon had been only one hundred metres short of the ambush site when they decided to stop and return to the LAVs. Had the troops continued their sweep of the area south of the highway for another few minutes, they would have stumbled upon the Taliban and hit them from an entirely unexpected direction.

"That would've fucked up the Taliban along Highway One far more than us driving through their ambush zones and shooting them up," Jurkowski thought, shrugging philosophically. "The Soviets never did that; they never got out of their vehicles."

Many of the Taliban commanders had learned their trade as mujahedeen insurgents fighting the Soviets in the 1980s and their tactics were designed to fight the Cold War–era Russian army. They were learning the hard way that the Canadians did not fight like the Soviets. Where the Russians tended to stick to the tactics in which they had been trained, following orders and plans largely without deviation, the Canadians were far more flexible. From the outset of the mission, the junior officers, sergeants and even corporals or privates of Task Force Orion were encouraged to use their initiative when faced with new threats and rapidly changing situations. The Soviets rigorously discouraged such independent actions by their small-unit leaders and changes in plans had to wait for approval from the top, slowing their reaction time to a crawl. Ian Hope's force was faster on its feet, did not follow any set pattern of movement or attack and used precision air and artillery strikes to trap the Taliban's fighters within minutes of the start of a firefight, pinning them down and killing or capturing them through their enormous superiority in firepower.

Jurkowski led the patrol from the ambush site to the nearest village, a tiny collection of mud huts and walls that showed signs of disrepair and poverty, even by Afghan standards. The ambushers had left an obvious trail of blood, drag marks and discarded equipment that clearly indicated they had retreated down one of its narrow streets. As the patrol entered the centre of the village, Jurkowski called for the village elder. Speaking through a translator, he began to quiz the man about the previous night's events. "Why are you letting these guys come and go through your village? To attack us?" he asked, careful to keep his voice level and calm.

The man claimed he knew nothing of the Taliban and had seen no one passing through his village last night. Some of the villagers even claimed not to have heard the fierce exchange of fire on the highway, just a few hundred metres away. Jurkowski shrugged sceptically. He had not really expected the Afghan to volunteer information that could endanger him and his family. Instead of grilling the villagers further, Jurkowski smiled and turned to point out the soldiers who had accompanied him on the patrol, all of whom had emerged unscathed from the previous night's ambush. He also pointed out the LAVs visible at the edge of the village. "These are the vehicles the Taliban tried to destroy," he said, his words relayed by the Pashtun translator. "You can see that they didn't succeed."

The elder's weathered face was impassive, but his dark eyes examined the LAVs and the Canadian soldiers standing nearby. Jurkowski smiled to himself as they left the village to return to the 530 Compound—at least in this village, the Taliban's fearsome reputation had been taken down a notch or two.

Charlie spent the next ten days and nights patrolling Ambush Alley, but never came closer to catching the Taliban ambush cell than they had on their first night out. The ambushes on the dangerous stretch of road, however, stopped entirely.

But the Taliban were still out there. Jurkowski discovered this for himself one night on a mission to help extricate a vehicle stuck in the soft sand of the Arghandab wadi, not far from the compound. After Charlie's three LAVs managed to tow the trapped vehicle free, the convoy headed back to the compound along the wadi, using its wide expanse of sand and gravel as a highway through the middle of the Panjwayi. The cars were running without lights, as they usually did, the drivers having flipped the night-vision goggles clipped to their helmets over their eyes.

Jurkowski had his goggles up and was watching the darkened skyline from the commander's hatch of his LAV with his naked eye. Out of nowhere, he saw the lights of a helicopter flying overhead, very fast and very low.

"If I don't have my lights on, why would a helicopter?" he asked himself, craning to watch as the light flashed overhead and then began to arc down towards the ground.

That seemed even odder. "No reason to land here," he mused, still watching the sinking bright light. "And there's no noise from the blades from the helicopter."

Jurkowski shrugged. "Pilots," he thought dismissively.

He asked the rest of his crew on the LAV's intercom if they had seen the helicopter, which had by now vanished into the darkness. None of them had and Jurkowski began to get suspicious. A few seconds later another bright light flew towards the convoy from the distant north shore of the wadi, its slow curving trajectory bringing it directly towards the line of Canadian vehicles.

With a jolt, Jurkowski realized that what he had seen soaring overhead was no helicopter. "RPG incoming! PUNCH, PUNCH!" he shouted into the radio, the signal to all the drivers in the convoy to step on their accelerators and avoid the rocket-propelled grenade hurtling towards them.

The three vehicles quickly scattered and Jurkowski tried to judge where the grenade would land as if he were playing a deadly game of dodge ball. "Go left, right, straight, no—left again," he barked into the intercom to the driver, out of sight in his separate compartment in the front end of the vehicle. "Now go, go!"

The grenade hit the ground harmlessly and there were no further attacks. By the time they scanned the distant tree line from which the RPG had been launched, the Taliban were long gone.

After several days of constant patrolling along the vulnerable stretch of highway, Charlie knew the ground well enough to mount a full-scale hunt for the ambushers. On June 3, Jurkowski pulled in his day patrols and organized a counter-ambush for the entire company, laying out a trap for the Taliban along a one-kilometre section of the highway where he felt certain they would strike next. The company was to set up a series of kill zones along the most likely paths the Taliban fighters would take to get into one of their favourite ambush positions. If all went according to plan they would hit the ambush cell when they least expected it, before they could attack their target on the highway.

The soldiers were familiar with ambush patrols, a mission they had practised hundreds of times on training exercises. The job required stealth, particularly when such a large group of men was moving into position in complete darkness. They would use hand signals to communicate and move carefully to minimize noise. Doing this on a base in Canada was one thing; doing it in the complicated urban clutter of the Panjwayi, with the possibility of Taliban fighters around every twist and turn, was something else again. For one thing, the soldiers had practised the complicated manoeuvres in the isolated forest or fields of training areas like Wainwright, Alberta, where contact with civilians or the enemy was not a factor. In The Panj, farmers and labourers were everywhere and the troops had no way of knowing which ones were actually Taliban fighters who had hidden their weapons or which would report their presence to the enemy. And there were other hazards roaming the landscape as well, including the huge Afghan dogs who usually gave soldiers a wide berth, but whose barking could alert the locals or the Taliban to their presence. There were also several varieties of poisonous snake and one soldier in Charlie had already been bitten by a viper during a patrol (without serious injury).

Once the soldiers had reached the ambush site, they had to move into positions carefully chosen by their platoon and section commanders to cover the area where the enemy was expected to pass. Machine gunners were positioned at either end of the kill zones to cut off any routes of escape. Then, the waiting began.

Jurkowski knew he had to lead more than sixty soldiers, with all of their weapons and equipment, over that difficult terrain at night, then get them into place and ready to spring their ambush, all without being seen or heard by their enemies. But he could still hardly restrain his grin: this would be the first company-sized ambush patrol by the Canadian Army since the Korean War, more than fifty years ago. "Holy fuck, I'm doing this for real now," he kept telling himself.

The company crowded into the backs of their LAVs in the 530 Compound just before sunset and were driven a few kilo-metres to the Arghandab wadi, then along its rough gravel and sand bottom to a point just south of where they were to lay their trap. The soldiers tumbled out of the vehicles and pulled on their twenty-five kilograms or more of body armour, ammunition, water and other kit for the long hike to their ambush site. Although it was only two kilometres away, it took hours to get there. Deep irrigation ditches slowed down the patrol consider-ably as each soldier had to slide down a steep two-metre-deep embankment, wade through foul-smelling, waist-deep water and pull their already heavy boots out of clinging mud to clamber up the other side.

Jurkowski looked down at the water at the bottom of the first deep ditch and made a face at the smell, grateful they were crossing at night and couldn't see what they were wading through. "That's not just water," he said softly, smelling the raw sewage that filled the bottom of the ditch.

Although they only had to cross two such canals, at several points in the march the men were forced to balance precariously on paths winding along the tops of low mounds of earth. The walls marking the boundaries between fields had to be scaled, one of them more than two metres high, and one grape orchard with its dozens of metre-high mounds of hard-packed earth took more than an hour to cross.

The residual heat from daytime temperatures that had approached 50°C made the night air uncomfortably warm long after sunset, and it was hard going for the troops. Jurkowski found it almost impossible to keep the lenses of his night-vision gear from fogging up with the exertion and stopped briefly on the edge of one deep ditch to flip them up from his eyes and wipe them clean.

When he pulled the goggles back over his eyes, the contrast between the profound darkness and their eerie green illumination disoriented him. He stumbled backwards, his feet slipped on the edge of a precipice and he was propelled backwards into the mud- and water-filled ditch. He landed on his back with a thump that winded him and a muffled splash.

In a daze, Jurkowski heard his radio operator at the top of the ditch softly call the entire company to a halt. "The OC just disappeared. Hold up the patrol."

A minute later he looked up to see a dozen faces, all wearing the one-eyed night-vision equipment, peering down curiously at him. "OC's back in sight," the radio operator reported drily, speaking in little more than a whisper. "Fell three feet into a ditch."

"You didn't have to tell everyone THAT," Jurkowski grumbled as hands reached down to heave him out of the hole.

Charlie finally reached their objective and Jurkowski called a brief halt to "RV" or rendezvous with his three platoon commanders. Craig Alcock was the first to arrive and the men each went down on one knee up against the outside wall of a small compound. A dog was barking furiously on the other side of the wall, but no one inside was paying any attention. The two friends grinned at each other in the darkness.

"How cool is this?" Alcock said in a barely audible whisper. "RV by barking dog."

"Just a couple of buddies out setting up an ambush," Jurkowski replied, his grin broadening. "Just another day out in the field."

When the other two platoon commanders joined them, Jurkowski quickly and quietly ordered each platoon to move silently towards its designated ambush site. Within a few minutes the entire company was spread out over a kilometre, covering every route in and out of the spot they suspected the Taliban would be using to hit targets on the highway. But after a few hours of silent, restless waiting, it became clear the enemy was not coming out that night. Jurkowski gave the command to pull out of the ambush zone just before the first faint light of dawn began to show the silhouette of the knife-edged ridge of rock to the east.

The local farmers were just leaving their homes to work their fields and orchards when the muddy, dust-covered soldiers climbed out of their hiding places and filed onto the road. The Afghans stopped and stared open-mouthed as more than sixty troops—helmeted, armoured and fully armed and equipped—appeared to grow out of their fields. The soldiers noticed the stares, nudged each other and smiled, some of them even swaggering a little as they casually strolled back to their LAVs. The enormous vehicles had roared to life from hidden positions on the outskirts of the village, drawing even more astonished looks. Jurkowski couldn't resist joking with the local farmers, many of whom he suspected were sympathetic to the Taliban if not actively supporting them. He gave all of them a big wave and a toothy grin as he walked past.

"Hey, how are you? Good day to work, eh? Anyway, been here all night. It should be safe for you," he told them cheerily, not minding that they almost certainly spoke no English. "Have a good day."

The real message was unspoken: that dozens of Canadian soldiers had spent the night in what the Taliban considered to be their backyard without being seen or heard by anyone. Jurkowski smiled broadly at the astonished look on the weathered face of the village elders. "Spread the word, motherfucker," he added under his breath, still smiling.

On June 10, Charlie was taken off counter-ambush duty for an assault on a new, larger concentration of Taliban, which Captain Massoud's sources had seen gathering in the centre of the Panjwayi area, well to the west of where they had been hunting the ambush cell. Within forty-eight hours of the company pulling out of the 530 Compound, the ambushes began again.

PART 3

Seyyedin
June 12, 2006

SEYYEDIN JUNE 12, 0830 - 1030 hrs

ANP
SEYYEDIN
Seyyedin
B
ANA
NALGHAM
Arghandab River
C
ANA
ZANGABAD
N
0
km
1
Dismounted infantry
Armoured infantry
Reconnaissance
Engineers
Platoon
Company
Battalion
Taliban
Active patrol routes
Roads a
tracks

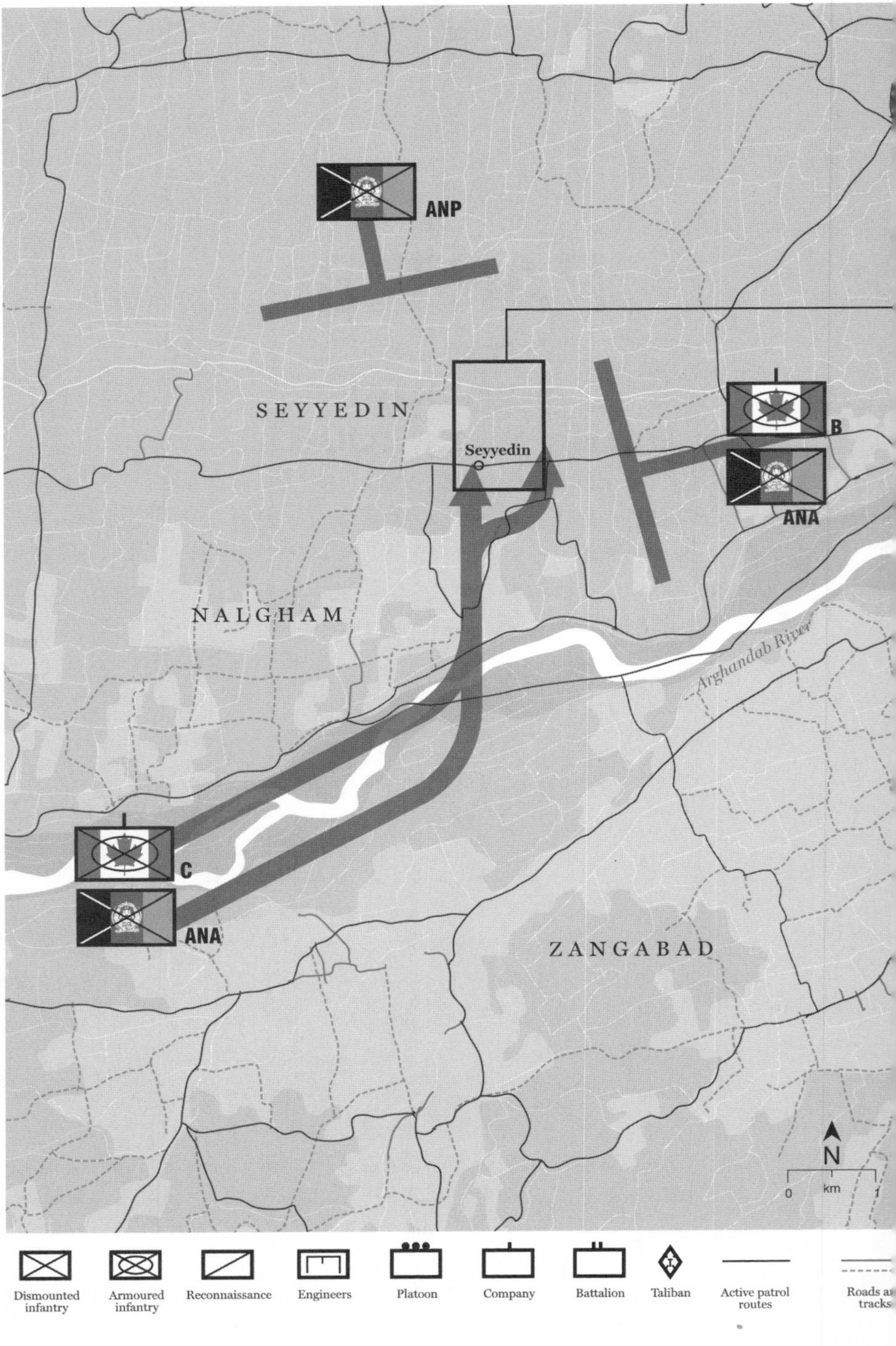

SEYYEDIN JUNE 12, 1100 - 1700 hrs

N

0 metres 100

CHAPTER EIGHT

"Nowhere to squirt."

Pashmul
June 9
0900 hrs

Ian Hope sat cross-legged on a ridge overlooking the Panjwayi District Centre, sipping hot, sweet *cha* with Captain Massoud and three unusual guests. The men were all lifelong residents of the Panjwayi, two of them in the traditional white khameez and Pashtun turbans and their leader wearing the blue-grey uniform of the ANP. All had thick, black beards and lined, weather-beaten faces. They eyed the Canadian lieutenant-colonel curiously as they sipped their tea in the shade of an old, burned-out Soviet T-62 tank. Hope treated them deferentially, listening closely, frequently asking their opinions through his translator and solicitously offering more tea whenever the level of steaming amber liquid in their glasses got low. The men were all in their late middle age but looked older, faces and bodies wracked by years of hardship and war. All three were former mujahedeen, veterans of the long civil war against the Soviets, and Hope had brought them to Panjwayi Centre for his own private battlefield tour.

Like all old soldiers, these loved nothing better than an attentive audience, and they soon warmed up to the ferrenghi colonel with the strange, pale eyes. Their leader was an Afghan police officer, an acquaintance of Captain Massoud who had spent nearly ten years as a guerrilla fighter, ambushing Soviet troop convoys and fighting them on the ground. Hope wanted to hear all about their battles, particularly in the Panjwayi—a hotbed of mujahedeen activity during the war and an area which the Soviets had never successfully pacified. Towards the end of the war in 1989, Russian troops did not even dare to venture into the region. Hope, a student of military history in all time periods, had a hunch that he could learn much about the Taliban by exploring how the mujahedeen had fought the Soviets.

The three former mujahedeen sipping tea with Hope quickly got over any reluctance to talk and were soon chattering excitedly about their battle for Panjwayi in September 1982, speaking almost too quickly for the translator to keep up. Even the burned-out tank they were using for shade became a subject for discussion, and some argument, among the three veterans over who had knocked it out and when. "That tank was dug in," their leader eventually told Hope. "We fired a lot of RPGs at it." They volunteered to walk the Canadian colonel around the district centre and show him how they had attacked, infiltrated and eventually captured it. The Soviets had sent a brigade—up to five thousand soldiers, with tanks and armoured personnel carriers—to recapture the town, resulting in a fierce battle that cost the Soviets hundreds of casualties. Hope marvelled at the mujahedeens' ingenuity as the men showed him how they had moved into the town in secret by knocking holes through the walls of adjacent compounds until they had an effective secret tunnel into the district centre.

Hope casually asked about the rest of the Panjwayi, particularly Pashmul, the collection of villages and farm compounds just to the west of the district centre where his soldiers had been fighting the Taliban since May. The mujahedeen veterans nodded enthusiastically: "Pashmul was a great area to hide in," one said, pointing to the low buildings of the villages just visible from the town. "We could go anywhere we wanted from there, even to Kandahar."

Hope's eyebrows raised a fraction. The former mujahedeen went on to tell him that not only had Pashmul contained plenty of food and water, but it was difficult if not impossible for the Russians to penetrate. It also gave the Afghans easy access to both the Arghandab River and to Highway One, where they frequently ambushed Soviet convoys or vehicles from the Russians' puppet Afghan government. Hope nodded encouragingly as they explained which routes they'd used to connect with their bases of support in Pakistan and neighbouring Helmand Province.

After touring the town on foot, Hope asked the three veterans if they were interested in taking a flight over Panjwayi on a U.S. Black Hawk helicopter, to which they eagerly agreed. Their leader, who had carefully trimmed his beard and put on his cleanest police uniform for the meeting, sat beside Hope next to the helicopter's open door and showed him the exact ambush positions and movement routes they had used. "We'd fire at them from there and there," he said, pointing to the same fields and orchards where Charlie had been hunting the Taliban's ambush cells for the past week. "Then we'd escape that way or that way."

Hope recognized the area from Ryan Jurkowski's reports on Charlie's counter-ambush patrols and realized with a start that the Taliban were not just using the mujahedeen's tactics, they were in many cases using the same villages, the same buildings, even the same ditches and walls and trees for cover. "These bastards are using exactly the same places," he thought, carefully noting the positions in his field message pad.

When the helicopter landed and the mujahedeen had parted company with many handshakes and grins, Hope returned to his command LAV, sat atop the turret and pulled out a cigar. Massoud's warnings about the Taliban's plans for the Panjwayi made perfect sense to him now: they were trying to do what the mujahedeen had done twenty years earlier and turn the dense terrain of the Panjwayi into a base for large numbers of fighters. All within a few minutes' drive of Kandahar.

Hope's suspicions were confirmed when he sent patrols to the firing positions that the mujahedeen veterans had pointed out from the air. His soldiers found fresh cartridges from AK-47s and the telltale water bottles that were a sure sign the Taliban had been in the area. In one large building the mujahedeen had pointed out as one of their former command posts, the Canadians discovered a Taliban first-aid facility, hastily abandoned as the patrol approached. The only difference between the mujahedeen and the Taliban was that "the muj," as Hope called them fondly, could move freely among the villagers and farmers of the Pashmul while the Taliban often had to threaten the local populace into supporting them.

Hope took a puff on a freshly lit cigar, pulled out his maps and began making plans. The next day, he launched Operation Jagra, from the Pashtu word for "fight." It was a plan to use Charlie as a hammer that would trap the Taliban in one village and crush them before they could escape. The village he chose was in the heart of the Panjwayi, part of the clutch of villages known collectively as Nalgham. The locals called it Seyyedin.

While Lieutenant-Colonel Hope was touring the Panjwayi with the old mujahedeen fighters, Major Bill Fletcher was landing on the hot, dusty airstrip at KAF, finally back from his mid-deployment leave. He was chagrined to find that he was now the least experienced soldier in the entire company. The soldiers all elbowed each other and laughed when they learned that the OC was on his way back into theatre. Nobody wanted to tell the notoriously gung-ho Fletcher about their many firefights over the past two weeks.

"Man, he asks me, I'm just going to say it was nothing special," a grinning Mike Denine told his friends. "I don't want to be the one to tell him what it was like. He's going to be so pissed he missed it."

But Fletcher had little time to feel left out. Soon after he landed back at KAF, Hope informed him that his company was headed back into the Panjwayi. He had just over twenty-four hours to familiarize himself with what Charlie had been doing over the previous weeks, the enemy's activities and the region's convoluted and crowded landscape. He sat down with Ryan Jurkowski in a quiet corner of the BAT and grilled him for more than an hour. "You've been there; you've been shot at. Tell me what I need to know," he asked.

At the end of the long briefing, Fletcher shook his head and thought, "This enemy is a lot more crafty than we gave them credit for." The next morning, Hope gave Fletcher his orders in the plywood-walled shack that served as the battle group's briefing room. He told him that the Taliban were reportedly massing in the centre of the Panjwayi, near Seyyedin, and Charlie was going in to take them out. And, Hope added, they had precious little time to do it: the company was being ordered out of the Panjwayi for a large U.S.–led operation.

"We've got three days to do something that's going to last," Hope said, "at least until we can get back into the Panjwayi."

Fletcher could tell that his diminutive boss was getting impatient with the weeks of cat-and-mouse fights. "He's tired of dicking around," he told himself, scanning the map of the Panjwayi spread out on the long table where the colonel was giving his orders. "He wants to go get these guys."

Fletcher approved wholeheartedly, but realized the task would not be easy. He spent a sleepless night sketching out his plan for the operation, drawing on advice from his senior sergeants, warrant officers and the officers who had spent the past three weeks in the Panjwayi. Bravo Company would be to the north of Seyyedin, waiting to block any escape, while Charlie moved in from the south to pin down the Taliban cell and capture or kill them. "Every time we squeeze these guys, they squirt out and get away," he said, glaring at the map in front of him. "So this time, we're not going to give them anywhere to squirt."

On June 11, the soldiers loaded up their equipment and bundled into the back of their LAVs. The entire company pulled out of KAF in a long convoy and headed through the city and onto Highway One. Charlie made no attempt to disguise its move. In fact, Fletcher wanted the Taliban lookouts in the area to report the departure of so many Canadian vehicles. The company raced through Ambush Alley, past all the major roads leading into the district and disappeared in a cloud of dust to the west while a pair of U.S. Apache attack helicopters roared overhead, escorting them for most of their trip.

To all appearances, Charlie was bound for neighbouring Helmand Province, where they had already spent several weeks in April helping beleaguered American forces. But when the convoy was well out of sight of the Panjwayi, nearly at the border with Helmand, Fletcher stopped and ordered the LAVs off the road. They pulled into an empty patch of sand and rock just off the highway and formed a defensive "leaguer"—the vehicles arrayed in a rough, widely spaced square, pointed outwards, with Fletcher's command LAV and the unarmoured support vehicles in the centre. The soldiers piled out of the vehicles and began making preparations to spend the night, unrolling their air mattresses and sleeping bags on the dusty ground behind the LAVs.

It was a short night. The soldiers were up and getting ready to move out long before dawn on June 12, and as Fletcher watched them roll up their bedding, check their weapons and pack away their kit he noticed a difference in his young troops. Earlier in the tour, they would have been chatting with their friends, scrounging for coffee or cigarettes—"jokin' and smokin'" in army lingo. Now, they were all business, moving purposefully in the pre-dawn darkness and filing into the back of their vehicles with little fuss or bother. "Look like they mean business," he thought, watching from the top of his command vehicle.

Captain Hugh Atwell's 7 Platoon pushed off first, almost half an hour ahead of the other two platoons, racing back towards Panjwayi along the highway they had travelled the day before. Atwell's soldiers were to link up with a detachment of ANP and set themselves up in positions to the east of Seyyedin to cut off the Taliban's retreat in that direction. The other two platoons, accompanied by a small contingent of Afghan Army troops, left the highway to swing down into the Arghandab River wadi and bounced along its meandering course until they were just to the south of their target, in position to sweep north on foot.

Fletcher pushed the LAVs of 8 and 9 Platoon to move as quickly as possible, hoping to catch the Taliban off guard. (In fact, Charlie's "button-hook" did surprise the Taliban, and threw its commanders into a panic.) But it was already growing light by the time most of Charlie was rolling down the gravel-bottomed wadi and Fletcher could make out the occasional lone figure of a farmer in the fields overlooking the broad riverbed.

Then, Atwell broke in over the radio. There was no sign of the Afghan police they were supposed to meet at a station on Highway One. "We're here and we got no cops," the young captain said drily.

Fletcher cursed and slowed the rest of his company to a crawl, knowing he had to coordinate his arrival at the village with Atwell's. Eventually, more than an hour late, two pickup trucks carrying fifteen policemen showed up at the ANP station. But the damage was done. Wary of bringing his approach to the village to a complete stop—never a wise idea in Taliban territory—Fletcher had decided to swing north and rejoin Atwell's platoon.

By the time Charlie began moving again, urged on by its impatient commander, the sun was well over the horizon. When the LAVs finally reached the point in the wadi due south of the village of Seyyedin and lowered their rear ramps to unload the soldiers in the back, the blinding Afghan sun was already beating down mercilessly.

At 8:30 a.m., Atwell's platoon, with its Afghan police contingent in tow, again left first, the soldiers clambering up the banks of the wadi and onto a small track leading north. Within minutes they caught sight of a long line of women, children and old men walking south away from Seyyedin. They carried small children or bundles of their possessions as they headed out of what they obviously expected to turn into a combat zone.

Back in the wadi, Fletcher heard Atwell's report on the radio and knew he had lost the element of surprise. The Taliban routinely ordered the local population out of villages where they intended to fight, not for humanitarian reasons but to maintain some semblance of good relations with local villagers. If word spread through the Panjwayi that the Taliban brought firefights into every village they entered, endangering women and children, they would be welcomed in very few communities, regardless of how much intimidation they brought to bear.

"This is not a good sign," Fletcher overheard one soldier telling his fire-team partner. "If we thought we were getting into something today, it looks like we were right."

"Just keep your wits about you," the other soldier replied quietly.

It was nearly 9 a.m. by the time the bulk of Charlie trudged out of the wadi and headed towards the village of Alizi, a smaller community astride their path towards the Taliban that were reportedly holed up in Seyyedin. The area had to be cleared of any Taliban before the company could push forward to its main target and soldiers walked warily towards the village, made more cautious than usual by its deserted streets and compounds. They searched almost every building, but aside from the usual collection of goats and sheep found only two inhabitants:

an elderly man and his teenaged son, who sat under a tree and watched impassively as the Canadian troops approached and split off into smaller teams to scour the village.

While most of his soldiers cleared the village, Fletcher headed for the tree. He was accompanied by a translator and his radio man, Corporal Keith Mooney—an irrepressible twenty-eight-year-old from the Newfoundland fishing port of St. Mary's who had been shadowing Fletcher for the entire tour. Mooney's job was to carry the heavy radio that kept Fletcher in touch with his company and to keep up with his fast-moving OC. His unofficial, self-imposed task was to keep the major out of trouble, which Mooney quickly discovered was a full-time job. As company commander, Fletcher was supposed to stay back from the front lines and coordinate the battle, sending reinforcements or calling in artillery or air strikes where and when needed. But his aggressive style drew him inexorably to the action and more than a few times during the six-month tour Mooney had been forced to grab the much larger officer by his belt and pull him back from an exposed position in the very front of an attack.

Fletcher introduced himself to the two Afghans through the translator and sat down next to the older man. The first thing he asked him about was the Taliban. "Oh no, there's no Taliban here," the elderly farmer replied, through the translator. "They left yesterday."

It was a typical response and Fletcher shrugged it off. "Well, we saw everybody leaving the village: why did they go?"

"Oh, they're afraid of you. Whenever you come they think there's going to be fighting."

The old man said he had remained because he was too feeble to walk the kilometre or more to the next village. Fletcher also suspected he was too stubborn to leave his fields untended. He continued to chat amiably with the man while his soldiers searched the village. Eventually, the Afghan sent his son into their nearby home to produce a bowl filled with a suspicious white fluid. The old man offered it to Fletcher, insisting that he take a sip. It was curdled goat milk, something of a local delicacy, but the smell alone made Fletcher's stomach churn.

He looked to Mooney, appealing to him to try it, but the stocky blond corporal shook his head firmly. "I ain't doin' it," he said. "You're the company commander: you try it."

Even the Afghan translator turned down the offer, so Fletcher sighed and lifted the bowl to his lips. "I guess that's why they pay me the big bucks," he muttered to himself as he took a tentative sip of the thick, lumpy white liquid.

He regretted it immediately. The drink tasted as bad as it smelled and Fletcher's stomach knotted up immediately. He forced a wan grin onto his face as he stood and thanked the elderly Afghan, then staggered away to join the rest of the soldiers, who had finished sweeping the village and were forming up to continue on to Seyyedin. As he walked deliberately forward, one step at a time, there was only one thought in his head: "Let's try not to throw up in front of the troops."

While most of his company moved forward on foot, Fletcher ordered Charlie's fifteen LAVs to take up positions to support their sweep through Seyyedin. Vaughn Ingram led one group of vehicles to the west, positioning them along a road running parallel to the wadi to seal off that escape route from the village. The rest of the LAVs were moved up behind the advancing troops, ready to use their 25-mm cannon to help deal with any attackers that threatened the dismounted infantry. But the area's narrow roads and rickety bridges and culverts made it all but impossible for the LAVs to get any closer than a kilometre away from the village. A frustrated Captain Marty Dupuis, who had taken charge of the LAVs after the soldiers dismounted, radioed Fletcher with the news.

"Roger that," Fletcher replied. He was already jogging to catch up with 9 Platoon, which was in the lead moving out

towards Seyyedin less than a kilometre to the north. A swearing
Mooney hurried behind, both men sweating profusely in the rising heat. It was nearly 10 a.m. now and the temperature was
over 40°C. Fletcher moved up until he was walking with the
leading section of 9 Platoon, on the point position in the company's careful approach to the village. He liked to be with the
leading troops in any advance, not only because it gave him a
first-hand view of what was ahead but also, he admitted with a
mischievous smile, because it let him "torture the platoon commander a little bit."

The company had been on the road for only a few minutes,
marching down a dirt lane partly shaded by a handful of trees,
when the popping of distant gunfire echoed off the mud-brick
walls followed by the rattle of a machine gun. Fletcher's head
snapped around: the firing had come from ahead and to his
right, where Atwell's platoon had been moving into their cut-
off position to the northeast of Seyyedin. "Contact, wait out,"
came Atwell's voice, crackling over Mooney's radio.

Fletcher couldn't see what was happening to Atwell's soldiers ahead on his right flank, and stewed while waiting for
more information. The firing died away quickly and he climbed
up onto the roof of a nearby hut in an attempt to see what was
going on. After a few minutes, he impatiently waved Mooney
over and grabbed the radio's handset to call Atwell and demand
a report.

After several minutes which Fletcher spent pacing back and
forth restlessly on the mud roof of the hut, Atwell called back to
explain. His soldiers, accompanied by the fifteen ANP, had
almost reached their cut-off position without incident. They
were approaching the foot of the high mound of earth overlooking Seyyedin, when three men in black khameez and turbans suddenly appeared at the top. Both sides watched each
other for a second, frozen in surprise. Then the Afghans atop
the berm swung up the AK-47 rifles they had been holding

behind their backs and started spraying fire. Atwell's troops immediately dropped to the ground and began firing back.

They were only able to fire off a few rounds before the Afghan police officers startled Atwell by suddenly charging the hill. With their allies between them and the Taliban, the Canadians were forced to stop shooting. The young captain, flat on the ground, watched in disbelief as the ANP scurried forward firing wildly as they went and the Taliban disappeared behind the mound of dirt. The ANP reached the top of the berm, fired a few more badly aimed shots over its top and began making their way back to Atwell and the Canadians.

"We've fired off all our rounds. We want to go home now," the senior policeman told Atwell after his soldiers had managed to corral all the ANP straggling back from their wild charge. The platoon leader argued and pleaded, but the Afghans were adamant: their fight was over for the day and they began walking south, away from Seyyedin. By the time Atwell began deploying his soldiers onto the berm he was almost an hour behind schedule and the Taliban were nowhere in sight.

Once briefed on Atwell's situation, Fletcher got the rest of Charlie moving again. He knew that the three gunmen Atwell had encountered were almost certainly lookouts for a much larger group of Taliban who were by now making preparations for the Canadians' arrival. What worried him most was that the enemy would use the warning to slip away, so he pushed his platoon leaders to get their men moving quickly, despite the growing heat. A group of LAVs off to Fletcher's left had shut down that escape route and Atwell's platoon had them cut off on the right, but Bravo Company was more than a kilometre to the north, too far away to ensure the Taliban could not escape in that direction. "Push forward! Push forward!" he urged the men on, eager to get close enough to the enemy to force a fight.

The soldiers inched cautiously forward, each platoon moving

in a column up the deeply rutted road leading to Seyyedin, paired off in fire teams to cover each other's backs as they walked. It took the company more than an hour to get to the village's outskirts, but once they arrived they found the Taliban almost immediately.

Pat Tower's section was in the lead, preparing to move into the village and begin clearing its dozen or more buildings, when the veteran sergeant came around a corner and suddenly found himself face to face with a man in a turban and the loose-fitting traditional khameez that the soldiers descriptively called "man jammies." The two men stared at each other for a second, stunned by the unexpected encounter. Tower had rounded the corner quickly, his rifle at the ready, and the man began to back away slowly. The veteran sergeant watched him carefully over his rifle's sights. Suddenly, the man pulled an AK-47 from beneath his voluminous dark robes and began firing. A line of bullets stitched the mud-daubed wall just to Tower's right and several more kicked up dirt all around him. Tower began firing his C7 rapidly, pulling the trigger methodically and sending bullets flying towards the Taliban gunman in quick succession. But the impact of the enemy rounds had raised a cloud of thick dust that almost instantaneously surrounded both men. Tower quickly lost sight of his target and although he emptied his 30-round magazine, and the Taliban fighter fired just as many times, somehow both managed to miss. His magazine empty, Tower threw himself headlong behind the wall, pulled out a grenade, tugged out the safety pin and lobbed it in a straight-armed throw at the Taliban fighter. By the time the grenade went off in a thudding explosion and a shower of metal fragments, Tower had reloaded and the rest of his section had caught up with him, huddled together behind the cover of the wall.

But the Talib was still there. Keeping low, Corporal Paul Rachynski stepped out around the corner and was immediately greeted by a bullet whining past his head. He quickly rolled back behind the wall. "Whoa, that was close," he said, breathing heavily.

Tower got up and raced out from behind the wall, crossing the small laneway to a wall on the opposite corner. He came up with his rifle at the ready, aimed at the spot where he had last seen the enemy fighter. But by then the man was a distant figure running full speed past the village towards a grape orchard and a squat, massive grape drying hut a couple of hundred metres to the north. Quickly, Tower and his section charged up the laneway after him, past the village to the edge of a grape orchard just north of Seyyedin's handful of houses and walled compounds, throwing themselves down behind a rough wall at the edge of the field for cover. Their arrival, and that of the rest of 9 Platoon close behind them, was met with a shower of bullets and a handful of rocket-propelled grenades coming from the thick-walled hut on the other side of the orchard.

To Tower, the firefight that quickly enveloped his men seemed like an exercise back in Canada. He watched his soldiers working in pairs, taking turns at standing up to fire over the chest-high wall at the flitting shadows, silhouettes or flashes from the Taliban's AK-47s. If a soldier fired too long from one spot on the wall, Tower barked a reminder to aim and move. "Fire a few rounds, then shift over," he told them. "Don't let them get a bead on you."

He was also concerned about his troops' supply of ammunition, knowing that a prolonged firefight could quickly exhaust the 350 or more rounds each soldier carried. Tower moved from one fire team to the next calmly reminding them to "Control your rate of fire; take aimed shots." His concern was well founded. By the end of the day, 9 Platoon had used up almost all of its ammunition.

Farther back in the advancing Canadian column, Fletcher began to run as soon as he heard the first shots, ignoring the by-now-blistering heat and his fatigue to head towards his forward troops. Using the buildings and low walls around the nearby fields for cover, he moved steadily ahead, with Mooney just behind him, and tried to pinpoint the location of the enemy fire. He could make out Pat Tower and the rest of 9 Platoon spread out along the wall separating the grape orchard from the village, returning the fire that had erupted from the thick-walled hut just over one hundred metres away. Fletcher smiled at the sight of Tower walking calmly along the platoon firing line, cuffing the young soldiers in the backs of their helmets and shouting "Remember your drills!"

Fletcher glared at the hut intently for a moment, estimating the Taliban strength at anywhere from fifteen to twenty-five fighters. Then he called for his FOO. Fletcher pointed at an open area to the northwest of the grape-drying hut, the only avenue of escape left to the Taliban. "I want you to close the door on those fuckers," he said. "Can you put some rounds in there? Keep it intermittent—just some sporadic fire to let 'em know they can't get away."

Captain Bob Meade, who had temporarily replaced Nich Goddard as Charlie's FOO, nodded grimly and got on his radio, shouting to make himself heard over the gunfire and explosions. Within minutes, the 155-mm shells were bursting almost exactly where Fletcher had pointed, sending up showers of dust and dirt in the fields behind the Taliban's stronghold. The fire was so close to the Canadians that Hugh Atwell's platoon, blocking the enemy's escape to the northeast, heard shell fragments whistling overhead. The booming explosions of the artillery continued every few minutes, adding to the growing din of the battle.

Tower and his platoon were joined at the wall by the Afghan troops, who had been advancing behind them, and spent almost an hour unleashing a hurricane of rifle, machine-gun and M72 disposable-rocket fire at the grape-drying hut with no apparent effect. The soldiers threw hand grenades and aimed rifle-launched grenades into the trenches between the lush grapevines, and piles of empty magazines soon began growing behind them.

With 9 Platoon keeping the enemy busy, and Atwell's platoon and sporadic artillery preventing an escape, Fletcher scanned what he could see of the battle shaping up ahead of him and quickly worked out a plan of attack. He had noticed a shallow, weed-filled ditch off to his right that appeared to lead straight north, past the grape-drying hut. He grinned fiercely and thought: "We've got 'em."

He found Warrant Officer Ron Gallant, the acting commander of 8 Platoon, and pointed out the ditch, which was lined by a low, partially crumbling wall. "We're going to go right up that ditch and close with them," he explained.

The warrant's eyes widened: he understood immediately what his OC wanted. He planned to lead 8 Platoon and the Afghan troops on a two-hundred-metre end run to the right, bringing them close enough so that they could fire down the long rows of grapevines and into the opening at one end of the hut. It was a classic infantry manoeuvre, called a right flanking attack, and it would bring the Taliban under devastating fire from two directions, killing them or forcing them to surrender or flee.

Gallant smiled. "We're actually doing this," he said, half to himself. "This is for real: holy fuck."

But when Fletcher ran over to the Afghan major in charge of the ANA soldiers and told him what he wanted them to do, the man drew himself up and insisted that his men should instead attack from the left, or west, while Fletcher's troops came in from the right. Fletcher bit his tongue and diplomatically pointed out that such a manoeuvre would end with the Afghans and Canadians firing at each other.

The Afghan officer waved dismissively. "That's OK, we won't aim at each other," he said, speaking through a translator.

Fletcher took a deep breath. "Thanks for the input, but this is how it's going to happen," he said patiently. "I've got my firebase set up, all my pieces are in place."

The Afghan officer scowled. "Well, if we aren't using my plan, I'm not taking my men."

Fletcher clenched his jaw. "You don't have a choice. You're working for me, so get your guys up and let's go."

"I'm not doing it."

Fletcher resisted an almost irresistible urge to punch his Afghan counterpart. Until today, his dealings with the ANA had been overwhelmingly positive. Their soldiers, trained by teams of American or other allied nations' troops, had impressed him with their toughness and their fearless pursuit of the enemy. They were invaluable in dealing with local inhabitants, who almost universally respected the national army, and the Canadian and other coalition troops respected the Afghan soldiers' ability to almost literally smell out the Taliban's hiding places. The only problem Fletcher usually had with his Afghan counterparts was that there was never enough of them to go around.

But this particular unit was a headquarters company, not front-line troops, and their commander was clearly more interested in his status than in fighting the Taliban. "Fine. Fuck you," Fletcher brusquely told him. "I'll deal with you later."

The translator didn't speak—he didn't need to. Fletcher's black expression said volumes. The Afghan major turned on his heel and barked out orders to his soldiers. A moment later, the ANA began trickling to the rear, taking up comfortable and safe positions well back from the fighting.

Fletcher didn't even notice. He was already getting 8 Platoon into position for its dash up the Taliban's flank.

CHAPTER NINE

"Do I look Afghan to you?"

Alizi
June 12
1200 hrs

About a kilometre behind the firefight, Sergeant Mike Denine had spent two hours jockeying his seventeen-tonne LAV back and forth like a bumper car, bouncing off walls and buildings as he searched feverishly for a road that would lead to Seyyedin. Still confined to his LAV by his sprained ankle, Denine was worried about the seven soldiers in his section who were "mixing it up" somewhere in the distance. "These are all goat tracks," he muttered, looking down at the military map in his lap. It showed two routes up from the wadi to Seyyedin, neither of which actually existed.

After several false starts, Denine finally found a road that was both broad enough for the LAVs and had bridges or culverts that could bear the vehicle's weight. He signalled to Captain Marty Dupuis, who was in charge of Charlie's LAVs while Fletcher and the troops were on foot, and led them up the winding narrow track towards Seyyedin. They made slow progress, forced to halt occasionally for the hundreds of civilians who were trudging towards them, fleeing the Taliban-held village.

They had just pulled past Alizi, the first village cleared by the troops that morning, when they heard the rattle of gunfire from up ahead. Dupuis immediately called Fletcher to ask if he wanted the LAVs to move into a support position, but Fletcher's voice came back over the radio telling them to stay put. "No," he said brusquely. "Wait out there. I need you to cover my back." The LAVs were the only reserve force Fletcher had—the only thing protecting his line of retreat back to the wadi, where the company's headquarters was set up.

Denine also heard the exchange over the radio, as well as the calls back and forth between the soldiers up ahead, and he fumed in his turret. His boys were in an all-out firefight and he was stuck in the rear.

By the time Fletcher was ready to begin his flanking attack on Seyyedin, it was after 1 p.m. and the temperatures had topped 45°C. Although his soldiers were in peak physical condition, he knew the weight of their equipment, ammunition, and body armour combined with the strength-sapping heat from the merciless Afghan sun was rapidly pushing many to the limits of their endurance. He wanted to get this fight over quickly.

Fletcher scrambled over a low wall, out of sight from the Taliban who were still firing furiously at 9 Platoon, and scuttled towards the ditch leading to the grape-drying hut, with Mooney and the rest of the attacking platoon close behind. He was ready to lead the rest of the way up the ditch but Sergeant Chris Mavin, whose section was leading the attack, grabbed his arm and held him back. "Sir, you don't want to do that," he said, shaking his head. "Put the C9 [machine gun] in front."

Fletcher firmly believed in leading his soldiers from the front and his men adored him for it. But while he knew exactly where he wanted the attack to go in, he also knew that if he was killed or wounded, Charlie would lose not only its commander but its momentum as well and possibly the firefight. He nodded reluctantly and watched as Private Brent Ginther shifted the big C9 machine gun onto his shoulder and took the point, with Corporal

Kory Ozerkevich and Mavin behind him, moving at a quick walk.

Although the ditch narrowed and grew more shallow as it approached the grape-drying hut, there was a wall shielding the advancing Canadians from the Taliban positions. The soldiers had gone about seventy-five metres when Fletcher heard an explosion of machine-gun fire from his left, coming from very nearby. He instinctively fired two quick snap shots in the direction of the fire and dove to the ground—the "double tap and drop" that every infantryman learned in basic training. He cursed under his breath when he looked up and saw a gap in the mud-brick wall separating the ditch from the orchard. The Taliban had used the gap to good advantage, firing through the crumbled section of wall as soon as the Canadians had come into view.

From his position in the dirt and weeds at the bottom of the ditch, Fletcher realized his soldiers were in trouble. Ginther had disappeared into a waist-high clump of weeds and the major could hear Oz off to one side moaning, "I'm hit, I'm hit, I'm hit!"

Mooney rushed up to Oz and began doing first aid, while Mavin crawled forward until he was next to Fletcher. "Where's Ginther?" he asked breathlessly.

"Go find him, I'll cover you," Fletcher shouted. He heaved himself onto one knee and brought his rifle up to his shoulder to begin squeezing off rounds through the gap in the wall. He was certain he wasn't hitting any Taliban, but hoped he was at least forcing them to keep their heads down. As Mavin crawled ahead through the weeds to search for Ginther, Taliban bullets continued to snap through the air and kick up dust on the opposite bank of the ditch. After a brief, desperate search, Mavin discovered Ginther face-down and semi-conscious, shot through both legs and bleeding profusely. The machine gunner had been hit twice, first by the bullet that tore through his legs, shattering his femur and missing his major arteries only by centimetres. A second bullet had hit the hardened plate on the back of his protective vest. It had knocked him over, but the body armour had done its job and stopped the slug.

When Mavin cut away the young private's blood-soaked pants, he saw that his legs were badly mangled. As enemy fire continued to slam into the dirt around him, Master Corporal Peter Chaisson crawled up to help Mavin get a tourniquet on Ginther's other leg. The platoon medic, Tim Ferguson, was just behind Chaisson and tried to get an intravenous plasma feed into Ginther. But blood loss and dehydration had taken their toll and Ferguson couldn't find Ginther's shrunken veins.

Ginther came to as Mavin was putting the tourniquets on the wounded soldier's legs, tightening the strap around each limb to cut off the flow of blood gushing from the wounds, which would hopefully keep him from bleeding to death. The wounded soldier looked down at his blood-soaked uniform and began shouting: "Get me the fuck out of here!"

Mavin, Chaisson and two other soldiers rolled Ginther on top of a body bag, then strained to drag him out of the ditch, the bullets still flying, and roots, branches and bushes getting in their way.

Oz had been less badly wounded, taking an "in and out" bullet in his shoulder just beneath the protection of his body armour vest. But he was still bleeding heavily, and after Mooney had spent several minutes trying to patch him up, both men were covered in blood.

As he watched his men helping the wounded soldiers, occasionally snapping off shots at the Taliban gunmen who were still firing at the small knot of Canadians, Fletcher called up the rest of the platoon to give covering fire and ordered smoke grenades thrown towards the grape-drying hut to obscure the Taliban's aim. He waved Mooney over and grabbed the handset of his radio, taking a deep breath and forcing himself to sound calm.

"We've got wounded," he told Jurkowski, still a kilometre back from the firefight. "Get the LAVs up here now. We need LAVs here."

He replaced the handset and continued to fire back at the grape hut, mentally trying to calculate how long it would take for the LAVs to arrive. A moan from the ground beside him—from Oz—interrupted his thoughts. "I've got a sucking chest wound: I'm gonna die!"

Fletcher looked down at Oz and quickly assessed the situation. "You don't have a fucking sucking chest wound," he snapped. "You aren't going to fucking die, so shut up."

Oz shut up. Fletcher knew his soldier was in as much danger from shock as from his wounds and hoped his brusque response would shake him out of thinking he was going to die. It worked. By the time the medical evacuation helicopter came to take Oz and Ginther out, Oz was walking under his own steam and joking with his company mates at the command post in the dry riverbed.

There were no collapsible stretchers available at the front of the firefight, so several soldiers dragged Ginther and carried Oz back along the ditch to where they had started, lifting them over a low wall as gently as possible and lowering them down the other side, bullets whistling overhead the entire time.

"Well, this plan has gone to shit," Fletcher told himself, then ordered the rest of the platoon back to the wall where the rest of the company was still firing away at the well-protected Taliban. The entire incident had put Fletcher in a foul mood. Not only had the plan failed, but the Taliban "had the gall to shoot at my guys," he explained later.

"All right, you fuckers, now it's really on," he said, sending orders through Mooney's radio. It was time to redeploy his platoons and bring more fire down on the enemy. "You aren't going anywhere."

Mike Denine rolled his LAV forward the minute he heard Fletcher's radio call announcing casualties. "I can get 'em up there," he called to Marty Dupuis, whose LAV was a few metres away. "Let me go."

Dupuis gave Denine the go-ahead and the sergeant led four vehicles towards Seyyedin at top speed, racing down lanes so narrow there was little room to spare between the LAVs' armoured flanks and the walls and buildings on either side.

The ANA soldiers who were waiting in the shade behind the firefight, as their major had ordered them to do, jumped up and raised their arms over their hands in triumph when they saw the LAVs roll past. Denine watched with a sour expression as his LAV bounced over a rut in the road. "Afghan face to an Afghan problem, huh?" he asked his gunner. "Do I look Afghan to you?"

Dupuis, meanwhile, had pulled his LAV up until it was level with the wall where 9 Platoon had been firing, at the right end of the long line of soldiers. But with all the dust, smoke and confusion, he couldn't tell from where exactly the Taliban were firing. He stood atop his turret seat, exposing more than half his body, and scanned the ground around him closely, looking for a target for his LAV's powerful main gun. So intent was he on locating the enemy that he failed to notice the bullets whipping all around him, and the engine and firing noise drowned out the shouts of the soldiers on the ground to his left, trying to warn him of the danger. Finally, the booming voice of Warrant Officer Tim Turner, Charlie's company quartermaster who had been called up to fill in as sergeant-major, cut through the background noise and caught Dupuis' attention: "Sir! Get the fuck down!"

Dupuis realized with a start that he was standing in the midst of a hail of bullets and that the fire was coming from the grape-drying hut just over one hundred metres in front of him.

"Oh, crap," he said, dropping abruptly into his seat, safely behind fifteen millimetres of hardened steel armour.

While Dupuis rotated his turret to bring the LAV's guns to bear on the grape-drying hut, Oz and Ginther were carried into another LAV, which immediately reversed away from the fight and roared back to the wadi, where the company's support vehicles were waiting to carry them to the patrol base. Ryan Jurkowski had already radioed a request for a medical evacuation helicopter, and within minutes the two wounded soldiers were loaded aboard a U.S. Black Hawk for the brief flight to the Kandahar field hospital.

Dupuis ordered Denine and Master Corporal Randy Smith's vehicles to pull up on his right, slightly ahead of the firing line formed by 9 Platoon. All three vehicles opened up nearly simultaneously with their automatic cannon and coaxial machine guns. The booming bass of the 25-mm cannons brought grins to the dirt- and carbon-covered faces of the foot soldiers, who slumped down behind the wall, exhausted.

Denine had pulled his LAV right up to one of the low, partially crumbling walls separating the grape field from the road. The vehicle's blunt nose nudged up against the thick mud bricks and the barrel of its 25-mm cannon was slung over the wall, pointed directly at the hut. Denine looked up through his open hatch at the leaves of a mulberry tree hanging above him and cocked his head. The sun was filtering down through the leaves from a nearly cloudless, azure-blue sky—"a pretty scene," he thought distractedly. He watched the leaves fluttering gently in the wind for a few moments, then frowned. "That's weird," he thought, both transfixed and puzzled by the image. There hadn't been so much as a puff of breeze to break the brutal Afghan heat all day.

Time seemed to crawl at a fraction of its normal speed as Denine admired the picture-perfect scene overhead. But when one of the branches suddenly snapped off, it took only a few seconds for Denine to snap back to attention. It wasn't the breeze that was making the leaves flutter—it was Taliban bullets. "You want to play?" he thought as he looked through his sites at the enemy. "Well, all right then." He began firing his LAV's 25-mm cannon at the nearby hut. "Those are my guys you lit up."

A few metres to Denine's left, Dupuis and his gunner, Corporal Sutherland—whom everyone including Fletcher called simply "Suds"—were also firing non-stop at the grape-drying hut. But the metre-thick mud and stone walls were absorbing their high-explosive rounds with little damage. "It's not going through!" Suds shouted. "It's not going through!"

With the flick of a switch, the gunner changed the LAV's ammunition to armour-piercing discarding sabot rounds—a high-density slug surrounded by a lighter "shoe" designed to penetrate harder targets. The sabot rounds punched completely through the thick walls, but left a hole only two or three inches across. "Switching to HE [high-explosive]," Suds yelled, his forehead still pressed up against the LAV's gunsight.

Dupuis, watching through his own sight, saw the high-explosive shells burst around the small hole and immediately widen it. "That's it—that made it bigger," he said into his head-set. "Keep putting HE in there."

Denine and Smith were firing as well, and from their side of the line they could pump dozens of shells into the hut's thinner end walls. "No one's getting out of that building," he said determinedly. "Not alive, anyhows."

The three LAVs spent almost forty-five minutes firing at the hulking building and the furrows between the grapevines that the Taliban were using as trenches. Each vehicle fired almost one hundred shells from its cannon and hundreds of rounds from the coaxial machine guns, while the artillery continued to drop high-explosive shells behind the hut, cutting off the Taliban's retreat. But while the Talibs' fire slackened off, they continued to fire back sporadically, including with some rocket-propelled grenades launched at the LAVs.

Fletcher had had enough. He waved over FOO Bob Meade and stabbed one finger at the grape-drying hut, now barely visible through the dust and smoke of the LAV rounds exploding against its walls. "I want to close this down," he shouted over the noise. "I want you to bring some rounds on these guys."

Meade told him he could order artillery fire at a moment's notice, but that there was an even better option. "We've got some air stacked up over us now," Meade replied, referring to the ground-attack jets that were in holding patterns far overhead, loaded with precision-guided bombs that could be dropped within a metre or less of a target. "You want to use them?"

"All right," Fletcher replied. "What do I need to make that happen?"

Meade understood Fletcher's question immediately: the company commander was asking how far back his troops would have to move in order to be sheltered from the effects of the bomb. "I need 700 metres," he answered.

Fletcher looked over the wall at the hut, less than 200 metres away, and turned back to Meade. "I can give you 300 or 400."

"OK, I'll make it work."

The burly major called out to his platoon leaders, ordering them to get their men behind walls or into ditches—any kind of cover available. Moments later, a warning came over the radio: a Royal Air Force (RAF) Harrier jet was in-bound with a 500-kg bomb, ETA five minutes. The LAVs had also been told to pull back, which Mike Denine acknowledged with a cheerful, "Better safe than sorry!" He fired one last 25-mm shell at the grape-drying hut before ordering his driver to reverse. The LAV backed up a few metres then lurched to a stop, shuddering as its eight wide wheels spun ruts into the hard dirt. The vehicle had run up onto a stump—one of the thick trees that dotted the edges of the grape fields all around the village had been struck by a Taliban RPG that had sheared off all but the bottom two metres of the trunk. Now the thick splintered mass of what was left of the tree was wedged under the rear of the LAV, gluing it to the spot.

"Punch it, punch it!" Denine shouted into the intercom that connected him to his driver, well aware that he needed to get much farther back from the incoming bomb.

The roar of the LAV's engine went up an octave as it strained against the obstacle. Then a blast shook the vehicle and it shot backwards, finally free of the stump. A second Taliban rocket-propelled grenade aimed at Denine's vehicle had instead hit the tree trunk, shattering it into thousands of splinters and freeing the trapped LAV. "That was nice of them," Denine said, laughing inside his turret as he wheeled back out of range.

The troops were told that the air strike would arrive in two minutes and the warning to take cover was passed along the Canadian line. Fletcher and Mooney huddled against a wall like the rest of the soldiers as the dark outline of the Harrier swooped in low and fast over the grape-drying hut, dropping a black speck that separated from the fast-flying jet and arced gracefully towards the long, squat structure. A second later there was a loud crump that the soldiers could feel almost as much as they could hear. The world seemed to turn upside down, shake itself out and turn right side up again. There was a flash from the explosion and a blast wave rolled through the grape orchard and the fields and streets of the village like a tsunami, washing a tidal wave of hot air and dust over the troops.

Fletcher was shifted six inches away from the wall and immediately looked over at Mooney to ensure his young radio operator was all right. "That was the fuckin' coolest thing ever!" the tow-headed corporal shouted. "Jesus Christ!"

In the shocked silence that followed the explosion, Captain Meade offered a dry observation: "I don't think we need that fire mission anymore."

They didn't. A mushroom cloud of thick black smoke hung over the hut, which had been partially collapsed by the impact of the bomb, and the Taliban gunfire had died away completely. Fletcher ordered his exhausted troops to their feet, walking down the line, hauling some of them up himself. The hours of fighting and the strength-sapping heat made the simplest tasks an ordeal and most of the soldiers found that even taking a step forward took all their strength. But Fletcher needed them to complete one more task: to sweep forward to the hut and deal with any Taliban left alive by the RAF bomb.

The soldiers formed a line and swept laboriously through the grape orchard, its hard-packed dirt embankments churned and broken and the leafy grapevines perforated by thousands of bullets, grenades and high-explosive shells. They found two men sitting dazed between the rows of grape furrows, neither of them armed, and a stockpile of weapons not far from the hut. Both men were detained, their hands bound with the "zap straps" most soldiers carried with them—thick plastic zip-lock ties that served as light, unbreakable handcuffs when tightened around the crossed wrists of a prisoner.

Once the hut was clear, Denine climbed out of his LAV to take a look at the structure into which he had fired more than one hundred cannon shells. He marvelled at the carnage. There was blood everywhere. He couldn't see how anyone inside had survived the hours of Canadian fire and the powerful blast from the bomb. "It's like someone dropped a can of stewed tomatoes into a blender in there," he said after surveying the shattered interior of the hut. "Whatever was inside, we killed."

As he watched his men plod through the fields around the hut, Fletcher knew they were at the end of their strength. The adrenaline rush of combat had used up their reserves of endurance and some were already throwing up from the inescapable heat and dehydration. He got on the radio and ordered Dupuis to find them a safe place to recuperate, at least for a little while.

The young captain found an abandoned compound a few

metres up the road from Seyyedin, with shade from a handful of trees inside its high walls and a well in the middle. There was plenty of room in the surrounding fields to allow the LAVs to form a defensive cordon, but the only entrance was a narrow but solid-looking gate of iron and sheet steel. Dupuis solved the problem by ramming the wall with his LAV and knocking down enough of it to allow the soldiers to walk inside easily.

The troops trudged into the compound and collapsed almost as soon as they found a patch of shade, guzzling down water by the bottleful and lying on their backs breathing in gulps of air. Most were amazed to have survived the day-long fight unscathed, although many discovered cuts and scrapes and didn't remember how they'd acquired them. Someone drank a full bottle of water, then looked down at his torso expectantly, joking that it should come squirting back out from multiple bullet holes.

The two prisoners were sat down under a tree near the middle of the courtyard and given water. They were bruised, scratched and still somewhat stunned from the blast of the bomb, but otherwise all right. Sergeant Vaughn Ingram squatted down next to them and began asking questions, taking careful notes on a small pad he produced from his tactical vest. One of them was a teenager, an obvious "madrassa kid." A search of his clothing produced wiring and other bomb-making materials sewn into the lining of his long vest, but he had little useful information.

The second prisoner was an older man who Ingram guessed was in his late thirties. Speaking through the company's Afghan translator, the man insisted he was a farmer caught in the wrong place at the wrong time. "No, I'm not Taliban; I'm not al Qaeda," he insisted. "I'm just a farmer. I got caught in the fighting."

The muscular sergeant nodded sympathetically. "Where's your farm? Which fields are yours?" he asked quietly. "Was that your grape orchard we were just in?"

The man paused, then admitted his farm was in another part of the Panjwayi. He was in Seyyedin to help his cousin, he said. "So, which farm is your cousin's?" Ingram asked. "What's his name?"

As the questioning continued, the answers became more vague. The cousin was only a friend and the prisoner didn't want to give his name and get him in trouble. Ingram smiled and nodded encouragingly, finally asking, "So, how many Taliban were there? How long were they here and what were they doing?"

The man shook his head emphatically. "No, I'm not Taliban," he repeated.

Ingram smiled again and pointed to a tattoo visible on the man's forearm—the crossed scimitars and Arabic script of a jihadist emblem. "Then what's this?" he asked blandly.

The man looked at Ingram and smiled back, then stopped talking. "All right, then," the sergeant said with a shrug.

Ingram waved over two sentries and the man was zap-strapped again and blindfolded. The next day, the prisoners were handed off to Canadian military policemen, and although Charlie never learned who the older man was, Ingram, at least, was convinced they had captured a mid-level commander. "That guy was no foot soldier," he said afterwards. "That was a cell leader at least."

After a brief rest in the compound, most of the company moved back to Pashmul to hook up with Bravo Company and spent the night catching a few precious hours of sleep on the rocky ground next to their LAVs. They spent the next two days carrying out gruelling sweeps through several villages and compounds in and around Seyyedin, but found nothing.

Still, Fletcher wasn't fooled into thinking that the firefight had put an end to the insurgents' activities in the area. "You'd have to be an idiot to think there aren't more of the bad guys there," he told his officers a couple of days later. "They were consolidating with some sort of purpose in mind: this was just a snapshot."

Despite the Canadians' efforts, they didn't succeed again in pinning down the Taliban as thoroughly as they had at Seyyedin: the enemy had learned to be wary of the Canadians. On June 14, Charlie was once again ordered out of the Panjwayi, and this time they were told to expect to be gone for nearly a month.

CHAPTER TEN

"I don't want to hear that!"

Kandahar Airfield
June 15

After the exhausted soldiers returned to KAF, Ian Hope brought his senior officers together for a final briefing on the big divisional operation for which they were being called away from the Panjwayi. He was not happy, although he tried to conceal his discontent as his subordinates filed into the spartan briefing room next to the Canadian Tactical Operations Centre (TOC), a plywood-walled, roughly constructed box that served as the nerve centre for the Canadian operations in Kandahar. Part of a military officer's professional code is to swallow any misgivings or complaints and give one's orders one's best effort. And that's what Hope intended to do.

Despite the disturbing signs of a Taliban build-up in the region and the boldness and aggression of their fighters in meeting the Canadians head-on, the American commanders in faraway Bagram were not convinced of the seriousness of the threat. Instead of continuing their work in the Panjwayi, Task Force Orion was ordered to join Operation Mountain Thrust, a major coalition offensive that spanned the five southern and several eastern provinces. The operation would be planned and directed by the U.S.–led coalition task force that commanded all allied combat units in Afghanistan.

Mountain Thrust involved dozens of American, British,

Afghan and other coalition units, more than ten thousand soldiers in all, spread across thousands of mountainous kilometres. The operation was designed to flush the Taliban out of the strongholds where the U.S. generals were convinced they were hiding. The Canadian role in the mission was relatively minor, a series of moves through the mountains north of Kandahar City, and Hope could barely contain his frustration at being forced to leave the ongoing battle in the Panjwayi.

Listening to Hope's briefing, Bill Fletcher could tell his commander was angry, much as he tried to hide it. "We know damn well the enemy up there doesn't want anything to do with us," he thought, looking at the large-scale map that laid out the planned movements of the Canadian battle group through the mountains. "We're being sent up there and our work down here's not finished."

The situation was particularly irritating for Hope for a few reasons. After a month of on-again, off-again fighting, the Canadians were finally beginning to see results from their running battle with the Taliban in Panjwayi. Seyyedin had been the longest and most intense firefight to date, and although a handful of Taliban had managed to slip out of Charlie's grasp, fleeing the grape-drying hut just before the bomb hit, all had been hurt. Charlie Company had killed, captured or seriously wounded an entire Taliban cell. Furthermore, for weeks Hope had been telling everyone in the Canadian and U.S. chain of command who would listen about the danger in the Panjwayi. Even before the more than two weeks' fighting that climaxed in the battle at Seyyedin, Hope had personally told Major-General Benjamin Freakley, the general in overall command of coalition forces in southern Afghanistan, about the Taliban's build-up in Panjwayi. He had gotten nowhere: the Americans just weren't listening.

Hope had returned to KAF on May 29, straight from more than a week of fighting in the Panjwayi, to brief Canadian brigade commander, Brigadier-General David Fraser, about the fighting in his area of operations. He alit from his LAV as soon as it rolled to a stop in the Task Force Orion compound, a small corner of the sprawling base where the Canadians parked their vehicles and kept most of their ammunition and supplies. Clutching a roll of maps in one hand, Hope marched directly to the two-storey white building built out of converted sea containers that served as brigade headquarters. His hands and face were coated with dust and his camouflage uniform was stiff with sweat and dirt from nearly a week of constant wear. He trotted up the rickety metal stairs to the second-floor office of the brigade's chief of staff, Colonel Chris Vernon, and without preamble, unrolled his map of the Panjwayi on his desk.

Vernon, a telegenically handsome British Army officer with a crisp public school accent and a shock of wavy grey hair, had a reputation as a keen military mind. Moreover, he was an experienced soldier, having served in the U.S.–led Operation Iraqi Freedom. He and Hope got along well and had a mutually high regard for one other, so Vernon listened closely as the Canadian pointed out the dozens of places his troops had made contact with the Taliban and described each in detail. Vernon frowned with growing concern at the picture Hope was painting: clearly there were more Taliban in the Panjwayi than anyone at the brigade or U.S. headquarters had suspected.

"Wait here," he said after Hope had finished, scowling at the map. "The general is in camp on a visit: he ought to hear this."

Hope knew who Vernon meant: Major-General Freakley, the commander of the U.S. 10th Mountain Division and the direct superior of Canadian Brigadier-General Fraser, Hope's immediate boss. He sank wearily into one of the office chairs and waited, running a hand through his thinning hair, which had taken on the consistency of bleached steel wool.

Freakley had a reputation as a general who kept his staff running hard to keep up. His role as commander of the Mountain

Division had created in him something of a fixation with Afghanistan's mountains as the natural sanctuary for the Taliban. And his previous experience had only hardened this opinion. In 2002, he had been part of Operation Anaconda, a failed attempt to trap and destroy the last major pocket of Taliban and al Qaeda fighters in the rugged mountains of eastern Afghanistan. Anaconda had cleared the insurgents out of the Shahi-Kot Valley, but most of the Taliban and their al Qaeda allies had escaped due to poor coordination between the coalition forces and Afghan troops. One of that operation's mistakes was the failure of American intelligence to properly locate the enemy, incorrectly predicting that they occupied several large villages in the valley. In fact, the valley floors were empty when coalition forces began swooping in by helicopter and many troops—most of them American—were caught in Taliban kill zones that were swept by fire from positions in the mountains and hills. Ironically, Anaconda was the first major combat operation that included a Canadian unit—the 3rd Battalion of the PPCLI—and among the soldiers protecting the troops on the valley floor was a Canadian sniper team, armed with a .50-calibre long-range sniper rifle. During the operation, Corporal Rob Furlong, of Newfoundland, set a world record for the longest sniper kill in history when he shot a Taliban machine gunner at a distance of 2,430 metres.

Freakley was determined to succeed where Anaconda had failed, and his staff had put together an ambitious series of operations that would send the Canadians all over northern Kandahar Province looking for Taliban. As Hope waited for the general, he wondered how Freakley would take the news that the enemy was much closer than he thought.

A few minutes later, Freakley strode into the room trailing a small crowd of staff officers in his wake. Vernon and a handful of Canadian brigade officers brought up the rear. The general was a big man with a booming voice, blunt features and a personality that took up all the space in a room. Hope was immediately conscious of his own shabby appearance and ripe smell—it had been days since he had had a shower. But Freakley smiled broadly and enclosed Hope's hand with his own when the Canadian colonel rose to his feet. He waved him to a chair near the head of a long plywood table and eased into one himself. "Tell me everything," he said.

Hope turned his map of Panjwayi around so it was facing Freakley and repeated what he had told Colonel Vernon about the obvious build-up of Taliban in the Panjwayi and the Canadian battle group's attempts to disrupt them. "There are probably two hundred enemy fighters there," he said, and watched as a sceptical frown formed on the general's face.

Hope pointed out five villages where Charlie and Bravo Companies had separately contacted large groups of Taliban within the space of a few hours: obviously they couldn't be in that many places at once. Freakley remained silent, but his frown deepened. Clearly, nobody had told him about the Taliban's build-up in Panjwayi.

Hope carried on, detailing the ANA and ANP operations in the area and finally laying out what he had gleaned from Captain Massoud and his network of informants. "The Afghans are saying that the Taliban have chosen to build a base of operations in Panjwayi for one of two purposes: either to conduct multiple pin-prick attacks every day along the routes into Kandahar and in the city outskirts itself, disrupting us and causing worry amongst the locals, or to conduct one large-scale spectacular attack into the city."

Hope took a deep breath. "They want to seize something symbolic—like the stadium, the palace, or the [United Nations] compound—and fight a bloody battle in the streets of Kandahar that they would lose, but which would have an effect similar to the Tet Offensive."

The words had barely left Hope's lips before Freakley

became visibly agitated. "I don't want to hear that!" he barked dismissively. "That's a bad analogy: don't use those words again."

The 1968 Tet Offensive, a series of attacks launched by North Vietnam deep into the southern half of the country, was still a sore point with many U.S. Army officers. The Vietnamese had coordinated attacks by regulars and Viet Cong guerrillas throughout South Vietnam, hitting U.S. military bases, South Vietnamese government installations and even the U.S. Embassy in downtown Saigon, which had been considered impregnable. Although a resounding military defeat for the communist North Vietnamese, Tet was a public relations victory. The American public had been told that the North was losing, but televised images of fighting in the heart of Saigon helped shift public opinion against the war, and it is now considered a turning point in the conflict.

Despite Freakley's discomfort, Hope believed the analogy was entirely correct. The Taliban wanted to attack Kandahar not to take and hold the city, but for the psychological effect such an attack would have on public opinion in Canada and other NATO nations. He was taken aback by Freakley's reaction and paused for a moment until the general calmed down. After a minute, Freakley's attention returned to the map in front of him and he began quizzing Hope in detail about the Taliban's activities and locations in the Panjwayi. Hope was puzzled. The American general seemed genuinely surprised to hear about such a large massing of the enemy almost literally under the coalition's noses, but for months now the Canadians had been sending in regular reports on their operations and what they were up against. He and Vernon exchanged looks. Was it possible the information wasn't making its way to Freakley? Hope glanced down the table at the general's staff officers. From the looks on their faces, Hope surmised that Freakley's staff were not happy with what their general was hearing, and even less happy that it was coming from a Canadian.

Freakley told Hope that he needed to watch this build-up by keeping forces engaged in the districts. The Canadian colonel pointed out that Task Force Orion was due to be withdrawn from the Panjwayi in just over two weeks in order to embark upon Operation Mountain Thrust. He gently suggested that the general alter his plan and allow the Canadians to remain in Panjwayi. Freakley thought this over, then countered with a suggestion of his own: the Canadian battle group could leave the bulk of its attached ANA troops in the Panjwayi to keep an eye on the Taliban, taking only a few Afghan troops with them when they went north.

Hope paused, wondering just what the general had been told for the past few months. The Canadian task force had been complaining almost daily about the shortage of ANA troops assigned to their area. "Sir," he said carefully, "we only have a maximum of fifteen or twenty ANA there with us now."

Freakley exploded. His face reddened and he slammed his fist down on the table. "Why the hell am I only finding out about this now?" he shouted at everyone in the room.

Hope snuck a look at Vernon, who was keeping his features carefully neutral. The British colonel had personally penned a letter to the general more than a month earlier, requesting that an Afghan Army battalion be attached to Task Force Orion. It had clearly never reached Freakley's desk. Hope cleared his throat and carried on with his briefing, outlining where the Taliban had been active and what his battle group had been doing to counter them. He paused and pointed out that the general's plans for Operation Mountain Thrust would draw the bulk of the Canadian task force—still the largest and most powerful combat force in the restive southern provinces—far away from the Panjwayi and the alarming build-up of Taliban forces.

Freakley listened to the rest of Hope's briefing with a deepening expression of unhappiness. "Well, it's not the first time that I have seen an operation change from the bottom up," he

said after Hope had finished. "I want you to be ready to com-
mence Mountain Thrust on time, and therefore you need to go
back into Panjwayi and deal with this threat prior to the start of
Mountain Thrust. In preparation, I will have 2-87 Infantry
Battalion [a U.S. Army unit] stop and assist you for two or three
days en route to their operation area in northern Helmand. You
can expect them between the 4th and 6th of June."

Freakley got up to leave, not nearly as jovial as when he had
arrived. The expressions on the faces of his staff hurrying after
him were similarly bleak. Hope didn't care: the general's aides
had clearly been managing the information he was being given,
either out of fear or a desire to shield him from bad news.
Reports from Canadians in the field that contradicted what the
general's staff had been telling him were "spin doctored" to
downplay the importance of what was happening in the Panjwayi.

A little over a week later—just before Charlie pinned down
and destroyed the Taliban cell in Seyyedin—Hope received a
final, terse order from the divisional headquarters in Bagram:
despite his desire to remain in the Panjwayi, the Canadians were
to move north as scheduled on June 14. The promise of the U.S.
infantry battalion had evaporated. "I am sure that other influ-
ences, more powerful than mine prevailed," Hope said later of
the decision. While Bravo Company remained in the Panjwayi,
Charlie and Alpha were sent on a series of manoeuvres across
the Arghandab Mountains to the north, roaring along remote
mountain tracks in areas where their LAVs were not designed to
operate. They spent most of their time cordoning off and clearing several of the villages that dotted the deep valleys between
the black spires and ridges of the mountains.

It was a far cry from Panjwayi. Alpha Company had been
operating in the mountains since the beginning of the tour and
knew there were few Taliban to be found. The insurgents'
weapon of choice in the mountains was the IED, bombs jury-
rigged from old Soviet or Chinese land mines or artillery shells,

buried along a road and detonated by a well-concealed "button man." The soldiers found this tactic nerve-wracking and frustrating: there was no telling when an IED would engulf their vehicle in flames and a concussive blast from the explosion. And when it did, there was no way to strike back, except on the rare occasions when they were able to spot the trigger man. But even these contacts were few and far between. For the most part, Charlie spent its time driving up and down winding mountain roads and the soldiers soon took to calling Mountain Thrust "Operation Waste of Time."

PART 4

**Pashmul
July 8–10, 2006**

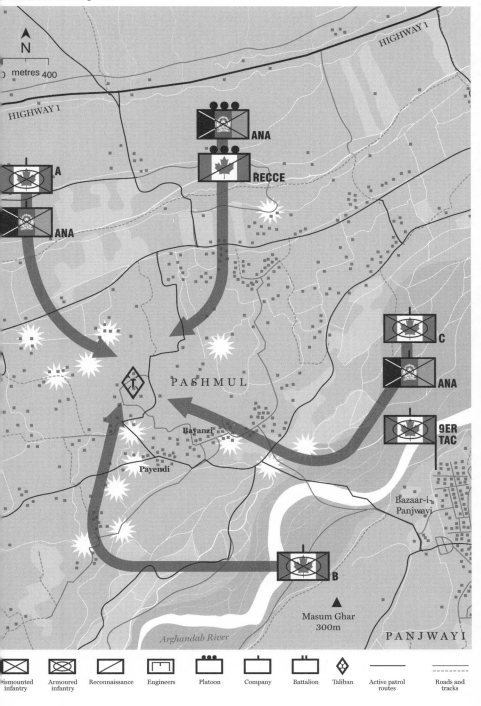

N

0 metres 400

HIGHWAY 1

HIGHWAY 1

ANA

A

RECCE

ANA

C

ANA

9ER TAC

PASHMUL

Bayanzi

Payendi

B

Bazaar-i-Panjwayi

Masum Ghar
300m

Arghandab River

PANJWAYI

| Dismounted infantry | Armoured infantry | Reconnaissance | Engineers | Platoon | Company | Battalion | Taliban | Active patrol routes | Roads and tracks |

CHAPTER ELEVEN

"A little surreal."

Kandahar Airfield
Early July

After three weeks of "Operation Waste of Time," Charlie Company was called back to KAF. The American commanders had finally acknowledged the growing Taliban threat in Panjwayi and the Canadians were being let off the leash, at least temporarily, to deal with it.

What had changed the minds of General Freakley and his staff in Bagram was an abortive raid by a U.S. special forces team into Pashmul—the jumble of walls, huts and compounds in the eastern end of the Panjwayi where the Taliban had been so active for the past two months and where Hope believed they were establishing a fortified base from which to attack Kandahar. The American commandos had launched the raid on June 24 against a fortified compound on the outskirts of Pashmul's cluttered collection of small villages. Their goal was to capture an HVT—likely a senior Taliban or al Qaeda leader. The operation went south almost as soon as the commandos hit their target. They ran into far more resistance than expected and found themselves deep inside Taliban-dominated country, on foot, with many of their number wounded.

Major Nick Grimshaw quickly deployed his Bravo Company, which had remained in the Panjwayi during Operation Mountain Thrust, and managed to extricate the special forces teams from the Taliban's clutches. Ian Hope heard through the military's informal grapevine that when the American special forces soldiers had returned—with one sergeant killed and several special forces soldiers seriously wounded—they reported to Bagram in no uncertain terms that something was brewing in Panjwayi. The message sent up to Major-General Freakley was frank: "Things are bad down there: the Canadians aren't wrong." It was a report the divisional staff could not minimize or deflect. Until the disastrous special forces raid, the Americans had believed that the "inexperienced" Canadians were seeing ghosts in the Panjwayi, exaggerating minor contacts with the enemy and wholly imagining others.

That would have been news to the soldiers of Bravo Company, who had had a busy three weeks patrolling the Panjwayi while Charlie and the rest of the battle group was roaming the mountain peaks and plunging valleys of northern Kandahar. They tried to restart several aid projects in the district that had been abandoned or delayed by the fierce fighting that began in May, but were handicapped by CIDA's continuing moratorium on operations in Kandahar.

Bravo Company did what it could with the army's own small, underfunded in-house aid agency. But the Taliban routinely attacked such reconstruction work, burning out rebuilt schools or medical clinics and threatening local villagers with death if they participated—and they were not about to let the Canadians work in the area again without a fight.

On June 23, Bravo Company had established a patrol base at last light in the Arghandab River wadi just north of a school in Mushan, Panjwayi. Mushan was situated just west of a cluster of villages that included Seyyedin, where Charlie had trapped the Taliban ten days earlier. Bravo was planning a medical outreach program for the next day, a sort of travelling clinic that brought military doctors and medics to outlying villages that otherwise had little or no access to medical care. Soon after dark, the gunners in the protective circle of LAVs spotted groups of Taliban in their night-vision sights, moving into position to attack. The soldiers were quietly roused and put on alert, so that when the Taliban began firing, the LAVs already had them in their sights. They opened up a devastating fire and forced the insurgents to flee in panic. But in the end, the Taliban got what they wanted: the medical outreach program scheduled for the following day was cancelled.

When Hope and the remainder of the battle group returned to KAF from the northern half of the province in late June, a terse message from divisional headquarters in Bagram was waiting. "Task Force Orion will be supported to conduct operations in Panjwayi," the new orders read. "You will be the main effort." Bagram had also given Hope more resources than had been put at the Canadians' disposal for the entire tour: more than 150 ANA troops, and 100 troops from the ANP; combat engineers; air support from Apache attack helicopters and UAVs (Unmanned Aerial Vehicles); and even a troop of British Household Cavalry equipped with Scimitar armoured reconnaissance vehicles.

But the news wasn't all good. Once again, the Canadians were being given only a few days to knock the Taliban back on its heels. The British Army, newly arrived in Helmand Province, was in trouble. The soldiers of the British 3 Parachute Regiment—"the Paras"—were suffering daily attacks on their bases in the Helmand River valley and found themselves isolated and running short of supplies. Operation Mountain Thrust was switching focus to eliminate the Taliban threat on the British, and the Canadian battle group was to be part of the new offensive. Although Hope was practically rubbing his hands with glee at the prospect of having all of his troops together for the first time, he knew he would have to move quickly to have an impact. Immediately, he began planning Operation Zahar, named after the Pashtun word for "sword."

The Taliban, however, seemed determined to interrupt him. On June 30, soon after sunset, the colonel was meeting with a group of brigade staff officers at the Canadian compound in KAF when he heard the scream of a rocket whistling overhead. It was quickly followed by the crump of an explosion nearby. Hope abandoned his conference, grabbed a nearby first-aid kit and ran towards the noise.

A Taliban rocket, fired by a remote detonator from the scrub and sand fields beyond the edge of the base, had slammed into the main mess tent where hundreds of Canadian, U.S. and allied soldiers and civilian staff ate every day. As Hope rushed to the tent, he had to force his way through a crowd of panicked civilian contract workers fleeing in the darkness.

He and the other Canadian and American soldiers who arrived at the scene found the wounded and helped carry them through the chaotic scene to the field hospital a few hundred metres away. Two Canadians and eight other coalition troops were wounded by the razor-sharp metal fragments from the exploding Chinese-made rocket. The Taliban had been lobbing such rockets at the sprawling KAF base for months, crudely aiming the explosives by propping them up against piles of rocks and hooking them to a cellular phone and a car battery so they could fire from a distance. In more than a dozen such rocket attacks on the base in the past year, this had been the only one to cause casualties.

Hope refused to let the Taliban attack distract him. A few days later, on July 5, he called his senior officers into the base to give them their marching orders. Bill Fletcher had raced in from Charlie's new base in Spin Boldak, more than an hour's drive south of Kandahar, to make it in time. He sat in the briefing room and watched the diminutive colonel pace back and forth in front of a satellite map of the Panjwayi, chewing on one of his thin cigars. On the map, three large coloured arrows converged on a small clutch of buildings marked "Objective Puma."

Fletcher recognized it as Payendi, one of the largest of the inter-connected knot of villages that made up the Pashmul area. Each arrow represented one company and each company was to capture and clear a sector of the village. Fletcher exchanged glances with Grimshaw and Major Kirk Gallinger, the commander of Alpha Company. The plan was unorthodox. "If I presented this plan at staff college they'd flunk me," Fletcher thought.

According to the army's "book," it was axiomatic that commanders did not aim their forces at each other. The fear was that their soldiers would accidentally hit one another with their rifle and heavy-weapons fire. As well, the ricochets and stray shots from weapons such as the LAVs' 25-mm cannons could carry a long way, potentially landing amid friendly troops. But Hope had complete faith in his company commanders and the soldiers of the battle group, and he didn't hesitate to trust them with such a risky manoeuvre.

Hope's plan was to have his three companies completely encircle one of the five large Taliban groups operating in the Panjwayi—more than two hundred enemy fighters in all and growing every day as reinforcements slipped across the Pakistani border. In Hope's words, his company commanders' job was to "disrupt and defeat them." Captain Massoud's network of informants and other sources of information—called "HumInt," or human intelligence—had reported a disturbing range of Taliban activity in Pashmul: weapons and ammunition caches hidden in cemeteries, a medical clinic for their wounded in a local "doctor's compound," and drug processing labs. To decide which hot spot to target, Hope had sought the advice of Grimshaw, whose company had been operating almost continuously in the Panjwayi since arriving in Afghanistan five months earlier. The Bravo Company commander chose a large cemetery just outside Pashmul, where his instincts told him a Taliban cell was protecting something of value to the insurgents.

Operation Zahar was scheduled to begin late on July 7 with an elaborate series of moves by all three companies of Task Force Orion. The opening gambit was designed to confuse the Taliban, who were known to keep watchful eyes on the gates leading into the main coalition base at KAF and along the major highways leading into the Panjwayi. But Hope knew he was being watched and made a point of regularly moving his companies in and out of both the main base and the smaller patrol bases in an elaborate game of hide-and-seek, all the while listening in on the enemy's cellular and walkie-talkie conversations. This Electronic Warfare component of Canadian army intelligence—or "EW," as the secretive work is known within the military—was something of a Canadian specialty within the NATO force. EW vehicles could be seen occasionally on the Kandahar base or parked on high ground in the surrounding area, bristling with antennae that could listen in on enemy radio, satellite and cell-phone chatter.

In Afghanistan, where there are almost no land-line telephones, the EW crews provided a gold mine of information on the Taliban's movements and intentions. The only way the enemy could communicate was by cellular phone or on cheap, Pakistani or locally purchased short-range radios that were intercepted relatively easily. The Canadians' ability to listen in was so good that whenever Hope sent his troops into a suspect area he would drive his LAVs past the target village or compound, firing their 25-mm main guns or calling in artillery rounds. He'd then listen closely to the resulting burst of Taliban radio or cell-phone transmissions. The more transmissions there were when the LAVs passed a certain area, or when shells exploded nearby, the closer they were getting to the Taliban's hideout. In the end, though, it always took infantrymen advancing on foot to pinpoint the enemy's exact location in the Panjwayi's confused terrain.

Although Hope was pleased to have all three companies together for Operation Zahar, only one of Charlie's three platoons was available for the mission—Captain Jon Snyder's 8 Platoon. Seven Platoon was to stay behind in KAF, where it was the designated quick-reaction force for the brigade, and 9 Platoon was posted to Spin Boldak, where it was finally getting familiar with the area Charlie was supposed to have taken charge of at the beginning of the tour. The ranks of many of the platoons were also depleted by mid-deployment leave. The leave plan, a standard for Canadian Forces' overseas missions, left Task Force Orion with up to a third of its fighting strength absent for most of the battles of May, June and July. At one point early in the fighting in Panjwayi, Hope considered asking National Defence Headquarters in Ottawa to cancel the remaining leaves because the situation on the ground was becoming so serious. After consulting with his sergeants and senior NCOs, however, he decided against it, largely because it would have been unfair to the half of his soldiers who had not yet taken their three weeks off. And by July, the troops had been almost constantly in the field, usually in action against the Taliban, and needed all the rest they could get. To bolster Charlie's depleted manpower, they were "loaned" Alpha Company's 2 Platoon, under Captain Sean Ivanko, which joined Charlie's 8 Platoon for the operation.

Payendi
July 7
1900 hrs

On July 7, soon after sunset, all three companies swung into motion. Alpha Company drove to Patrol Base Wilson, a new Canadian base on the side of Highway One, where Bravo Company had been stationed for the past three weeks. Alpha made it look like a routine "relief in place" for the benefit of their Taliban watchers, but instead of returning to KAF, Bravo drove southeast into the Panjwayi District Centre. There, they met up with Charlie, which had rolled out of Kandahar as quietly as possible, running up the Arghandab wadi with their headlights blacked out. Charlie and Bravo formed a long column and rumbled down the dry riverbed to take up their positions to the southwest and southeast of Payendi. Because the LAVs rode on wheels, instead of the noisy metal links of tracked vehicles, and because of their quiet engines, the column made surprisingly little noise as it bounded down the wadi, the drivers picking their way around gravel beds and sand dunes.

Meanwhile, soon after Alpha's arrival at the patrol base, the company had moved out again, this time driving south into the heart of the target area. Recce Platoon was already in place, having moved stealthily into position eight hours earlier. All of Task Force Orion was converging on Objective Puma.

In the back of some of Charlie's LAVs, the soldiers had been joined by ANA troops. The men spoke almost no English, but cheerfully accepted the Canadians' cigarettes, with broad grins lighting up their dark, bearded faces. Normally, the Afghans drove everywhere in tan-coloured pickup trucks, the soldiers crowded into the back, but the vehicles were not able to handle such rough terrain in the all-encompassing darkness. Hope had split most of them up among the Canadian LAVs, Nyalas and other vehicles and the Afghans were thoroughly enjoying the ride. They were much more lightly equipped than the Canadians, eschewing bulky and heavy body armour and even forgoing helmets in favour of green berets. The ANA prized mobility over protection. Despite this bewildering and often lackadaisical approach to safety—not to mention their unfortunate habit of closing their eyes when firing their AK-47 assault rifles—most of the Canadian soldiers got on well enough with the ANA, and were impressed by their often reckless courage. The Canadians knew that their Afghan colleagues could fight.

As the LAVs made their way through the warm night, Mike

Denine stood on the crew commander's seat, half out of the hatch, watching the shadowy trees and walls that were just visible over the lip of the wadi. It wasn't long before he saw a familiar sight—the silhouettes of a long line of men, women and children leaving the village. Once again, the Taliban was forcing civilians out of the areas they considered their turf. "Well, we know we're heading into the shit now," Denine said quietly, watching the escaping civilians lugging small pieces of furniture, in one case even a bed, towards the government-run refugee camps outside Kandahar.

It was just after midnight on July 8 when Denine's LAV veered north and led the column up the small rise that separated the wadi from the fields and compounds of Pashmul. Charlie was still nearly three kilometres from its "line of departure"—the point on the map at which Operation Zahar was supposed to begin—and Bravo Company had yet to push past Charlie and cut to their left in order to hit the target village from the southwest.

Bill Fletcher's command vehicle was just ahead of Denine's LAV and had barely rocked forward from its steep climb onto the flat ground ahead when Fletcher's gunner, Corporal Sutherland—Suds—spoke softly into his headset: something was moving in the line of trees ahead. "I've got heat signatures," the young corporal reported, squinting into the infrared gunsight, which showed the outlines of a handful of men, their body heat glowing green in the LAV's sights.

Before Fletcher could reply there was a sound like a train being shot out of a cannon, followed by an explosion off to one side of the LAV. "What the hell was that?" he shouted, half-deafened by the blast.

"I think it was an RPG, sir," Suds answered.

"Roger that. Go ahead and engage them," Fletcher said, sounding calmer than he felt.

Suds had already pressed the trigger. A split second after the major gave the order, the booming reports of the 25-mm gun drowned out the chatter of Taliban machine-gun fire aimed at the Canadian column and the whoosh and crump of RPGs exploding nearby.

Denine's gunner had seen the same group of Taliban in the trees ahead and opened fire a fraction of a second earlier, when the sergeant saw one of the distant gunmen reaching for his RPG launcher. "Hit 'em," Denine said calmly and a violent fireworks display abruptly lit up the night.

While hundreds of machine-gun tracer rounds and cannon shells tore into the enemy position, Fletcher was trying to simultaneously command his LAV and run his company. He got on the radio and ordered the rest of his company forward to make room for the line of Bravo Company vehicles still in the wadi behind them. Fletcher never took his eyes off the spot where the gunmen had opened fire, watching the high-velocity shells from the LAV's main armament kick up dirt and splinter trees. After a few minutes, the Taliban fire died and Bravo's vehicles roared out of the wadi and turned left to head towards their starting positions. Fletcher deployed his LAVs to cover the trees and orchards to their front and ordered his troops to prepare to dismount and sweep through the tree line.

In his own vehicle, Denine's attention was drawn from the now shattered and scarred trees to a clutch of structures to his left, where a crowd was boiling out of a handful of buildings and scattering in all directions, fleeing the noise and fire from the Canadian vehicles. "Like cockroaches," he muttered to himself, slewing his turret around to watch the bizarre exodus.

Through his night-vision gunsight, Denine could clearly see the sparkle of weapons firing at the Canadian column, but he also saw women and children, even goats and dogs, among the crowd in his crosshairs. He swore under his breath: the Taliban were using the handful of villagers still in the area to shield their escape. He keyed his radio transmitter to warn the rest of

Charlie. "If they're shooting at us you can hit 'em," he said, "but be careful."

Just minutes after the firefight had died away, Fletcher's radio hissed to life. The rest of the battle group was reporting contacts. The Taliban had decided not to wait for the Canadians to get into place before opening the battle.

While his battle group was manoeuvring into position, Ian Hope had driven Niner Tac up a steep dirt track to the top of Masum Ghar, a small ridge overlooking the entire Pashmul area. It was a site from which he could easily communicate with both the brigade headquarters at distant KAF and his three companies. He had just positioned his LAV and his crews were setting up the radio antennae to relay broadcasts to headquarters when the blackness beneath him erupted into flashes of light and explosions, accompanied by the distinctive thumping booms of 25-mm chain guns. While Hope scanned the fields below with the LAV's night sights and his binoculars, reports began flooding in: all three companies and Recce Platoon had come under fire within a few minutes of each other. A handful of soldiers from Bravo and Alpha Companies were wounded, one seriously, and Recce had taken three prisoners.

The Taliban had been surprised by Task Force Orion's nighttime moves, but had recovered quickly. Small "early warning groups" of four or five fighters had been posted along the roads and tracks leading into the Pashmul to delay the Canadians' advance and to forewarn the larger groups of Taliban deeper inside the maze-like area.

Hope watched and lit the first of many cigars, glancing up at the moonless night sky. The crews of the handful of vehicles in Niner Tac watched and exchanged glances. Sunrise was hours away and it was already clear that this was going to be a long day.

The first faint light of dawn had begun to illuminate the battle-field. Bill Fletcher was preparing to order his troops out of their LAVs when a burst of gunfire and explosions erupted to his left. Bravo Company had been ambushed by another group of Taliban sentries less than a kilometre to the west and the soldiers of Charlie could see volleys of RPGs bursting in the air around the vehicles as they advanced towards Payendi in the semi-darkness. Fletcher was standing in his turret, scanning the fields and walls ahead for more signs of trouble, when Suds tugged on one leg to get his attention.

"I've got five guys moving left to right," the corporal called up from his gunner's seat. "They're not in traditional garb, but they're carrying weapons."

Fletcher frowned and dropped down into the turret to peer through his scope at the men Suds was tracking. The five were wearing western clothing, walking casually across the front of the Canadian position several hundred metres away, their AK-47s slung over their shoulders or dangling from their slings.

"You want me to light 'em up?" Suds asked, his forehead still pressed up against the sight.

"No, stand down," Fletcher answered slowly, watching the distant figures etched in the green and black of the sight. "I don't want to shoot up any ANA."

Fletcher did not know exactly where the ANA attached to Bravo Company were deployed and did not want to risk a friendly-fire incident. He raised Bravo on the radio and asked if any of their ANA or ANP were in the area. While he waited for the reply, Fletcher watched the small group of men trotting across his sights closely: they moved quickly and easily over the rough terrain, unlike the hurried, panicky movements of most Taliban fighters. To Fletcher, their actions screamed "veterans." A few minutes later, his radio crackled to life and Bravo Company reported no friendlies in front of Fletcher. But by then, the five had moved out of sight. They were almost certainly foreign fighters for the Taliban—jihadists from Chechnya, the Arab countries or Pakistan, a sure sign that the enemy was moving its most experienced fighters into the Panjwayi.

As soon as there was light enough to see, Fletcher ordered his men to dismount and clear the ambush site. The soldiers walked steadily forward into the trees, finding no Taliban hiding in the line of walnut and mulberry. For once, however, they did find bodies. Three of the gunmen had been hit by 25-mm rounds from the Canadian LAVs, one of whom had been completely decapitated by a high-velocity shell, his head nowhere in sight. The second Talib had taken a large fragment of metal in the chest but was somehow still alive. A few soldiers performed first aid on the badly wounded gunman, while others argued over who was going to get the gory job of searching the headless body, which was covered in and surrounded by blood, turning the dirt and undergrowth around it black in the grey pre-dawn light. The wounded prisoner died soon after the soldiers found him and a short distance away they found the dismembered remains of a third Talib. This man had been struck in the centre of his chest by a 25-mm shell and torn to pieces. "Not a lot left of him," Fletcher said dispassionately, when he came forward to see the bodies. He turned over a PKM machine gun lying next to one of the dead Taliban with the toe of his combat boot. The thick barrel of the Russian-made weapon had been cut cleanly off by a 25-mm slug.

Most of the soldiers were now used to the gory aftermath of a firefight, shrugging off the blood and bodies with a philosophical "That's what they get for shooting at us," as one private told Mike Denine. But it was so rare to find a Taliban body that most of the troops found an excuse to go and see the three in the field. Fletcher took the discovery as a good sign: the Taliban had been so surprised by the Canadians' advance that they didn't have time to do their usual "battlefield cleanup." Reports from the other companies and Recce Platoon indicated that they, too, had caught groups of Taliban hiding and come upon others that were clearly taken by surprise.

Soon after clearing the tree line, Charlie Company mounted up and continued pushing north, brushing up against Taliban cells every few hundred metres. The enemy laid ambushes along the tracks they thought the Canadians were most likely to use, but Charlie had learned a lot over the previous months. They knew almost as well as the Taliban where the next trap would be sprung. Still, Mike Denine noticed that these Taliban were a little different than those the battle group had been fighting in the Panjwayi off and on all summer. "These guys know what they're doing," he told himself. "They know how to ambush, they know fire and movement. They know everything we do."

Fletcher estimated that there were two or three groups of Taliban in front of him, each with fifteen to twenty-five men. They were attacking and ambushing aggressively and moving quickly back and forth to come at the Canadians from different directions. The Taliban tried repeatedly to find a way to out-flank the Canadians, but the presence of all three companies made that almost impossible: there were too many soldiers closing in. By early afternoon, Charlie had advanced to within a kilometre of Payendi, slowed by the crazily winding roads, the cross-hatching of walls and irrigation ditches, and the Taliban's pin-prick delaying attacks. At a relatively rare patch of open ground, the company was stopped by a fusillade of fire from a grape-drying hut outside the village that forced both platoons to take cover and spread out, returning fire.

Fletcher took stock of the situation in a glance. The Taliban had decided to make a stand using the thick walls of the grape-drying hut as a bastion against the firepower of the LAVs. He jumped out of his vehicle and waved urgently at Golf Thirteen, the nearby artillery LAV, and signalled the FOO to follow him. "Come on with me!" he shouted, straining to make himself heard over the incoming and outgoing gunfire. His FOO, Captain Andrew Charchuk, nodded, pulled himself out of his commander's hatch and clambered down from the height of the turret, trying to ignore the bullets snapping past. Charchuk, who had been sent to southern Afghanistan only a few days earlier, pounded on the rear door of the LAV and shouted for his master bombardier to shoulder his radio and come along. Master Bombardier Jeff Fehr had been riding in the back of the vehicle for most of the day. He went pale when he stepped out of the vehicle and looked around. The LAV was stopped just a few metres from the spot where it had been hit by an RPG on May 17, killing Nich Goddard.

But there was little time to reflect. Fletcher had already loped ahead of them, headed for a small compound nearby. Clutching their radios and other gear, the gunners scrambled to catch up with the company commander and the ever-present Mooney, who, as usual, was hurrying along just behind him. Charchuk climbed up a short flight of mud-brick stairs to the top of a wall overlooking the neighbouring compound, which was sparkling with the muzzle flashes from Taliban weapons and the zipping tracers from the Canadians' machine guns. "Can you hit that?" Fletcher asked, pointing at the thatch-and-mud rooftops just visible beyond the high walls of the compound.

Charchuk took out his laser range-finder, a small scope that bounced an invisible beam of light off the nearest wall, and read from its reflection the precise distance. The cluster of buildings from which the Taliban were firing was exactly eighty-nine metres away. "In theory, we should be okay," he said, but recommended one platoon move back, to be on the safe side.

Charchuk called up the troop of guns located near Patrol Base Wilson, several kilometres away, and fed them a set of coordinates for the compound. A few minutes later, a single shell came whistling in more than three hundred metres from the target. After a series of corrections were called in by radio, using the laser to pinpoint exactly where the round had exploded, a second single shot from the artillery's M777 howitzers exploded within fifty metres of the target. Charchuk made a slight adjustment to their aim and radioed in the order: "Fire for effect."

There was a few seconds of silence before the air and ground around the compound erupted in fire and smoke as dozens of high-explosive shells burst, sending shock waves rippling for hundreds of metres in all directions. The gunfire from the walled-in buildings behind the grape-drying hut stopped abruptly and the Canadians cheered: even Fletcher flashed a brief smile before ordering his soldiers forward.

Charlie and the rest of the task force advanced steadily into Payendi, occasionally skirmishing with the Taliban as they methodically cleared the village one building and one compound at a time. But the raw power of the artillery seemed to have taken the fight out of the insurgents and they spent most of their efforts trying to escape the ever-tightening circle of Canadians.

By sunset, Payendi was clear and all three companies and Recce Platoon were setting up their defences at HQ for the night. They had endured more than twelve hours of almost constant contact with the enemy, made all the more difficult by the baking Afghan summer heat. The village was a ghost town, now occupied only by the Canadians and the handful of prisoners they had taken during the day's fighting. In the fading light, Bill Fletcher and Kirk Gallinger strolled over to Nick Grimshaw's command LAV to talk over the next day's operations. It took just a few minutes over their heavily marked-up satellite maps to sort out which areas would be each company's responsibility. With routine matters such as passwords and arcs of fire settled, the three majors sat on the LAV's rear ramp for a rare moment of relaxation. One remarked that this was the first time all three of them had been together in the field since the tour began five long months earlier.

The Bravo Company headquarters was set up near a large cemetery complex just outside the village—several acres of rock-covered Afghan graves, each marked by its own thin branch or pole from which fluttered tattered streamers of coloured cloth. The three men sat silently for a moment, watching the ANA troops searching the graveyard for the major Taliban arms stockpile that Massoud's informants had insisted was somewhere near the village. The ANA were just silhouettes against the setting sun, moving through the graveyard like ghosts flitting among the dipping and waving banners.

"A little surreal, isn't it?" Fletcher said finally, as the Afghan soldiers gave up their fruitless search.

The three men got to their feet and trudged back to their respective commands, the next day's work just a few short hours away.

CHAPTER TWELVE

"The man who wouldn't die."

Payendi
July 9
0430 hrs

The night passed quietly enough. Most of the troops slept curled up in their combat uniforms and many did not even bother taking off their body armour. They simply doffed their helmets and the tactical vests that went over top of the protective gear, carefully laid their rifles within easy arm's reach, and fell asleep on the nearest patch of level, rock-free ground. The only enemy that penetrated the defences were tiny sand fleas, a constant annoyance to the soldiers whenever they had to sleep on the ground. About the size of a black fly and just as voracious, they could hop up only to about knee level and weren't able to bite through the Canadians' sand-pattern camouflage uniforms. During the day, the fleas weren't a problem. But whenever the troops lay down, the insects would swarm, leaving exposed faces peppered with bites. For some reason, Mike Denine was immune. As the men around him woke long before dawn, scratching and rubbing at their bites, he cheerfully cried, "They just don't like the taste of me, boys!" Then he mounted his LAV and prepared to lead Charlie out of their night base and into Payendi.

Charlie had been given what was expected to be a fairly easy job—to clear several grape fields and a handful of hulking grape-drying huts to the south of the village. No Taliban was expected in the area and the task was estimated to take no more than a few hours. Because there were no good roads through the corrugated fields on the outskirts of the village, Denine and the rest of the company's LAVs would remain to the rear, while the bulk of Charlie marched down the narrow paths on foot.

Eight Platoon was in the lead, leapfrogging ahead of the Alpha Company platoon while it cleared a grape-drying hut with Fletcher close by. The popping of weapons fire snapped the burly major's head around and a second later Mooney's radio came alive: "Contact, wait out." It was Captain Jon Snyder, the 8 Platoon commander.

Fletcher had no intention of waiting. He sprinted forward, headed for the group of buildings that the lead platoon had been sent to clear out with Mooney just behind him, cursing as always while he tried to keep up. By the time they arrived, a small knot of troops, including Snyder, was pulling a soldier back into cover, dragging him along the ground to a spot clear of the bullets splashing in the dirt just behind them. Despite his bulky body armour, the prone and motionless wounded soldier looked frail and Fletcher's heart sank as he motioned to his platoon commander, waiting for an explanation.

As 8 Platoon approached the buildings, they had stumbled upon a man wearing an ammunition belt. The man, who had been walking nonchalantly out of the compound as the Canadians came up, spotted the soldiers and fled inside. Snyder had ordered his platoon to prepare to clear the compound, moving his lead section into a "stack" outside the gate, ready to pour inside once the door was kicked open. As they charged into the compound, several long bursts of gunfire had ripped into the closely packed group. A Taliban gunman firing from the roof of the complex had hit Corporal Tony Boneca, an Army reserve soldier from Thunder Bay, Ontario, in the chest, just above the thick ballistic plate that provided most of the protection. The rest of Boneca's section had dragged him around a corner of the high wall that surrounded the compound. The stricken soldier now lay bleeding in the dust while one of his comrades worked frantically to revive him and the rest of his friends looked on helplessly.

Snyder looked around. "Where's his rifle? Where's his kit?"

In the confusion of the firefight, Boneca's rifle and helmet had been left behind and were now lying in the middle of the area swept by bursts of enemy rifle fire. "You've got to go get his kit," Snyder said insistently.

The soldiers looked at each other for a moment. "Well, fuck it then," Private Mike Charlish finally answered, rising heavily from one knee. "I'll get them."

Charlish sprinted into the open area, grabbed Boneca's rifle and bolted back around the corner, ducking the sporadic Taliban fire from the roof. "Fuck it," he muttered, breathing heavily as he sank to the ground, dropping Boneca's equipment near to where another soldier continued to work.

Fletcher ordered his second platoon, 2 Platoon from Alpha Company, to move up and bring more firepower down onto the compound, then watched silently for a moment as the medics continued their efforts. One of his comrades was performing mouth-to-mouth on the young soldier, pausing between breaths to spit out blood.

"Sir," Mooney spoke softly from Fletcher's side, "there's fuckin' no way."

"Yeah, I know," Fletcher answered quietly, "but don't say anything. They've got to try."

Tearing his eyes away from the scene in front of him, Fletcher turned his attention to organizing an assault to take the compound. Although he estimated it was defended by only a handful of Taliban, he knew they were determined. They were returning fire from their well-protected rooftop position, despite steady fire from the Canadians and a handful of RPGs launched by the ANA soldiers attached to Fletcher's command. A team of

Canadian snipers on a rooftop six hundred metres away could see two men shooting at Fletcher's troops, but the Taliban gunmen were sheltering behind a series of low walls on the building's roof, and to their frustration, the snipers could not get a shot. Marty Dupuis, whose LAVs were nearly a kilometre back from the compound, was also attempting to get a clear shot at the roof, but his line of sight was blocked and the way forward barred by the thick grape fields and a maze of walls and ditches.

As Fletcher sized up the situation, an American captain and sergeant who were attached as military trainers to Charlie's ANA troops jogged up and volunteered to lead another assault on the compound. "Let's go in and get 'em," the captain said bluntly, casting a sideways glance at Boneca and the medics.

Fletcher nodded in approval and deployed his two platoons to cover possible escape routes. But he wasn't about to let the Afghans go in alone: Fletcher intended to personally lead the assault on the Taliban who had killed one of his soldiers.

One of 8 Platoon's three sections quickly moved up to the compound walls and prepared to lob hand grenades into the small yard just ahead of the ANA's attack. On a signal from Fletcher, he and two other Canadians pulled the safety pins from the baseball-sized grenades and hurled them hard over the wall. So hard, in fact, that one of the three injured his knee and had to be helped back to safety behind the Canadian firing line, which was snapping off shots to keep the Taliban's heads down.

Fletcher waited the handful of seconds that it normally took for a grenade's fuse to burn down, but only one explosion echoed off the compound's walls—two of the grenades had been duds. "Son of a bitch," he said angrily. "OK, boys, in we go!"

The eight soldiers burst into the courtyard through the narrow gate and pelted across the few metres of open ground to throw themselves up against the building where the Taliban had installed themselves. Breathing heavily from the sprint, Fletcher felt a wave of relief: the gunmen on the roof hadn't even had the chance to fire on them as they ran. He watched the Afghan soldiers edge along the wall towards the stairs leading up to the roof, while he and the two Americans flattened themselves against it under a crude awning of branches and twigs. The three were now almost directly beneath the Taliban on the roof and Fletcher watched the Afghan soldiers brace themselves, then rush up the stairs. The brief set of stairs, enclosed in a stucco-covered stairwell, made a right-angle turn halfway up before emerging on the top of the building. As soon as the ANA soldiers reached that point, a Taliban gunner at the top of the stairs sent a cloud of bullets into the stairwell. The Afghans were driven back amid spatters of chipped plaster and brick.

"We could do this," Fletcher thought as the ANA reeled back from the sudden burst of fire. "We could end this in a few minutes, but we'd lose guys doing it."

The stocky major decided he wasn't going to lose any more of his men to this one small compound. He was about to order the ANA and the two Americans back the way they'd come when the ground around him came alive with bullet impacts. One of the Taliban fighters, either hearing or seeing Fletcher and the two Americans beneath him, had leaned out over the edge of the roof and held down his trigger, pumping in a flood of fire that kicked up the dirt around Fletcher's feet. The Americans instinctively hugged the wall for cover, but the Canadian major turned and dove headfirst towards a small wooden door that led into the interior of the house, not realizing that the door had been chained and padlocked shut, and that its wooden frame was deceptively strong. Fletcher's helmet struck the door like a battering ram and bounced off it, propelling him backwards onto the ground where the Taliban bullets had just been kicking up the hard-packed earth.

Fletcher lay on his back, the wind knocked out of him, looking up at the thin layer of thatching that was all there was between him and the Taliban. All he could think was, "I'm going to die and I'll look like an idiot."

Fortunately, the two Americans had raised their rifles to fire up through the awning, forcing the Taliban to pull back from the edge of the roof. The U.S. sergeant helped Fletcher up and, realizing for the first time that the company commander had followed them into the compound, bluntly asked, "Sir, what the fuck are you doing up here?"

Fletcher just shook his head and ordered everyone out of the compound. Before he raced out of the courtyard, however, he stopped long enough to raise one booted foot to kick the small wooden door that had almost been the death of him until it was splintered off its frame. "Goddamn thing," he growled.

Once the Afghans and the Canadians had cleared out, Fletcher stalked angrily back to Charlie's firing line, sweat streaming down his face, and called over Charchuk. "Well, we tried it the old-fashioned way," he told the FOO. "Let's just level the place."

Charchuk nodded and radioed the pilot of a U.S. attack chopper that had been circling nearby, waiting for the Canadians to call him in. The AH-64 Apache ground attack helicopter was used by U.S., British and Dutch forces in Afghanistan to quickly bring overwhelming and accurate firepower down on targets identified by ground troops. A pair of Apaches had been circling not far from the Canadians all afternoon, armed with a 30-mm chain gun and dozens of Hellfire and Hydra missiles. Charchuk gave the pilot the coordinates of the building where the gunmen were holed up. The helicopter screamed in low, pumping dozens of shells from its 30-mm automatic cannon into the Taliban-held compound, raising a vast cloud of choking, blinding dust.

Charchuk was trying to contact the battery of Canadian artillery when he heard an unfamiliar voice break in and offer to help. It was the controller of a U.S. Predator, an unmanned drone plane that had been circling overhead all morning, transmitting a stream of video images back to its home base in KAF. The spy planes were generally used for surveillance, but this Predator was armed with a Hellfire missile, a precision-guided rocket with a high-explosive warhead. The American controller said he could fire it right into the compound.

"Well, that sounds pretty cool," Fletcher said when his FOO relayed the offer. "What'll that do?"

"I don't know, sir, let me look it up." Charchuk flipped through the volume of manuals he always carried with him to find out how far back Charlie's soldiers would have to be when the missiles struck—no one in the Canadian army had ever seen a Hellfire strike, let alone guided one onto a target under fire.

After a few seconds, Charchuk concluded that most of them would be safe, but recommended that 8 Platoon pull back another 150 metres. While Fletcher ordered Jon Snyder to withdraw to a safer distance, Charchuk radioed the precise location of the troublesome building and gave the go-ahead for the missile launch. A few seconds later, the soldiers heard the roar of the missile streaking in over their heads and the compound was rocked by a shattering explosion that enveloped the buildings and the Canadian positions with a blinding cloud of swirling dust. When it cleared, the Afghan and Canadian troops cheered: part of the roof of the compound's main building had collapsed and a small fire was burning somewhere inside.

Fletcher ordered two sections from Sean Ivanko's 2 Platoon to get into position to storm the compound again. Once more, he joined the section of Canadians outside the gate into the small courtyard.

Two more grenades were thrown at the building, and again only one exploded. Fletcher shook his head in disgust. Problems with hand grenades had plagued the task force for months. The army had been warned more than two years earlier about problems with its Canadian-made grenades, some of which failed to explode at more than ten times the rate of the American model upon which they were based. But the Canadian Forces insisted the higher dud rate of its C13 grenades, manufactured under licence by SNC Technologies Inc., of Le Gardeur, Quebec, was the result of an isolated batch and had done nothing to address the problem. In the heat and dust of southern Afghanistan, the Canadian-made grenades failed at an alarming rate.

Fletcher had expected the Hellfire missile to take the fight out of the Taliban holed up in the compound, but when he and the dozen other soldiers tumbled through the opening and began their drills to secure it, sporadic bursts of gunfire from the roof made it clear that at least one Taliban fighter had survived the missile strike. A second attempt to storm up the stairs onto the roof was driven back by a long volley of AK-47 fire, and a frustrated Fletcher once again ordered the troops out of the compound.

Shaking his head in disbelief, he ran up to Charchuk. "We need some more stuff on this," he said, gesturing at the compound less than one hundred metres behind them.

"Again?"

"Yeah, again."

The artillery officer hesitated. The Canadian gun battery in distant Patrol Base Wilson was ready to fire volleys of shells onto the compound, but he also knew that Charlie's troops were only eighty-nine metres away, far too close for safety. He explained to Fletcher that they were sitting in the "beaten zone," the area which was likely to be swept by fragments of metal from the howitzer shells when they burst just above the ground. "Sounds good: let's do it," Fletcher replied grimly, determined to end this fight immediately.

Charchuk already had the gun battery on his radio. He ordered them to fire a single round and prepared to "walk" the artillery onto the compound as he had the day before, adjusting the aim after each shot. Each shell took a few seconds to travel the more than four kilometres from the patrol base to the target, and each time one was fired, Charchuk and Fehr, his

FOO tech, looked at each other and winced in anticipation of a high-explosive round landing on top of them.

The process of adjusting the fire had barely begun when a familiar American-accented voice came over Charchuk's other channel: the unmanned Predator was still circling far overhead and its controller had been watching the Canadians' assault on the small compound from the aircraft's high-resolution video cameras. He had seen a man trying to bolt out of the building, taking advantage of the Canadians' temporary withdrawal to make a run for another group of compounds several hundred metres away.

Fletcher and Charchuk decided to use the already zeroed-in artillery to discourage him, dropping half a dozen shells into the field ahead of the fleeing man. Charchuk listened to his radio closely for a moment, then gave Fletcher a thumbs-up. "Looks like he's wounded," he said, relaying the message from the Predator's controller. "He ran into the stairwell and collapsed."

Fletcher decided for the last time that he had had quite enough of the small compound and its handful of determined defenders. "Right, bring in the Apaches again," he told his FOO.

The angular profile of the attack helicopters swooped down on the buildings three times, firing their high-speed cannons on the first strafing run, and following up with a fusillade of rockets that exploded in waves against the mud-brick walls and started another round of fires inside the compound. The Apaches had scarcely begun their third pass when the ground heaved and an enormous explosion blew out part of a building: a fire started by one of the attack chopper's missiles or a lucky hit by a high-explosive cannon shell had ignited a stockpile of weapons and ammunition hidden in one of the compound's smaller structures. Charlie had finally found the Taliban's hidden arms cache.

Fletcher was kneeling in a shallow ditch with Mooney on one side of him and the American captain on the other when the arms stockpile exploded. The concussion from the blast sucked the breath from their lungs and sent a cloud of shrapnel, stones and dust whistling through the air in all directions. Mooney felt something hit his legs hard enough to bowl him over and when he looked down, was shocked to see blood spreading like an ink stain down the pants of his combat uniform. "I'm hit, I'm hit!" he shouted.

Fletcher glanced over and realized that, for once, the young corporal who had been his shadow throughout the entire mission wasn't there. Mooney was on the ground, shivering and staring at a growing pool of blood in his lap. Fletcher swore and grabbed his first-aid kit, pulling out his belt knife to cut away Mooney's pants and find the source of the bleeding.

The American captain who had been on his left was also wounded, hit in the leg with the same shrapnel that had felled Mooney and, incredibly, somehow managed to miss Fletcher. Charchuk, who had been just a few metres away, rushed over to begin bandaging up the American.

Mooney looked up at Fletcher as the major cut away at his pants leg to expose the wounded leg. "Are they OK?" he asked after a moment.

"What?" Fletcher answered, looking up at the young corporal's whitened features.

"Are my boys OK?" Mooney said, gesturing to his crotch. "Tell me my boys are OK."

Fletcher rolled his eyes and sighed. He shook his head and gingerly lifted the blood-soaked patch of tan-coloured cloth covering Mooney's groin, still not quite believing he was checking his signaller's private parts. "I don't know, Mooney," he said after a pause. "Is it always this small?"

The corporal looked at him, dumbfounded, and Fletcher smiled: "Yeah, yeah," he quickly added, "they're OK."

Mooney breathed a sigh of relief and let his head slump back. He was going to be all right. He knew his major well

enough to know that Fletcher wouldn't have been teasing him
unless his wound was relatively minor. The shell fragment that
tore into his leg missed any major arteries and by the time the
medics rolled him onto a stretcher and carried him back to be
evacuated to the field hospital in KAF, Mooney was making rude
jokes and swearing cheerfully.

But the U.S. Army captain that had been just to Fletcher's
left was growing pale as Charchuk tried to patch him up and
the artillery officer was worried that his patient was about to go
into shock. Then the American's sergeant came up behind them,
looked over Charchuk's shoulder and shook his head sadly. "Sir,
that's barely worth wearing a Purple Heart for," he said drily.
The captain choked out a dry laugh and brightened up almost
immediately.

Smaller explosions rocked the compound for more than half
an hour as ammunition and explosives stored inside continued
to "cook off"—ignited by fires that sent a plume of smoke into
the air that could be seen for kilometres around. The combat
engineers who examined the compound estimated that the muni-
tions cache had likely contained hundreds of pounds of land
mines and artillery shells destined to be turned into Taliban IEDS
or suicide bombs.

It was nearly an hour later when Fletcher clipped his bayonet
onto the end of his rifle and ordered all of his troops to sweep
into the now shattered compound. Instead of using the gate,
Fletcher hauled himself onto the top of one of the tall walls, its
surface cracked and blackened by the explosions. He had
planned to vault over it into the compound, but when he
reached the top, his weight, augmented by his body armour,
ammunition and equipment, proved too much for the weakened
structure and it collapsed in a cloud of dust, broken bricks and
plaster. For the second time that day, Fletcher was unceremoni-
ously dumped on his backside inside the courtyard. He looked
up to see a young private—a radio operator from Alpha Company

that he didn't know—looking down at him and struggling to keep a straight face.

"It's cool," Fletcher said with a sigh. "It's OK. You're allowed to laugh."

The private grinned at him and Fletcher added irritably: "Now fucking help me up."

Once on his feet again, Fletcher looked around at the inside of the compound, which was blackened and blasted almost beyond recognition. The soldiers cleared the buildings that were still left standing and found what was left of the two gunmen on the roof. The men who had held off the Canadians for so long had been badly mangled by the Apache's strafing runs and the resulting explosions from the arms cache. Of the third man, who had tried to dash out of the compound, there was no sign.

The soldiers searched inside the buildings and around the outside of the compound, but found nothing. Then a shout from the centre of the courtyard drew everyone's attention. An Afghan soldier was shouting and waving excitedly at the opening of a small culvert, a covered drainage ditch that ran the length of the small patch of open ground inside the compound. Canadian and ANA soldiers clustered around the opening trying to see what was inside. Finally, one of the sergeants kneeled and peered into the small, dark space and saw the bleeding, frightened face of the sole surviving Taliban looking back at him. The fighting had left him with a bad gash on his head and several smaller cuts to his face. He had survived by crawling into the cramped confines of the culvert while the explosions burst all around him and was now facing a small crowd of heavily armed soldiers, most of whom were astonished that anyone could have survived the destruction. "It's the man who wouldn't die," one private marvelled.

The man refused to come out of his hiding place, despite several minutes of orders and cajoling from the Afghan soldiers. Finally, an exasperated Canadian sergeant kneeled at the end of the culvert and pulled out a grenade. He showed it to the man and made it clear what would happen if he didn't come out voluntarily. At last, the Taliban fighter began inching out on his belly. The man was surprisingly young—in his twenties, Fletcher guessed—and despite everything was only slightly wounded. The Canadians bandaged his badly bleeding head and brought him to where an exhausted Fletcher was sitting in the shade.

When the major asked him, through the translator, who he was and what he was doing in the village, the man claimed to be a farmer. "I live here," he said. "I don't know what *you're* doing here."

Fletcher quizzed him about the two riflemen on the rooftop who had held off his soldiers for the better part of the day. The prisoner claimed he didn't know them and said he could not explain how they came to be in the compound.

"Why did you try to run?" Fletcher asked.

"I was scared of you. I thought you were going to kill me," he told the translator.

The story was familiar by now, probably a standard Taliban cover, Fletcher thought. When asked detailed questions about where he lived and which fields he farmed, the man began telling conflicting stories, at one point claiming he was from another village. He later told another interrogator he was Iranian, which the Afghan soldiers claimed was probably true, based on his accent.

Exhausted from the strain of fighting in the stifling heat, Fletcher just shrugged. He ordered the man handcuffed and taken back to Ian Hope's command post for further questioning. He was clearly an insurgent leader of some kind and Fletcher radioed Hope with the information and made arrangements for the prisoner to be picked up. By now, Fletcher could see that the ANA troops were growing hostile to the prisoner and he ensured that at least a pair of Canadians were at all times between the Afghans and the prisoner until he was taken away. It was not unheard of for Afghan soldiers to take prisoners into an isolated field and administer their own rough justice by shooting them in the back of the head. Fletcher sighed: it was just one more complication.

After they finished their search of the compound and the surrounding fields, Charlie was pulled back to Payendi and the company settled into the same defensive positions around the village that they had occupied the night before. Most of the troops collapsed beside their LAVs and fell asleep immediately, not even bothering to strip off their tactical vests and helmets.

Bone-weary as he was, Fletcher found it impossible to sleep. He had never lost one of his soldiers while in command and Boneca's death affected him deeply. During the day's fighting he had been busy coordinating the attacks and in the immediate aftermath he had had his hands full organizing the clearance of the compound and the move back to Payendi. But now, in the darkness of the village, Fletcher sat in the back of his command LAV second-guessing his every move and questioning all his decisions. "Did I do something wrong?" he asked himself. "Could I have done anything different, to make it turn out different?"

Fletcher didn't think he'd made any major mistakes during the long, hot day of fighting. What was really on his mind was whether or not the soldiers blamed him. The men in his company were his whole reason for being in Afghanistan—for everything he did—and he dreaded losing their respect more than almost anything.

He needn't have agonized. The soldiers who were still awake, sitting in pairs in the turrets of the LAVs on sentry duty or talking quietly among themselves, had concluded that Boneca was the victim of plain bad luck. "Nothing you could do about it," Mike Denine said after the fight, summing up the consensus view. "Like the boys say: when your luck's in, your luck's in. You've got to go."

By the next day, there were no reports of Taliban anywhere

near Payendi and after an uneventful morning searching empty huts and fields, Charlie and the rest of the battle group pulled out of the Pashmul area and headed back to base.

They had all but destroyed one of the largest groups of Taliban to gather in the Panjwayi since the fighting had begun in the spring. During the day-long fight, as many as one hundred insurgents had been killed, captured, wounded or forced to flee the district.

Despite the success, Hope knew that the threat had not been eliminated. The Taliban would be back—the Canadians had only delayed their plans for an attack on Kandahar.

But Hope's task force was once again being ordered elsewhere. British forces in neighbouring Helmand Province were in trouble, their bases surrounded by hostile local inhabitants, under daily Taliban attack and running short of supplies. Charlie Company got only a few hours rest before they were ordered to mount up again and make the long drive west to the Helmand River valley.

Corporal Tony Boneca's helmet and body armour had been left behind when his body was carried away from the fight, and the equipment lay in the open when Fletcher ordered the compound bombarded and strafed. The other soldiers in Boneca's section retrieved it and later presented the helmet, burned and crushed by explosions and fires, to the Lake Superior Scottish Regiment, Boneca's home unit.

The battered helmet and a photograph of Boneca, who was only twenty-one when he died, are on display in the Army Reserve regiment's armoury in Thunder Bay, Ontario.

PART 5

The White Schoolhouse
August 3, 2006

THE WHITE SCHOOLHOUSE AUGUST 3

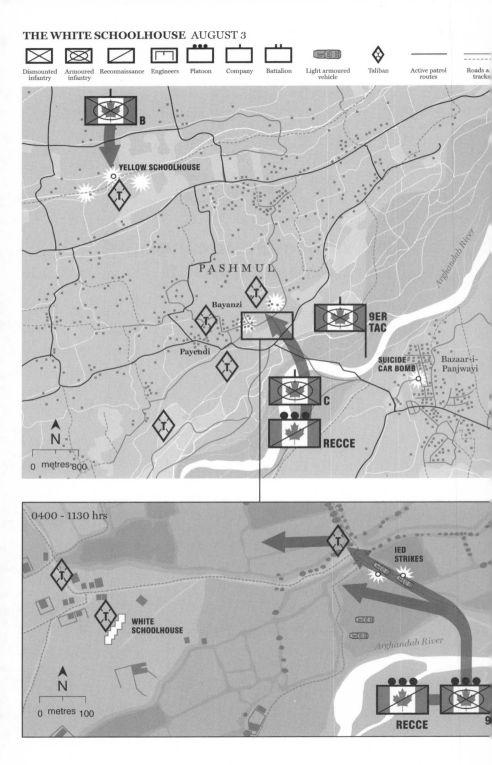

Dismounted infantry	Armoured infantry	Reconnaissance	Engineers	Platoon	Company	Battalion	Light armoured vehicle	Taliban	Active patrol routes

Roads a. tracks

YELLOW SCHOOLHOUSE

B

PASHMUL

Bayanzi

Payendi

9ER TAC

SUICIDE CAR BOMB

Bazaar-i-Panjwayi

C

RECCE

N

0 metres 800

0400 - 1130 hrs

IED STRIKES

WHITE SCHOOLHOUSE

Arghandab River

RECCE

9

N

0 metres 100

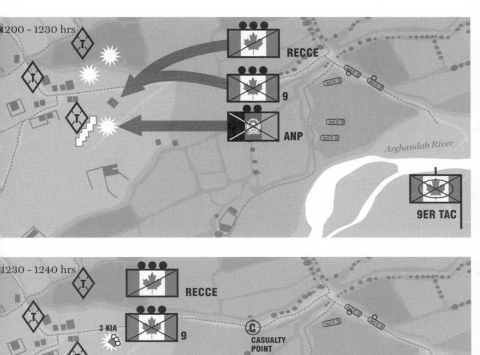

1200 - 1230 hrs

RECCE

9

ANP

Arghandab River

9ER TAC

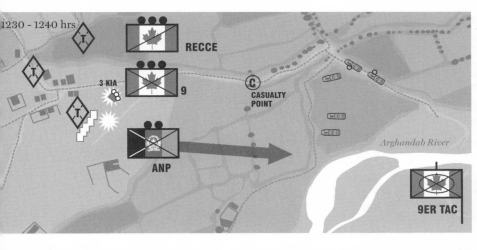

1230 - 1240 hrs

RECCE

9

3 KIA

ⓒ CASUALTY POINT

ANP

Arghandab River

9ER TAC

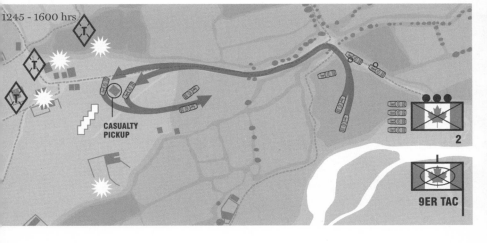

1245 - 1600 hrs

CASUALTY PICKUP

2

9ER TAC

CHAPTER THIRTEEN

"You know what to do."

Spin Boldak
July 30

In their new base in Spin Boldak, one hundred kilometres south-east of Kandahar, the men of Charlie Company thought they had finally left the grape orchards and lush marijuana fields of Panjwayi behind. The company that Ryan Jurkowski had, mostly jokingly, called the battle group's homeless now had a permanent base—a large and relatively comfortable compound on the outskirts of the border town. They had earned a little comfort. After rescuing the British soldiers of 3rd Para in Helmand, Charlie spent nearly two weeks in almost constant contact with the enemy. They lived out of the backs of their battered LAVs, fighting the Taliban for control of the area's towns and villages.

Now, ensconced in the relatively peaceful Spin Boldak area and with only two weeks left before the end of their tour of duty, Fletcher knew his soldiers were beginning to "wind 'er down," already thinking ahead to the flights that would soon begin to ferry them out of southern Afghanistan's heat and dust towards home.

The last few weeks had seen changes in the entire mission—changes set in motion at levels far above Fletcher and Charlie Company's "boots on the ground" in Panjwayi. In two days' time, Major-General Freakley was to hand over command of all coalition military forces in Afghanistan to British Lieutenant-General

David Richards, a move that would mark the end of the U.S.–led Operation Enduring Freedom. All coalition troops in the country would henceforth fall under the command of NATO's expanded International Security Assistance Force (ISAF)—including the Dutch, British, American and Canadian soldiers fighting in the southern region, including Kandahar. A change of command ceremony was set for August 1 and the hundreds of staff officers in Bagram and KAF were preparing for what they insisted would be a seamless transition.

But Hope was restless. The Taliban was well aware of the August 1 handover date and Hope knew from Bravo Company's almost daily clashes with the insurgents that they were still active in the Panjwayi, and still present in unprecedented numbers. Hope suspected their plans hadn't changed, despite his battle group's best efforts to disrupt them. A further complication also loomed on the horizon. The Afghan national Independence Day celebrations were approaching on August 19—the day the country had won its independence from the British in 1919—and Hope remained convinced that the Taliban were planning an attack on Kandahar timed to coincide with the festivities. There had been a recent and sharp increase in clashes with Taliban fighters across all five southern provinces, but especially in Kandahar and Helmand. One week earlier, on July 22, a double suicide bombing on the outskirts of Kandahar City had killed Corporal Francisco Gomez and Corporal Jason Warren—two soldiers returning from the fighting in Helmand. Hope saw the increased activity as a potentially ominous sign that the enemy was building up to the spectacular attack Captain Massoud had warned him about three months earlier. Task Force Orion was soon to be replaced by a battle group based on Ontario's Royal Canadian Regiment (RCR) and Hope knew that the Taliban would see the change, along with the transition from U.S. to NATO command, as an opening—a situation they would not fail to exploit.

Hope decided to strike first. On July 30, he made the one-hour trip from KAF to Spin Boldak and explained his plan to Fletcher. He proposed a two-pronged attack into the maelstrom of the Pashmul area, with Charlie as one end of the pincer movement and Bravo Company the other. Their targets were two schoolhouses, buildings that Afghan informants had identified as gathering points for the growing number of Taliban fighters flowing into the Panjwayi. The Yellow Schoolhouse—located on the northern edge of the Pashmul and nicknamed for its off-white paint scheme—would be Bravo Company's objective. The White Schoolhouse in the village of Bayanzi—well known to Charlie from its fighting there in mid-May—would be Charlie's responsibility. Since only one of Charlie's three platoons was available for the operation—one had to remain in Spin Boldak and another was doing duty in Kandahar as the brigade's quick-reaction force—they would be reinforced by the battle group's reconnaissance platoon. When Hope had finished his explanation, Fletcher volunteered 9 Platoon as Charlie's contribution to the operation, then paused.

"If you want a company headquarters, I'm available," he added hopefully.

Hope shook his head. "Won't be necessary," he replied. "I want you to stay and sort things out in Spin Boldak."

Five days later, on the banks of the Arghandab River, Hope would realize that decision had been a mistake.

The soldiers had settled in for the evening at the Spin Boldak base, picking up the same running poker games they had been playing since they began training together more than a year earlier. Sergeant Vaughn Ingram was losing, as usual: the muscular NCO was famous throughout the regiment as a terrible poker player, but one who doggedly kept returning to the game determined to win. Pat Tower was convinced that the same traits that made

Ingram a great soldier made him a born sucker at the poker table—betting aggressively on losing hands, bluffing madly or determinedly playing out hands he should have folded immediately. Kiwi Parsons was getting teased about a minor abdominal infection that had been plaguing him for about a week and had kept him on light duties. His friends jokingly accused Kiwi of milking the condition for all it was worth to avoid working for the final three weeks of the tour. "The war right now is perfect," he replied contentedly. "Air conditioning, good food, single rooms and sneaking over to the Yanks [at their nearby U.S. base] every night for a couple of glasses of horrible French wine."

When word came down that Fletcher wanted to see Warrant Officer Sean Peterson—9 Platoon's acting commander since a family emergency had forced Captain Craig Alcock home—the soldiers speculated that they were headed to KAF, where they could hit the base's Burger King and Pizza Hut. Some even gossiped hopefully that they were being rotated back to Canada ahead of schedule. But when Peterson walked into the barracks from the OC's office, a tight smile on his face, everyone knew they were going back into The Panj. "Holy fuck, here we go again," someone said wearily and the NCOs crowded into Peterson's small room to hear the details.

The warrant laid out the news: 9 Platoon was to head into KAF the next day to prepare for an operation in the Panjwayi. Kiwi swore under his breath. He realized immediately that his infection was going to keep him out of the mission. He wasn't exactly looking forward to a return to the region that had already claimed the lives of two of his comrades, but he wanted to finish what Charlie had started. Kiwi, like most of his company, wanted one more crack at the Taliban. More importantly, where the rest of his platoon went he was determined to follow. "There's no way in hell that I'm going to miss this," he thought grimly. "I HAVE to go!" As soon as the briefing broke up Kiwi went straight to the company medic to get his clearance.

The medic took one look at him and refused, but Kiwi argued and pleaded until the medic agreed to let him go at least as far as KAF, where a doctor could check him out.

The platoon lined up its LAVs early the next morning, bundled into them and drove to KAF, where they headed straight for the BATs and the battle group's compound to arm, refuel and load their vehicles for the mission ahead. Kiwi made a beeline for the field hospital. A military doctor poked and prodded his torso for several minutes while the master corporal tried not to wince at the pain. The young doctor looked suspiciously at Kiwi, but he smiled winningly and she signed the form clearing him for active duty.

The next day, August 1, marked the handover of command from the Americans to NATO. At dawn, Charlie pulled out of KAF and onto the road into Kandahar City. The soldiers' weapons had been cleaned and re-cleaned, equipment double-checked, and bottles of water and rations jammed into every spare corner. After an uneventful run through the nearly empty narrow streets of the city, the long line of LAVs and other vehicles headed over the ridge and across the small bridge that marked the beginning of the Panjwayi and the start of Ambush Alley.

By the time they reached Patrol Base Wilson, it was under attack. The convoy had to slow its approach while Bravo Company, which was occupying the fire base, drove off the Taliban who had crept to within a few hundred metres, before firing mortars and rocket-propelled grenades from the thick cover across the highway. The shooting was over by the time Charlie turned off the highway and raced through the gap in the fire base's high walls, but the soldiers exchanged raised eyebrows at the enemy's audacity. They soon learned that these "nuisance" attacks had become almost daily occurrences. The hit-and-run mortar or grenade attacks never did any serious damage—the Taliban launched its weapons from a considerable distance and fled after a few minutes of firing—but the enemy in the Panjwayi was clearly growing bolder.

Nine Platoon spent that day and the next watching the White Schoolhouse from the opposite bank of the dry Arghandab riverbed. The LAVs were positioned more than a kilometre away, sitting for hours while the blistering white heat of the Afghan sun turned their armoured surfaces into hot plates and strained the inadequate air-conditioning systems beyond their limits. Parsons, Ingram, Tower and the others took turns watching on binoculars, taking notes, sketching out maps and trying to memorize the layout of the area. There were no signs of life from the schoolhouse. Its windows, long emptied of glass, were boarded up with rough planks and there was almost no one in sight around the dozen or more buildings arrayed in a rough semicircle behind the school. Even the small market and surrounding farmers fields were empty—a sure sign that this was Taliban territory.

The platoon had one brief brush with the enemy when a small group of Taliban approached their lookout position and fired a few shots their way. Tower led his section out the back of his LAV and charged into the fields and toward the walls of the school-house after the fleeing gunmen. The veteran sergeant soon heard another group of Canadians coming up behind him, and looking back, saw Ingram's grinning face. "I wouldn't let you come down here on your own," he shouted at Tower cheerfully. The Canadians pursued the elusive Taliban for nearly half an hour, occasionally exchanging fire until the two sergeants finally believed they had one enemy fighter cornered behind a low mud-brick wall. Each pulled out a hand grenade, yanked the pins and on Ingram's nod lobbed them overhand behind the wall. A few seconds later, a single explosion rang out: only one grenade had gone off.

"Yours didn't go off!" Ingram said accusingly. "You must've forgotten to pull the pin."

"How the hell do you know which grenade didn't go off?"

Tower shot back. "I know how to throw a fucking grenade: I've thrown more than you!"

The two men bickered back and forth for a few seconds, huddled in the shallow ditch, until the absurdity of their argument finally sank in and Tower chuckled. "I still say it was yours that didn't go off," Ingram said as they moved up to check where the Taliban had been hiding. The gunman had vanished. The two men led their sections back to where the LAVs were still watching over the schoolhouse.

Patrol Base Wilson
August 2
1600 hrs

Captain Jon Hamilton and his Recce Platoon pulled into the crowded patrol base on August 2, along with Hope and Niner Tac. Somehow, they squeezed their LAVs, G Wagons and other vehicles into the dirt parking lot that took up most of the space inside the high walls and concertina wire of the converted Afghan police outpost.

Hamilton was a relative late-comer to the army. He had joined only six years earlier after kicking around the world working at various jobs in international trade. One—a stint with a sports-betting outfit in Venezuela—was part of what he fondly called his "interesting career" before the military. Hamilton didn't have the university degree the Canadian Forces demands of most of its officers. Instead, he'd signed a twenty-year contract with the army when he joined, and promised to obtain a degree within a few years. The thirty-year-old from the small town of Norwood, Ontario, just outside Peterborough, quickly made a name for himself as a no-nonsense, hard-charging junior officer who had an easy rapport with his enlisted men, most of whom called him "Hammy."

That may have been why he was given the coveted job of commanding Recce Platoon: a plum position for a junior officer because of its greater latitude and correspondingly greater responsibilities. Recce attracted some of the fittest and most experienced soldiers in the battalion, including its crack sniper teams, and Hamilton and his soldiers spent much of their time on their own, scouting out the battlefield and often taking orders straight from the battle-group commander or even higher up the chain. Recce was trained to be a mobile, fast-moving force. In Kandahar, that meant they drove the lighter G Wagons— four-wheel-drive jeeps with C6 7.62-mm machine guns mounted on top, a nimbler but less heavily armed and armoured vehicle than the seventeen-tonne LAVs.

Shortly after the task force had landed in Kandahar, Recce was given its own zone of responsibility. But due to the ever-changing Taliban threat and the constantly shifting demands of the coalition's southern command, Hamilton's soldiers, like Charlie Company, had roamed widely across both Kandahar and neighbouring Helmand Province.

Hammy had gotten a good look at the Taliban early in the tour and had not been impressed. The fighters he'd encountered in Panjwayi, Helmand and the mountains to the north of Kandahar City seemed to him to be "piss-poor soldiers"—good at intimidating unarmed local villagers but unable to do much in a fight against professional soldiers. So Hamilton shrugged off the fact that he was routinely outnumbered and outgunned. He had supreme confidence in his soldiers' ability to beat even the largest force the Taliban could muster.

Like the rest of Task Force Orion, Recce was short-handed. The platoon had landed in Kandahar with only twenty-four men, compared to the thirty-two soldiers in a full-strength platoon, and five months of continuous operations, injuries and leave had taken their toll. By the late afternoon of August 2, when he arrived at Patrol Base Wilson, Hamilton had just eighteen soldiers available for the planned assault on the White School-house. The shortfall didn't seem to bother him. "That's just the way it plays out," he would say philosophically. "You gotta do what you gotta do with the numbers you have."

Pulling into the base just behind Hammy was Sergeant Willy MacDonald. The stocky thirty-three-year-old from Regina had been Hamilton's right hand throughout the tour—acting as his fire team partner, covering his back, and more than once pulling him out of trouble. While Hamilton walked over to the small command post set up in one corner of the darkening patrol base, MacDonald organized Recce's brief stay and ensured his soldiers were settled in. Then he went off to scrounge a cup of coffee and some battle-group gossip from Charlie's NCOs.

Hamilton sat with the rest of the officers and NCOs in Hope's command tent, waiting for The Boss to issue his orders for the next day. He scoured the maps, satellite photos and intelligence reports on the two long, low buildings that would be the operation's targets.

After months of intermittent fighting, all the children were long gone from the two mud-and-plaster-walled schools. The single-storey, roughly rectangular structures, set about three kilometres apart, had become "centres of gravity" for the Taliban who had been trickling into the Panjwayi all spring and summer. According to Captain Massoud's cell-phone network, that trickle was now turning into a flood, and the schoolhouses were being used as gathering points for insurgent cells to prepare for ambushes or firefights, or to rendezvous and treat their wounded after the fighting ended. Hope wanted to use this information to the Canadians' advantage. The schoolhouses provided a perfect opportunity to catch the Taliban with their pants down when they were concentrated in one or two confined places, and to surround and destroy them. If the battle group was lucky, Hope told his officers and NCOs, they would catch a senior commander in their net.

Hamilton nodded as he listened to Hope's orders in the gravel parking lot, recognizing the feint his boss had in mind. "It was kind of showing the guy your left hand—B Company clearing the [yellow] schoolhouse—then giving them the right," he mused.

For the benefit of any Taliban watchers, both companies were to drive east down Highway One towards Kandahar before doubling back to hit the two schoolhouses from separate directions. Bravo Company would leave later, rolling west through Ambush Alley before pulling an abrupt U-turn just south of the dangerous stretch of road. They would hit the Yellow Schoolhouse from the west. Meanwhile, Charlie and Recce would swing further south along the Arghandab wadi and strike the White Schoolhouse from the opposite direction.

Even before Hope began issuing his orders, a pair of rocket-propelled grenades had whistled over the crowded patrol base, exploding well outside its perimeter. Hamilton barely bothered to look up from his maps and field message pad. Even the booming reply from the nearby pair of M777 howitzers went largely unremarked, despite the blasts of sound that echoed off the base's high walls. The artillery quickly zeroed in on a grape-drying hut less than a kilometre away and sent a volley of shells into it, bringing the Taliban's fire to an abrupt end.

Hope finished his orders and instructed his officers to get some sleep. Many of their soldiers were already dozing off. By now, the men were well practised in the art of stealing whatever snatches of rest they could, whenever they could. As darkness settled over the base, soldiers curled up in their LAVs and G Wagons or stretched out on the gravel and hard dirt of the compound.

While he was as tired, if not more so, than his troops, Ian Hope found it impossible to sleep. He was uneasy about the next day's operation, and had learned from bitter experience that his intuition was not to be ignored. He climbed on top of his command LAV and stretched out on the flat space behind the turret. He pulled out the small waterproof box in which he kept his supply of cigars and began smoking and thinking.

By 2:30 a.m., the compound was bustling. Charlie's and Recce's soldiers were mounted in their cars and Bravo Company was preparing for its own departure, scheduled for about an hour later. Like all the soldiers, Kiwi Parsons had a morning routine, in his case sitting atop his turret with his gunner for a cigarette and coffee, when he could scrounge a cup. "To ease the pre-mission jitters," he said with a grin.

The long convoy made up of Charlie's six LAVs, Hope's Niner Tac vehicles and Recce's G Wagons rumbled through the narrow gate leading out of Patrol Base Wilson. They made their way down the darkened and deserted highway, seemingly headed away from their objective and back to Kandahar City.

Hope led the Canadian convoy on an agonizingly slow ride up Ambush Alley, headlights off and drivers navigating via their night-vision goggles. In the turret of his LAV, just a few cars back, Parsons smiled to himself as he scanned the smattering of small buildings, trees and ditches along the roadside for signs of the enemy. "The colonel's hoping to get ambushed," he thought to himself. "He wants to kick their ass." Over the intercom he could hear his driver, Private Ben Weir, also chuckling at the convoy's snail-like pace. Parsons knew Weir was thinking the same thing.

But the Canadian column was too big and too well protected, and an ambush never materialized. The line of vehicles reached the Panjwayi District Centre without incident and swung onto a secondary road—a thin skein of potholed and haphazardly maintained pavement leading toward the dry, flat wadi. There, Hope's LAV pulled off to one side and the colonel himself clambered out to direct traffic through the narrow alleyway leading down into the wide, stoney riverbed.

In the front seat of his G Wagon, Hamilton almost laughed aloud as he passed Hope. The slight colonel reminded Hammy of a scene in the movie *Patton*, when George C. Scott as the famous U.S. general stood on an upended oil drum to untangle a traffic jam of tanks at an intersection in northern France. "Just like Patton," he laughed. "He's out there being the traffic cop."

The convoy bounced down into the gravel-and-dirt flood plain of the river and rumbled back eastwards toward their target in almost total darkness, the muted rumble of the LAVs' enormous diesel engines the only sign of their advance.

Although the sun had been down for more than eight hours, the air was still uncomfortably warm. Parsons and the rest of the LAV crews kept their air conditioning running full blast as they swept down the wadi in the nearly complete blackness, the silhouettes of orchards, marijuana fields and the occasional small building or walled compound sliding past.

In the backs of their LAVs, Pat Tower, Vaughn Ingram and the rest of the soldiers dozed, watched the small screen in their crew compartment that showed the view from the night-vision gunsights, or checked their weapons and kit for the umpteenth time. It was still pitch-black when they reached the point at which they were to turn north and leave Niner Tac to set up Hope's command post in the wadi. Soldiers nudged each other awake and watched the small screens inside the troop compartment intently, prepared to bolt out of the back at a moment's notice.

Hope's original plan had called for Recce to seize a small bridge over a long, deep irrigation canal, thereby clearing the way for 9 Platoon to push through and charge across the five hundred metres of deeply rutted dirt and low scrub to take the school. But after Hope's orders, when the soldiers had looked at the map and aerial photos of their target again, a potential problem emerged. The mud-and-stone bridge was a perfect site for IEDs. As well, it was at almost exactly the same spot where the

Taliban had set up a "sentry group" in July to fire on the advancing Canadians. Given the likelihood of problems, Sean Peterson, the acting commander of 9 Platoon, suggested to Hamilton that Charlie take the lead instead. The company's heavily armoured LAVs were sturdier than Recce's light G Wagons, and it made sense to have the armour up front from the start—the bridge was too narrow and small to allow the vehicles to jockey for position. "The plan was for the LAVs to zoom up as close as possible to the schoolhouse and the bazaar just beyond it before disgorging their soldiers to clear the buildings on foot."

So Charlie was once again in the lead when the convoy reached its jumping-off point and turned north out of the wadi onto the hard gravel road that led towards the schoolhouse. Almost immediately, the gunner in the lead LAV picked up a group of about a dozen men clustered around a low wall and a line of trees, invisible in the dark, starless night but lit up like daylight on the infrared gunsights. The contact was passed to the other LAVs in the convoy, which quickly spread out to either side of the lead car for a clear view. There was no sign of urgency or alarm among the Taliban insurgents: the LAVs' deceptively quiet engines had once again tricked the enemy into thinking the Canadians were still more than a kilometre away.

"They know we're here, they just don't know we're this close," Kiwi thought with satisfaction as he watched the Taliban fighters casually walking back and forth, their AK-47s and grenade launchers slung over their shoulders or propped up against the low wall. The men—sent out as sentries for the main group of enemy fighters—were in exactly the same spot as the ambushers who had fired on Bill Fletcher's advance into the area nearly a month earlier.

Charlie quickly received Hope's permission to engage and the LAVs opened fire. Their 25-mm guns and coaxial machine guns lit up the night with explosions and tracer bullets. Kiwi fired a long salvo with his machine gun and saw several of the gunmen fall as the rounds hit home. The LAVs hosed down the area with fire, frequently shifting aim to saturate nearby locations where more Taliban might be hiding. After a few seconds, the firing stopped. The ground where the would-be ambushers had been standing glowed on Kiwi's heat-sensing gunsight as warm blood spread over the cooler earth.

From the edge of the wadi, Hamilton watched as the deep orange flashes leaped out of the barrels of the 25-mm cannons and the tracers from the machine guns sprayed the distant trees, kicking up dust and smoke that was visible in flashes as the cannon shells exploded. "Not much of a fight," he thought.

The Taliban gunmen were gone—fled or killed in the deadly hail of fire from the LAVs. Once again, Hamilton and his men put their G Wagons into gear and followed the line of LAVs as it began to move forward. They didn't get far. A few minutes later, an explosion rippled through the convoy and the lead vehicles were swallowed in a cloud of fine-grained Afghan dust.

"Oh shit, we're getting RPGed now," Hamilton cried. His ears rang from the concussion of that blast—one he assumed was from a Taliban rocket-propelled grenade. He was wrong. The blast had come from a roadside bomb concealed just under the hard-packed dirt of the roadway and set off when the tires of the third LAV rolled over its pressure-plate activated trigger.

The explosion nearly blinded Kiwi Parsons and shook his seventeen-tonne LAV like a wet towel. While the rest of the vehicles immediately swivelled their turrets and fired into any nearby cover, hoping to kill the Taliban observers or "trigger men" who had laid the roadside bomb, Kiwi ignored the ringing in his ears and stood in his turret to scan the stricken vehicle a few cars ahead.

Through his night-vision goggles, Kiwi could see Sean Peterson's LAV still smoking and canted awkwardly to one side. The soldiers in the back had stumbled free of the vehicle and were helping to pull out the crew in the turret. Over the radio, someone called for a medic and Kiwi felt a knot growing in his stomach: two men were down.

The soldiers in the back of his own car tumbled out to help. Despite the danger of more bombs on the road ahead, Kiwi ordered his driver to pull up to the left-hand side of Peterson's LAV, putting the bulk of his armour between the disabled vehicle and the schoolhouse, where he suspected more Taliban were gathering.

A soldier jogged up to Kiwi's vehicle and wordlessly handed him a slip of paper. It was a note from Vaughn Ingram, who had scrambled out of his LAV minutes after the explosion and headed straight for Peterson's vehicle. Kiwi sat in his turret and stared mutely at the paper: Sean Peterson had been badly wounded by shrapnel and concussion. He would survive, but the blast put him out of commission for the duration, leaving Vaughn Ingram in charge. Although upsetting enough, it wasn't Peterson's injury that caused the knot in Kiwi's stomach to harden. Ingram's note also contained an order to call in a "nine-liner"—a radio casualty report. The driver of the crippled LAV, Corporal Chris Reid, was VSA—Vital Signs Absent. The bomb had detonated immediately underneath his compartment at the front of the LAV, killing him instantly. "Dead before what he knew hit him," Kiwi thought.

The lanky Reid, whose steady driving had gotten Kiwi's LAV through the night ambush on Highway One in May, was one of the best-liked soldiers in the platoon, notorious for his generosity to his comrades and valued by the NCOs as an older, steadying influence on the younger privates and corporals in the unit.

Kiwi pushed his shock aside and refocused on the task ahead, shifting his LAV to support the dismounted soldiers from 9 Platoon and Recce who were now spread out in a wide, irregularly shaped cordon around Peterson's blackened vehicle. The soldiers flopped onto the ground and lay motionless, using whatever small ruts or rises were around them for cover.

Within minutes, Reid's body and the still-unconscious Peterson were carried back to a Bison armoured vehicle that had been attached to Hope's Niner Tac for the day. The Bison, an earlier version of the LAV without a turret, was used for transport and secondary duties, including as armoured ambulances. Shortly after, an American Black Hawk medical evacuation helicopter, escorted by a pair of Apache attack choppers, swept into the flat section of the wadi to collect Reid's body and the wounded warrant officer.

The first glimmers of daylight warmed the ground around the stalled column of LAVs and G Wagons as the medevac took place. As soon as he could see without using his night-vision goggles, Hamilton gathered a handful of his Recce soldiers and pushed on to the small bridge that was to have been the starting point for the assault on the schoolhouse.

Hamilton was in a sour mood as he and his soldiers sprinted in relays up to the bridge, one team stopping to provide cover while the other scrambled forward. The operation had not even begun and already the Canadians had lost a man and one of their precious LAVs. And they were losing time. Hamilton had never been impressed by the ANP, who had been involved in planning the morning's attack, but now he suspected that some of them had tipped off the Taliban.

"Okay, they obviously know we're here," Hamilton muttered to himself. "We're not fooling anybody." He peered down the rough track that turned sharply to the left, leading towards the schoolhouse now visible in the growing light.

What Hamilton saw did not improve his mood. There were signs of the Taliban presence everywhere: an RPG launcher and several of its oblong black grenades lay on the ground, and yellow plastic water jugs were scattered along the deep irrigation ditches that lined both sides of the road. As usual, there were no bodies, but Hamilton took some solace in the numerous splashes of blood soaking into the dusty ground and leading towards the schoolhouse compound. The LAVs' guns had hit their mark. One of his soldiers also found a partially assembled roadside bomb near the bridge, an old Soviet artillery shell hastily covered with dirt and twigs, the fuse in its nose replaced by jury-rigged wiring.

A chest-high wall of rough mud bricks lined the north side of the road. Holes had been knocked into its thick surface every few metres, allowing ambushers to fire on anyone approaching. Behind the wall there were more signs of the Taliban. "Well, looks like they were lying for us," one soldier said sardonically, eyeing a collection of ammunition, cast-off weapons and partially assembled roadside bombs.

As the blistering Afghan sun peeked out from behind the long, knife-edged ridge that rose over Panjwayi, Hamilton and his men could make out distant figures darting around the schoolhouse compound. With his radio man behind him, Hamilton jogged back to the scene of the bomb strike to check on the rest of his platoon, still spread out in a circle to protect the disabled LAV. He then sought out Sergeant Alain Vachon, one of the combat engineers attached to the battle group and a specialist in disarming the Taliban's deadly IEDs.

Hamilton told Vachon what they'd found in the ditch ahead and the sergeant agreed to come take a look. Vachon looked down scornfully at the makeshift bomb the Recce troops had painstakingly uncovered and to Hamilton's astonishment gave it a quick nudge with one booted toe. "Yeah, we can take care of this no problem."

Vachon went back to his LAV near the middle of the convoy. He ordered his driver to fire up the engine and swerved around the vehicles in front of him to move up to Recce's position. The engineer's LAV got only a few metres down the road before another blast rocked the site, sending a column of powdery dust into the air and the soldiers huddling farther down into whatever cover was available. The bomb set the LAV ablaze and began "cooking off" shells from the vehicle's 25-mm main gun and machine-gun ammunition. Corporal Jason Joe, on loan from Charlie to act as the gunner in the engineer LAV, was first out of the burning vehicle, but quickly realized that the rest of the crew had not gotten free. He climbed back up onto the burning car and pulled out Sergeant Vachon and the driver, despite the flames and exploding ammunition. All three suffered burns and concussion from the explosion and Joe had minor shrapnel wounds from the exploding 25-mm shells.

Hamilton watched the events unfold with growing frustration. The planned mission for the day had clearly gone out the window. Two of the five LAVs were now out of commission and the main route into the schoolhouse was obviously mined. He called over Vaughn Ingram and the two men each went down on one knee to discuss the options. Ingram wanted to attack. Hamilton agreed, but the situation had changed dramatically. It was time to call Hope—still at his command post in the wadi just a few hundred metres behind them.

"Sir, we've got two vehicles down," Hamilton spoke into his radio. "We're going to have to re-cock."

"I'm coming up," Hope replied.

A few moments later, the lieutenant-colonel's slender form appeared over the lip of the wadi. The three men squinted at the long, low schoolhouse now clearly visible in the early morning light. Hope told them that he had just received a report from the intelligence cell in KAF. The Canadians had surprised the Taliban with their swift approach and had caught a senior commander hiding somewhere inside one of the compounds just behind the school. The question was how to proceed. The original plan of using the LAVs' armour and firepower to lead the attack was out of the question—so many roadside bombs in such a short stretch of road was unprecedented and the narrow track was now too dangerous. They couldn't risk losing more of the valuable armoured vehicles.

Hope looked over the fields at the schoolhouse and the dim figures which could now be seen moving around. "Looks like we'll have to do it the old-fashioned way," he said finally.

"Roger that, sir," Hamilton replied automatically. He knew what Hope meant: an infantry attack across the more than three hundred metres of scrub-filled fields and open ground between the Canadian positions and the school.

Bullets had already begun snapping overhead. It was badly aimed "harassing fire," but a harbinger of things to come. Hope didn't even duck as he strode back to the wadi where his LAV, Nyala and Bison vehicles were drawn up in a cordon around his mobile headquarters. He picked up his radio to report back to brigade headquarters, beginning the long, frustrating process of requesting air and artillery strikes to support his troops and ordering up recovery vehicles to haul away the badly damaged LAVs. One of Hope's cast-iron rules was that his soldiers were never to abandon a vehicle to the Taliban, no matter how badly damaged. He was determined to deny the enemy the propaganda value of showing a burnt-out Canadian LAV surrounded by jubilant Taliban fighters on CNN.

Hope took care of some other business as well. He called up his reserve force—the Alpha Company platoon still waiting at KAF, nearly an hour's drive up the highway—and ordered forward the battle group's EOD (Explosive Ordnance Detachment), the Canadians' bomb-disposal squad. His work was hampered by a breakdown in the satellite radio, his only dependable link with brigade headquarters at KAF—he could send but not receive messages. The conventional radio sets had limited range, which made it difficult for Hope to call for backup, or monitor a second firefight that was steadily building to the north where Bravo Company had found and trapped another large group of Taliban. Not for the last time that day, Hope found himself wishing he had taken up Bill Fletcher on his offer to come along.

The White Schoolhouse
August 3
1030 hrs

It was mid-morning, and the sweltering Afghan air soaked the soldiers in sweat beneath their body armour, and plastered hair against skulls under sand-coloured camouflage helmets. By the time Hamilton gathered his small Recce force for the renewed attack, the temperature was approaching 50°C and climbing. The heat sucked the energy from the heavily encumbered Canadians, most of whom had by now been up for hours. As they huddled in the steep-walled irrigation ditch that led towards the schoolhouse compound planning their attack, Hamilton and Ingram were grateful for the sliver of shade its dirt walls provided and for the thin relief given by the shin-deep muddy water at its bottom.

With the ranks of both Recce and 9 Platoon depleted by the IED strikes and the almost unbearable heat, the men decided to combine their small force into a single "scratch" platoon. Two groups, led by Hamilton and Ingram, would attack the schoolhouse along the axis of the road and the low wall that ran parallel to it for most of its length. A third group would be in reserve behind them, ready to move forward if needed. Charlie's four remaining LAVs would stand off in the relatively open field on the assaulting forces' left flank, where they could fire their powerful chain guns and machine guns to support the attack.

The gunfire coming from the schoolhouse and the compound behind it was still irregular and mostly badly aimed, but the number of bullets whipping past the Canadian troops moving into position was steadily increasing. Ingram deployed his dismounted soldiers along the ditch leading towards the schoolhouse, and a nearby wall, to begin returning some of the Taliban's fire. The LAVs were already providing what covering fire they could. Ingram hurried down the shallow trench to where Hamilton was organizing the attack.

Hamilton was always nervous in the minutes before a fight, worrying about what might go wrong or if he had forgotten something in his preparations. As he and Ingram lay against the dirt embankment on one side of the irrigation ditch preparing for their attack, they glanced up to see Private Andy Social, one of the 9 Platoon troops, climb out to the edge of the deep ditch, take aim at the compound, then suddenly stagger back into the ditch, struck full in the chest by a slug from an AK-47. Before either Hammy or Ingram could react, the young private picked himself up, looked down in amazement at the thick chest plate of body armour that had stopped the ricocheting bullet cold, and promptly bent over and began throwing up.

Their nerves stretched to the limit by the hours of danger, the bullets whistling overhead and the tension over the coming attack, Hamilton and Ingram looked at each other and burst into laughter. Somehow—and for some reason neither could have explained—the sight of the retching soldier struck the two veterans as hilarious. Social recovered, looked at his superiors with disgust, and continued firing over the edge of the ditch.

While Ingram and Hamilton were manoeuvring their troops into the jumping-off point for the assault, the promised contingent of ANP arrived. The captain eyed the small group of blue-grey uniformed Afghans sceptically. Captain Massoud had promised forty or more policemen, but when the Canadians had arrived at the schoolhouse compound in the early hours of the morning there were none in sight. Massoud was embarrassed and furious with the local police commander, whom he strongly suspected of collaborating with the Taliban gunmen who were now operating more or less openly in the Pashmul area. While the Canadians had been making their first advance towards the building, Massoud had spent an hour pacing back and forth in Hope's command post, shouting into his cell phone in Pashtu. Eventually he managed to produce fifteen policemen, carrying plastic-stocked AK-47s that some had covered in "jingle"—the colourful stickers, decorations and medallions that Afghans seemed to delight in plastering on their weaponry.

Hamilton did not have an especially high opinion of the Afghan police force, particularly those he had seen so far in the Panjwayi, and this group did not inspire any more confidence. They seemed reluctant about the coming attack, nervously eyeing the low buildings shimmering in the heat and dust. But Hamilton nonetheless split them up between his group and Ingram's, doubling the number of attackers to fourteen Canadians and fifteen ANP.

Hamilton launched the assault on the compound at 11:30 a.m., with a "caterpillar" attack. Split into fire teams of two or three soldiers, his tiny force moved and fired in turn, one team hammering away with their C7 assault rifles or C9 light machine guns while the other made a short dash up to their position. Then the first team rushed forward another few yards, and threw themselves onto the ground. When the team leader shouted "Covering!" the next team hurled themselves forward once again.

The caterpillar is slower than the leap frog—in which each fire team rushes past their covering partners to take up positions ahead of them—but is more deliberate and puts more fire onto the enemy position. With his troops already wilting in the blistering heat, Hamilton decided the less arduous approach was wiser.

The LAVs pumped dozens of high-explosive cannon shells into the schoolhouse to suppress the Taliban rifle and machine-gun fire, but to no avail. The enemy had either shifted to buildings farther back or laid low until the punishing cannon fire moved on to other targets. Almost as soon as the Canadians leaped out of the cover of the two ditches to begin their assault on the school, the Taliban began throwing out more fire.

Just behind the assaulting force, the reserve group, led by Sergeant Mars Janek, found themselves drawn into a firefight as small groups of Taliban gunmen filtered out of the buildings north of the school in an attempt to use the cover of the marijuana field to fire on the Canadians' flank. The Taliban skirmishers were quickly driven off, but the fight deprived Hamilton of even more of his shrinking pool of soldiers and used up his only reserve force.

While the Canadians advanced steadily towards the schoolhouse, the ANP contingent dashed ahead, firing their AK-47s wildly in the general direction of the enemy. The fifteen Afghans got as far as the school's outer walls but quickly drew a hail of gunfire from Taliban hidden in firing positions around the school and in the buildings beyond.

To Hamilton's disgust, the ANP immediately turned and ran back through the Canadian line to the relative safety of the road beyond. Resisting a brief urge to shoot the fleeing policemen himself, the tall captain just snorted and called Hope on the radio to report.

"The ANP's run away and the fight's obviously started," he said. "What do you want me to do?"

"You know what to do," Hope replied tersely.

"Roger that, sir," Hamilton answered again. With an inward sigh, he turned back to the attack.

While 9 Platoon led the first abortive advance up to the schoolhouse, Bill Fletcher was listening helplessly to the radio in his command post in Spin Boldak, more than 150 kilometres away. He hung on every broken or faint transmission he could hear coming out of the gathering battle in the Panjwayi. Fletcher had kicked everyone but the duty operator out of the room that served as his company headquarters. He listened to the report of the IED strike with a feeling of complete impotence. He could tell from the broken and static-filled snatches of radio chatter that his soldiers were in a fight—in some bursts of clear messages he could even hear the explosions and bullets whining past—but he was powerless to help.

The first report of a fatality indicated that it was someone from call sign Six—Recce Platoon's radio code name—and Fletcher felt a guilty pang of relief that it wasn't one of his men. It was short-lived: a few minutes later Corporal Chris Reid's zap number was read over the airwaves. Fletcher lowered his head for a moment, then strode out to call his soldiers together and break the news.

CHAPTER FOURTEEN

"Just like World War One."

The White Schoolhouse
August 3
1130 hrs

Kiwi Parsons had manoeuvred his LAV to within two hundred metres of the school. He'd turned off the mined road and crossed the field of scrub and dirt to position himself to the south of the attacking infantry, with his friend Tony Perry's vehicle nearby. With his head just above the rim of his turret hatch, Kiwi scanned the apparently abandoned school closely and kept a sharp eye on what he could see of the buildings in the village beyond. He felt his gunner tugging on his leg, slipped down into a sitting position, and looked into the gunsight at a group of more than fifteen men moving down a road in the village behind the school, carrying RPG launchers and rifles. Kiwi waited until they had cleared the corner of the building and then quietly told his gunner, "Engage." The cannon shells and machine-gun rounds struck in the middle of the group, exploding in a shower of dust, flames and smoke. Perry's LAV, seeing the shells hit the area behind the school, also opened fire until the dust made it impossible to see anything. While his gunner kept a sharp eye on the schoolhouse and the buildings beyond, Kiwi watched Ingram and Hamilton get their fifteen soldiers in position. Ingram turned and gave him a thumbs-up—the predetermined signal—and Kiwi ordered his gunner to fire into the open windows and doors of the school for thirty seconds. When the fusillade ended, he looked over and saw the ragged line of grey Afghan police scattering under a cloud of Taliban bullets and RPGs.

As dismaying as that sight was, a moment later Kiwi saw something that made him smile. Hamilton and Ingram's small band of tan-camouflaged soldiers were manoeuvring as if on a training exercise—one group at a time dashing forward amid a shower of bullets, dirt and dust. "Ain't that a sight," he said proudly, before returning his attention to his gunsights.

It took Hamilton and Ingram's small force an agonizing fifteen minutes to reach the pair of small buildings that were the closest part of the schoolhouse compound, but they finally sprinted over the last one hundred metres of open ground and led their soldiers into the two small huts. As Hamilton burst into one of the buildings, the ripe smell rising from its darkened interior told him that his men had captured the school's latrine. Since there were no low windows or openings to use as firing positions, he and Ingram quickly spread their troops around the exterior. The men used nearby walls and the whitewashed structure itself for cover and returned the Taliban fire with the chatter of bursts from their C9 machine guns and snap shots from their assault rifles.

Bullets flying around him, Hamilton took stock of the situation. Although his tiny command had finally reached their target, they had not passed through the deadly field of fire unscathed. Just as they reached the schoolhouse, Private Kevin Dallaire had been hit in the stomach by an AK-47 round, just beneath the lower edge of his body armour, and Hamilton could see in a glance that his injuries were severe.

Corporal Andy Gorman had been behind Dallaire in the dash for the schoolhouse, and had seen him drop his rifle and fall. He dragged the wounded man the few metres to the building. For Gorman, the run across the fire-swept ground had seemed to take forever and the twenty-three-year-old remembered thinking, "What the fuck am I doing this for? This is the stupidest thing I've ever heard of." But when the soldiers on either side of him hauled themselves to their feet, he followed as if on autopilot, ignoring the bullets crackling past his helmet and tearing up the dirt all around.

Gorman wasn't even supposed to be on this operation: he had been assigned to the company quartermaster for most of the tour, where he handled supplies, issued ammunition and weapons and made minor repairs to equipment. In a few short weeks he had watched his friends go from displaying gung-ho enthusiasm, avidly looking forward to their first "contact," to having the weary matter-of-fact competence of veterans. When he was offered the chance to fill an empty slot in 9 Platoon for what looked like the last operation of the tour, he jumped at it. Three days later, he found himself at the schoolhouse, hauling the badly wounded Dallaire up against a wall that offered at least some cover from the incoming fire. He tore aside Dallaire's body armour in a rip of Velcro and tried to give him first aid to stop the bleeding, but there was little blood coming from the wound. "We're all fucked," he thought desperately.

Bullets were now cracking overhead at an alarming rate and from every direction but the way the handful of soldiers had come. The Taliban's AK-47s and light machine guns were firing from rooftops, nearby buildings and the low walls that crisscrossed the entire sprawling compound. Hamilton knew his men were in a precarious situation: there were many more Taliban in the complex beyond the schoolhouse and around its grounds than anyone had realized. Hundreds of fighters were now pouring fire onto the eight Canadian infantrymen crouched around the small outbuildings at the north end of the compound. Worse, he could hear the familiar whoosh of RPGs passing overhead. Hamilton grabbed his radio's handset and began calling for an artillery or air strike to help his beleaguered soldiers.

264 | CHRIS WATTIE

Ingram took charge of the northernmost of the two small buildings. He rushed to position soldiers and weapons in the best of the sparse cover available, pausing occasionally to calmly snap off quick shots from his assault rifle. In the next building over, separated from Ingram by a long, high wall, Willy Mac-Donald was doing the same. Hunkered down behind a set of concrete stairs, MacDonald would pop up periodically to snap off five or six shots at whatever targets he could make out in the sights of his c7. Every time he did, MacDonald drew a burst of fire from several of the Taliban machine-gun and rifle positions less than one hundred metres away. The enemy fire was accurate and heavy, sending up chips of concrete or clouds of dirt all around him.

The outhouse's only windows were tiny and set high up on the walls, making them almost useless as firing positions. Instead, the soldiers sprawled up against the corners of the buildings, on either side of the wall running between the buildings, or near the two open doorways.

One of the privates near MacDonald was firing his rifle steadily from the doorway and paused to grin from beneath his dust-coated helmet. "Man, this is just like World War One!" he shouted over the roar of incoming and outgoing fire.

Crouched behind his own scanty cover, MacDonald couldn't help but laugh. "You're twenty years old—how the fuck would you know?" he shouted back.

Back in the wadi command post a few hundred metres away, Ian Hope was juggling calls on three radios. Major Nick Grimshaw of Bravo Company was reporting a successful firefight to the north, with more than fifty Taliban caught in a net around the Yellow Schoolhouse, and the noose slowly closing. Hope's calls for air and artillery support were not going nearly as well. His satellite radio was still only transmitting, so Hope had no way of knowing if his requests for fire support were being received. He impatiently waved over Major Steve Gallagher, the commander of his artillery battery, and told him to call KAF on his cellular phone. Were they hearing his calls and, if so, why wasn't there a high-explosive howitzer shell already on its way?

Gallagher called the TOC at the Kandahar base and reached a duty officer in the headquarters. After a brief conversation, he looked over at Hope and nodded curtly. "They hear you, sir," he said.

When the command centre in KAF finally did manage to contact Hope on the radio, the battle-group commander could hardly believe his ears. They refused to authorize an artillery fire mission on the Taliban positions in Bayanzi because the rounds could damage nearby civilian buildings. "The lawyers say we can't authorize a fire mission," said the voice from headquarters.

The icy demeanour Hope had maintained throughout a summer of fighting nearly cracked: the village that lay just past the schoolhouse had been deserted by all its inhabitants for several days. The only people in the area were the Taliban fighters who were firing furiously at Hamilton's pinned-down soldiers.

Headquarters also pointed out another problem: under new rules brought in when NATO had taken command of the Afghan mission from the Americans two days earlier, no "danger close" artillery fire was allowed—"danger close" meaning any fire missions within five hundred metres of friendly forces. Hope argued, but to no avail. Although he struggled to keep his voice calm, he was infuriated that a staff officer sitting in the safety of KAF was denying his soldiers the help they so desperately needed.

A salvo of explosions interrupted Hope's thoughts, and he squinted into the white-hot sky in the direction from which the sounds had come. The day before, an ANP colonel had helpfully pointed out a patch of high ground on the opposite bank of the Arghandab wadi, about a kilometre away. It was the perfect place, he said, for Hope to set up his command post. Hope had his doubts about this particular policeman's loyalties and had thanked him for the suggestion while making a mental note to keep well clear of that area. Stepping out of his command post into the blinding sun, Hope saw a fountain of dust shooting skyward from the exact spot the colonel had recommended: the Taliban had dropped an entire volley of mortars onto it. Hope nodded knowingly and returned to his radios.

Despite the heated fire being thrown at his troops, Hamilton wasn't panicked. His soldiers had been exchanging fire with the Taliban for more than an hour and were giving almost as good as they got. As his men snapped off methodical, well-aimed shots, Hamilton felt confident that a fire mission from the artillery or an air strike would either kill the enemy or force them to take cover. He was sitting up against the wall near the door of one of the outhouse buildings, trying to reach Hope's command post over the radio, when he heard an ear-shattering bang, smelled the sharp bite of cordite and felt a blast tear the handset out of his grasp. Stunned by the concussion, he barely noticed the sensation in his left foot, "like someone poking a stick." He rolled over to retrieve his radio before looking around.

An RPG had hit the wall of the outhouse just a few feet away and exploded, spraying razor-sharp fragments of metal through the small group of Canadians. Two soldiers in the small patch of hard-packed earth in front of him were down and not moving—Dallaire and Corporal Bryce Keller, his machine gunner. The dust and smoke from the strike was still swirling around the outhouses when Hamilton, still numb with the shock of the blast, saw Ingram's prone form a few feet away. The sergeant was still moving, although he had been badly wounded and was bleeding from shrapnel in his torso and legs. Hamilton watched as

Ingram crawled over to the unmoving Keller and began to administer first aid, pulling a plastic-wrapped field dressing from his tactical vest and slapping it on one of the stricken soldier's many wounds.

As he sat half dazed on the concrete floor next to the shattered and still-smoking wall, Hamilton saw Ingram's hands fall away from Keller's body. The veteran sergeant lay down his head and closed his eyes. "That's okay, Vaughn, you rest now," he thought, his ears still ringing.

Hamilton finally looked down at his tan desert combat boots and noticed one of them was dark with blood. "I'm hit," he called out to his second-in-command, who was still firing from the next building. "You'd better get over here, Willy."

Vaughn Ingram had been everywhere during the hour-long firefight, ignoring the bullets that were flying past or stitching holes in the dirty white plastered walls of the outhouses, to move calmly from one soldier to the next, pointing out targets, adjusting their position or just reassuring them with his presence.

Just before the grenade struck, Ingram had ordered Andy Gorman to look around the corner of the small building against which they were sheltering to see if the company's LAVs were coming up. Gorman had been right beside the barely conscious Dallaire, pressing a bandage onto his wound. He had squatted down and shuffled two steps over to the edge of the building to peer around the corner. He was about to turn back to the sergeant when the Taliban grenade hit, sending deadly fragments of metal coursing through the spot where he had been standing seconds before. The blast bowled Gorman over and when he climbed back onto his knees he could see that Dallaire had been hit again, this time in the chest. His ballistic vest had been opened to allow Gorman to bandage his wound and the young private had had no protection when he was hit a second time.

Gorman crawled over and took Dallaire's hand in his own. "I'm with you, buddy," he croaked, his throat choked by thirst and the clouds of smoke and dust.

Dallaire gave a faint squeeze in reply and Gorman felt a sharp stabbing pain in one of his hands. He glanced down and swore in surprise at the blood pouring out: a piece of the grenade had sliced into the fingers of his right hand.

The blast from the RPG strike knocked Willy MacDonald down and hurled him backwards into the building he and three other soldiers were defending, but the wall between the two outhouses protected his half of the small force from the projectile's deadly cloud of fire and metal.

"Holy fuck! What the hell was that?" he shouted, struggling to get his feet underneath him again.

For a moment after the RPG hit, the Taliban fire aimed at the two small buildings occupied by the Canadians slackened, then escalated further until it sounded like a hurricane of metal breaking against the walls. MacDonald swore under his breath. He knew the insurgents would love nothing more than to capture a Canadian soldier and would likely try to follow up the successful grenade hit by swarming the soldiers pinned down in the schoolhouse. He decided he wasn't going to wait for them to attack—he was going to attack them. He checked that all his soldiers were unhurt, then told them to get ready to charge.

Before he could make a move, MacDonald heard Hamilton's shout for help. He turned to the other soldiers firing from the scant cover of the building and told them to prepare. "Put fresh mags on your weapons and put a fresh belt on the machine gun, because they're coming," MacDonald told them grimly. "I've got to go help the other guys."

With that, MacDonald took a running leap through the doorway and scrambled around the wall and across the open ground between the buildings. As bullets whizzed past from every direction, MacDonald dove headfirst into the second outhouse and landed on Hamilton's shattered foot, prompting an outburst of swearing from the captain. The RPG had turned the darkened interior of the hut into a charnel house and MacDonald needed a moment to take it all in. Ingram and Keller were lying dead just outside the building and Dallaire was unconscious and bleeding heavily. The remaining three soldiers were all wounded.

MacDonald put a tourniquet on his captain's leg to staunch the blood flow and a field dressing on his shattered foot, apologizing the entire time for taking so long to get to him. "I'm sorry I took so long, Hammy," he said, his voice thick with emotion. "I'm sorry."

The stocky sergeant had been living and fighting alongside Hamilton for more than five months and the thought of letting down his captain when he had been wounded was almost too much. Hamilton reached up and grabbed the lapels of his sergeant's combat shirt, pulling his face down to within inches of his own. "Don't worry about it, Willy. You didn't take that long. It was only a few minutes, not even two minutes," he said. Hamilton let go. "Besides, I knew you'd come for me."

MacDonald swallowed a wave of emotions, nodded and continued to wrap bulky bandages around Hamilton's wounded foot. When he was finished, he brought up his rifle, shuffled the few feet to the open doorway and began returning fire while Hamilton tried to raise the command post on the radio.

As he calmly squeezed off shots, aiming at the muzzle flashes and occasional fleeting silhouettes that were all he could see of the enemy through the dust and smoke, the stocky sergeant felt a hand tugging at his ankle. He looked down to see Private Tim Qualtier, known simply as "Q" to the rest of 9 Platoon, crawling up behind him despite badly bleeding shrapnel wounds to both legs.

"Where's my gun? I want to fucking fight."

MacDonald shook his head in bewilderment: a pair of tourniquets were visible on the private's blood- and dirt-covered legs. "Man, you can't fight. You're all fucked up."

"I can still shoot," Q insisted. "Just put my gun in front of me and point me in the right direction."

MacDonald stared at the private for a second then sighed. It would take longer to argue with Q than to just do what he wanted. He reached over to grab Q's c7 and propped it up on the filthy floor in front of him. Qualtier grimaced and crawled forward until he could slide the weapon's butt up against one shoulder. "Crazy bastard," MacDonald said warmly as Q began to fire.

On the other side of the room, Hamilton had finally managed to get a transmission out and reported that he had two soldiers killed and several wounded. Finally, frustrated by the finicky radio, he shouted into the handset: "Get those fucking LAVs up here or we're all dead!"

A second later, his radio went out. Hamilton angrily jammed the handset back into its receiver.

While Ingram and Hamilton were launching their assault on the schoolhouse, Pat Tower had set up a casualty collection point in a small hollow about two hundred and fifty metres away, a sheltered spot where any wounded could be brought back for first aid. Tower had watched the grey-blue uniformed Afghan police running to the rear and barely had time to curse before the first of several heat casualties tumbled into his position. The men's faces were grey with overheating, and despite the blistering temperature and furnace-like air, they had stopped sweating as their bodies began to shut down in the relentless heat.

The blistering heat had begun to claim soldiers even before the attack was launched. Corporal Tony Nolan, who had been carrying the platoon's heavy portable radio in addition to his own gear and weapon, was brought back to Tower's position, pale and shaking. The signaller was barely able to move his arms by the time Tower half-carried him to the small hollow, but there was no time to administer first aid. Seconds later, a pair of Taliban gunmen who had crept out of the schoolhouse began firing at them from a ditch only a few metres away. The men flattened themselves on the parched ground as bullets began kicking up dust.

From his LAV turret to their right, Kiwi Parsons could see the Taliban fighters and he radioed Tower with their approximate position. "I'm going to use a grenade," the sergeant replied. "See if I can get their heads down."

Tower pulled the pin, crawled up to the edge of the shallow hole and hurled the grenade in a textbook straight-arm throw, despite the unnervingly accurate fire zipping all around him. He dropped back onto his belly, counted off five seconds, then swore—it was a dud. Tower pulled another grenade from his tactical vest and crept up again, trying to throw it in the same spot where he had dropped the last one. After another five seconds went by without an explosion, Tower swore again, more loudly this time. He pulled out a third grenade and threw it even harder than the first two. To his relief, it tumbled into the ditch and exploded, abruptly cutting off the Taliban fire.

By then, two more soldiers had succumbed to the heat, including Master Corporal Tom Cole, who had been left behind with the platoon's C6 heavy machine gun to cover the assault, almost halfway between Tower's casualty collection point and the schoolhouse. Tower could hear the rising crescendo of machine-gun and RPG fire aimed at the soldiers in the outhouses ahead and decided that he was needed there. Doubled over to keep a low profile, he sprinted up to Cole's position with the medic just behind him.

"If you want to go up onto the objective, that's where I'm going," Tower told Cole. "Do you want to come?"

"Oh, yeah," Cole replied, nodding vigorously despite the exhaustion writ across his face.

Tower, Cole and the medic jogged up the water-filled ditch towards the school. It didn't take long for the Taliban gunmen in the compound to spot them, and RPG and machine-gun fire was soon peppering their position, forcing the trio to dive for cover. Huddled against the dirt wall of the ditch, Tower radioed Hamilton, telling him help was on its way.

"Don't bother coming up, we're near the end of our effective strength," Hamilton's voice crackled over the airwaves. "We're all gonna be heat casualties soon. We're going to try to pull back to the ditch."

A few minutes later, Tower heard the blast from the RPG strike and Hamilton's desperate radio call. Now he had absolutely no doubt what to do. He turned to his two companions. "We're going up. They need a medic up there," he said, still panting from the exertion of their first dash towards the schoolhouse. "Come on."

The heat forgotten, Tower clambered up the bank of the ditch and sprinted across the one hundred and fifty metres of open ground to the two outbuildings where the rest of his platoon were sheltering. "Friendlies coming!" he shouted as he went. "Friendlies coming up!"

The hail of gunfire that had intensified after the RPG strike was now directed at Tower's small group hurtling across the clear ground towards the school. The fire was so fierce that all three men later found bullet holes in their uniforms or the ammunition and equipment pouches strapped to their chests.

Cole and the medic headed for the building on their right, where Hamilton and MacDonald were taking cover from the incoming fire, while Tower dove into the farther building. After checking on the handful of troops there—they were tired but still fighting—he called out over the dividing wall to MacDonald.

"Give me some cover fire so I can come across," Tower shouted, then flung himself out of the doorway. He raced around the wall between the two buildings and across the bullet-swept gap into the second outhouse.

MacDonald looked up at Tower with visible relief. "Oh good, we can get the fuck out of here," he said wearily.

"What do you mean?"

"Well, you've got the LAVs with you, don't you?"

"No," Tower said, shaking his head. "It's just me, Tom and the medic."

MacDonald's face fell and he swore bitterly. Tower looked around the dim, fetid interior of the building. Immediately, he noticed that Ingram was nowhere in sight.

"Where's Vaughn?" Tower asked, puzzled that his friend hadn't taken charge after Hamilton had been wounded.

"Pat, Vaughn's dead," MacDonald replied dully, nodding through the doorway at the bodies still lying outside in the dust.

For a moment, Tower was stunned. He stood stock-still, staring at the body—his friend's body—that he hadn't noticed in the rush across from the other building. When he turned back to MacDonald a few seconds later, he was all business.

"We've gotta get out of here, Willy." Together, they began to organize the handful of uninjured soldiers.

In the field outside the schoolhouse, just to the southwest of where Hamilton's force was pinned down, Kiwi Parsons had been shifting his LAV into different positions to keep the Taliban gunners from zeroing in on his vehicle—moving a few metres in one direction, firing into the school or the outlying buildings, then moving again. But the enemy was active from both sides now and his LAV was the focus of much of the fire. In the first five minutes after Hamilton's small assault group went into the schoolhouse, Kiwi counted more than sixty RPGs. His car was constantly rocked by explosions and rattled by bullets ricocheting off the armour.

He and his gunner had been firing almost constantly since Hamilton had stormed the school and had to be reloaded twice, once by Sergeant Mars Janek of Recce Platoon, who ran forward through the Taliban fire lugging briefcase-sized metal containers full of 25-mm shells.

Kiwi happened to be looking in the direction of the two outhouses when the Taliban RPG arced toward them, as if in slow motion, and exploded. "Holy fuck," he breathed, listening fiercely to the radio, as if willing Ingram or Hamilton to come over the air and say they were all right. Instead, he heard the wounded captain's desperate call for help.

Kiwi ordered his driver to reverse and swing the vehicle around so they would be in line behind Tony Perry's LAV, about one hundred metres away. Then he called Hope. "We can get to them, sir," he said. "Let us try."

"That road could be compromised," the colonel answered, "mines or IEDs. Are you sure you can make it?"

"We can make it, sir."

Kiwi could see the top of Perry's helmet on the commander's side of the LAV ahead of him. Perry's head was twisted around so that he was looking right at Kiwi, eyes just visible above the rim of his hatch. They looked at each other and Perry nodded.

After a long pause, Hope's voice came over Kiwi's headset: "Good luck."

By then, both LAVs were already rolling forward.

Back at his command post in the wadi, Ian Hope put down the receiver of one of the radios he was quietly but frantically working. He had managed to call in reinforcements from Kandahar. One Alpha Company platoon had already arrived and was deploying in the field between his command post and the schoolhouse, and a second platoon was on its way. Aircraft had taken off from the strip at KAF and were in-bound, but permission to bring in artillery fire was still being denied.

Hope could hear the rising storm of Taliban fire just half a kilometre away and knew his soldiers were fighting for their lives. His mind made up, he turned to Steve Gallagher. "Call the gun battery directly," he said. "We need a fire mission now."

He ordered Alpha Company to mount their LAVs and follow Kiwi and Parsons into the schoolhouse. Then he sat back and waited.

The road leading up to the school was too narrow for the LAVs to run side by side, so Kiwi followed behind Perry's vehicle. "You go to the west side, I'll take the east," he said over the radio.

As soon as the two LAVs began moving, the Taliban realized what they were doing and turned their sights on them. Dozens of RPGs exploded on or around the two vehicles, rocking them back and forth as they raced up the short stretch of road. Hundreds of machine-gun bullets bounced off the LAVs' armour plating, sounding to Kiwi inside his turret "like the regimental drum line was playing on the outside of my car."

They pulled past the two small buildings that Hamilton's tiny assault group had been defending for more than three hours, putting their bulk and armour between the Taliban and the pinned-down soldiers. Kiwi and Perry lowered their rear ramps and began rotating their turrets back and forth, firing bursts from their 25-mm cannons at their highest speed: two hundred rounds per minute. While the dead, the wounded and the handful of survivors scrambled into the back, the two LAVs fired more than four hundred shells from their main guns and hundreds of rounds from their coaxial machine guns, hitting at every Taliban firing position they could see. Kiwi was certain they were killing dozens of insurgents, but the dead and wounded were replaced quickly and the storm of incoming fire slackened only a little.

Andy Gorman had stayed with Dallaire during the entire firefight, pressed up against the wall of the outhouse for the little protection it offered and returning fire despite the pain in his hand. When the LAVs finally arrived, a medic had to practically drag him away. "You've got to get out of here!" he shouted at the young corporal.

"Fuck you!" Gorman screamed back. "He's still alive and I'm not leaving him."

The medic shook his head sadly and Gorman looked down at Dallaire, motionless and pale, and realized he was dead. The two men gently lifted Dallaire and carried him into the back of Perry's LAV, while Gorman raced back into the building's interior and continued firing back at the Taliban.

It took agonizing minutes to load the cars. By then, another pair of LAVs from Alpha Company had radioed that they were on their way to collect the rest of the pinned-down troops.

"I'm good to go!" Perry radioed when his vehicle was full.

"I've had enough of this place, too. Let's go," Kiwi answered, then hit the button to raise his armoured rear ramp.

The mechanism didn't respond, and when Kiwi looked back through the crew compartment he realized with a sickening lurch the thick steel chain that raised the ramp had been shot clean through by a Taliban RPG. Kiwi swallowed hard, then radioed Perry.

"I've got to go first, you'll have to cover me," he said, then pulled out.

Perry followed as closely as he dared, trying to use the body of his LAV to protect Kiwi's vulnerable open rear door. Even with his friend's vehicle close behind, Kiwi spent the twenty-minute drive back to the wadi expecting an RPG to come straight into his wide-open back hatch. If one had hit and exploded in the troop compartment it would have instantly killed the soldiers piled one on top of the other in the back, and likely destroyed the LAV. Neither Perry nor Kiwi breathed easy until they were over the bank of the wadi and out of the enemy's line of sight.

As Kiwi and Perry reached the command post, Hope was all action: calling in helicopters to evacuate his wounded and dead, ordering the Alpha Platoon forward to suppress enemy fire, and coordinating the retrieval crews that were to haul away the two LAVs disabled by the roadside bombs so many hours earlier. His work was interrupted by a salvo of Taliban mortar shells that passed overhead and landed in a fountain of dirt and smoke farther up the wadi. "Too close for comfort," Hope remarked quietly.

A moment later, the ground trembled and Hope saw a black mushroom cloud rise from the direction of the Panjwayi District Centre, less than a kilometre behind them. A suicide car bomb aimed at the convoy of vehicles of the recovery crews bound for Hope's command post had exploded. No Canadians were wounded, but the blast devastated the town's bustling bazaar, killing twenty-one Afghan civilians and seriously injuring thirteen more. To Hope, it was a worrisome sign. Clearly, the Taliban were in Pashmul in far greater strength than even he had suspected, and they were coordinating their attacks on the Canadians from several different directions. Hope's own estimates put the number of fighters in the village beyond as high as two hundred. In short, he was in danger of becoming surrounded and trapped. Hope grabbed the transmitter for his silent satellite radio and once more requested air support, all but begging for help.

As if in answer to a prayer, Hope heard an earth-shaking roar overhead. He looked up to see the extraordinary sight of a U.S. Air Force B1 bomber barrelling towards them, just above tree level. The dull grey, swept-wing bomber soared over the Canadians' heads in a flash with a roar like an express train, headed for the Taliban-held village to the north. As the huge aircraft passed over the insurgents' positions, the pilots turned on the afterburners of their four powerful jet engines, dumped raw fuel into the exhaust and lit it in a bomb-like explosion of power. The B1 crew had heard Hope's radioed pleas for assistance, and although they had already dropped their bombs farther north (to support Bravo Company's battle at the Yellow Schoolhouse), the American airmen decided to give the embattled Canadians a psychological boost. For the first time all day, Hope allowed himself a brief smile.

Just behind the American plane was a flight of French Mirage fighter-bombers, racing in to drop strings of bombs on the entire line of Taliban-occupied buildings. The enemy fire, which had been steadily snapping overhead, finally fell away to almost nothing. Hope grabbed another radio and spoke to the pilots of the medevac helicopters circling overhead. It was safe to land.

Pat Tower had had little chance to rest since diving into the last vehicle out of the schoolhouse, bullets pinging off the armour even as the wide ramp in the rear swung up behind him. Following the short but hair-raising ride back to Hope's command post, Tower was plunged into the role of platoon commander. He tried to reorganize what remained of his exhausted troops. After the toll from the heat, roadside bombs and enemy fire was tallied up, he was left with only eighteen of the thirty soldiers who had arrived for the pre-dawn attack nearly twelve hours earlier. He directed his men into the three remaining LAVs and asked them to prepare for whatever was coming next.

Tower was on autopilot, doing the job he had spent most of his adult life training for and which he knew so well he could do it in his sleep. He was deliberately not thinking about Ingram's body, lying a few feet away next to those of Keller and Dallaire.

Exhausted and numbed as he was, Tower burned to get back into the schoolhouse and beyond—to push past it and get at the Taliban who had killed his friend and three more of his comrades. Weaving his way through the stretchers and bodies that crowded the command post, Tower found Hope still working his bank of radios.

Hope turned to Tower and blinked in dismay at the blood and dust that covered much of his soldier's uniform and kit. "Where's Sergeant Ingram?" he asked quietly.

"Dead, sir," Tower answered matter-of-factly. "That's him there."

Hope looked down. For the first time, he noticed that one of the nearby bodies belonged to Vaughn Ingram, who had served with him years earlier in the Canadian Airborne Regiment. The colonel looked up, stunned and saddened, as Tower calmly reported that 9 Platoon was reorganized, all its soldiers and equipment accounted for and ready to rejoin the attack.

"We've got three working LAVs and nine dismounted troops: enough to take out a couple of compounds," Tower said. "Which one do you want us to attack, sir?"

Hope's voice caught in his throat and he took a moment to answer. "Take up defensive positions around the command post for now," he said finally. "I'll let you know."

Just behind Tower was Willy MacDonald with a similar report on the state of Recce Platoon and a more bluntly stated question: "We gonna go get those bastards, sir?"

Hope stared at the stocky sergeant, torn between laughter and admiration. He repeated the orders he'd given to Tower and turned to stare hatefully in the direction of the buildings where three of his soldiers had died. He tossed away the thin cigar he had smoked to a stub—only the latest in a long string that day—and made up his mind.

He had soldiers, artillery and air support, and his every professional and personal instinct was telling him to attack. But he did not have any ANA troops at his disposal and the police—who were at that moment lounging a short distance away in the shade of a small tree drinking bottled water—were worse than useless. "The only Afghan face on this operation is the Taliban," he thought bitterly.

He had no doubt his soldiers would drive the Taliban out of Bayanzi, no matter how many were dug in inside the village, but with no ANA and only the highly unreliable ANP, they would simply return a couple of days after the Canadians left. Hope glanced at his watch: it was 3:45 p.m. "We're pulling out," he told Randy Northrup. The regimental sergeant-major nodded and the command post began organizing the orderly extraction of the soldiers.

By 4:30 p.m., the Canadian vehicles had pulled out of the sun-baked wadi and the cluttered fields that had cost them four dead and eighteen wounded. The Taliban had suffered far worse: intelligence officers later estimated that dozens had been killed—including two mid-level commanders—and even more wounded, among them the unnamed senior Taliban leader who had been reportedly surprised by the Canadians' quiet and swift nighttime advance on a base he considered safe from attack.

Ian Hope's LAV was the last to pull out of Bayanzi. He made a point of stopping at the edge of the wadi and firing his 25-mm chain gun into the Taliban positions for a full fifteen minutes, daring them to try to hit him. "I want them to hear me firing," he said tersely. "I want to taunt them."

Spin Boldak
August 3
1630 hrs

Bill Fletcher heard the news over the radio in his command post in a daze. It seemed impossible that four of his soldiers were now dead, including the seemingly indestructible Vaughn Ingram. He took a moment to collect himself, then sent word for Master Warrant Officer Sean Stevens, the company sergeant-major, to call together the remnants of Charlie Company who were still in the Spin Boldak base.

When Fletcher marched out onto the open square, the soldiers were lined up in three ranks, their apprehension palpable in the late afternoon heat. They were already in shock over the death of the popular Chris Reid and the troops knew their OC hadn't called them out to give them good news. Fletcher stood ramrod straight in front of the ranks of camouflage uniforms and swallowed hard. "In the battle of Panjwayi there have been three more soldiers killed," he said, then pulled out a scrap of message paper on which he had scribbled down the names of Ingram, Kevin Dallaire and Bryce Keller. Fletcher started to read off the names and his voice caught after the first. He was barely able to choke out the rest of the list before he had to turn and walk away.

Many of his soldiers—tough, resilient men who had been through months of fighting and hardship—had tears streaming down their faces.

CHAPTER FIFTEEN

"A very bad day."

Arghandab Wadi
August 3
1530 hrs

Captain Jon Hamilton's last view of Bayanzi and the White Schoolhouse was from the air, in the medical evacuation helicopter that took him back to the field hospital's operating room. The LAV ride out of the schoolhouse had passed in a blur as Hammy sprawled in the back with the other wounded soldiers— covered in blood, dirt, soot and the acrid smell of gunpowder, listening to the tattoo of bullets rattling off the vehicle. He had been gingerly carried out on a stretcher and laid in the only scrap of shade available in the blistering heat of the wadi, where he waited with the other wounded for the U.S. Black Hawk to fly him out of the sand, dust and fire.

When his stretcher was lifted into the chopper for the short flight back to base, Hamilton turned his head and saw the group of ANP sitting well back from the gunfire that was still occasionally cracking overhead. The police, the same ones who had run away while his soldiers had charged into the schoolhouse, waved at him cheerfully. Hamilton stared at them for a second, then gave them the finger.

"At the end of the day, it took fucking two hundred of them to take on fourteen of us," he told himself. "They got four of our guys, but I can tell you right now they're hurting a lot more than we are."

Hamilton laid back and closed his eyes. "They tell me it was three hours," he said later, "which was a fucking lifetime, believe me."

When he had finished his pointed report to Lieutenant-Colonel Hope in his command post, Willy MacDonald hooked up with the other half of Recce Platoon, which had been engaged in its own firefight with the Taliban fighters who'd tried to slip through to attack the Canadians on their flank. He was almost immediately assaulted by Sergeant Mars Janek. Janek wrapped his arms around MacDonald and lifted him off the ground in a joint-cracking bear hug. The much shorter MacDonald was astonished to see his friend and fellow sergeant was almost in tears. "Don't you ever do that again!" Janek said gruffly. "I thought we'd lost you."

Willy didn't know what to say to that.

Kiwi Parsons managed to get the rear ramp door on his battered LAV closed manually before the Canadian force pulled out of Bayanzi, although it took nearly ten soldiers almost half an hour to lift the heavy armoured door and lock it into place. When Hope gave the signal to move, Parsons steered his battered LAV into the long line of vehicles snaking down the wadi on their way back to KAF. But the hundreds of kilometres of rugged terrain and thousands of bullets, grenades and other explosives had finally taken their toll. Parsons had gone only a few kilometres when one of the coolant lines in his engine blew. He got on his radio and informed Niner Tac that his battle-damaged car would not last long enough to make it to KAF and suggested he divert to another coalition camp in Kandahar City, just a few minutes away. Hope agreed and Kiwi turned away from the rest of the convoy, silently pleading with his LAV to hang on just a little bit longer. He entered the camp at 5:15 p.m. and pulled his car up in front of the vehicle mechanics bay. It promptly ground to a halt. "My wonderful, beautiful car died," Kiwi said.

He climbed out of his turret and trudged over to the mess tent, barely able to put one foot in front of the other. Kiwi sat down and tried to drink juice or cold water—tried to avoid thinking about all that had happened that day. Over the next few hours, he and his crew were approached by almost every other soldier on the base, mainly Americans, British and Australians, and all complete strangers. Every one of them was eager to pat the Canadians on the back or shake their hands.

"That really meant something to us," Kiwi said later. "We had fought the biggest battle for Canada since Korea."

After they returned to KAF, Pat Tower gathered the small group of 9 Platoon survivors around him. "Today's been a very bad day. A lot of bad things happened, but a lot of good things happened as well," he told the young soldiers, most of whom were staring back at him with dull eyes, still in shock over the day's fighting and the deaths of their friends. "You did amazing things and you should be proud of the way you performed."

The troops nodded glumly and returned to their work, unloading and cleaning weapons or straightening out the by now chaotic interiors of their LAVs. After a moment, Tower joined them.

Ian Hope spent the rest of the day doing after-action reviews of the battle for the White Schoolhouse, filling out paperwork and, finally, writing letters to the families of his fallen soldiers.

The next day, after some badly needed sleep and a long-overdue hot shower, Hope was back in his tiny office just off the TOC. He heard a knock on the 2x4 frame of his door and Brigadier-General David Fraser walked in through the open entryway.

Hope filled him in on the details of the previous day's fighting, including the surprising number of Taliban they had found in the Pashmul and his surmises about what they were up to. Fraser nodded and listened intently, watching his battle-group commander closely. He and Hope had known each other for more than fifteen years, including time served together in Bosnia during the vicious civil war of the early 1990s, and Fraser had watched his subordinate age visibly over the past few months. He had never looked so worn down and old before his time.

Hope repeated his concerns that the Taliban were massing for an attack on Kandahar within the next two weeks and suggested that Task Force Orion be kept in Afghanistan for an extra month to help the new battle group that was already arriving in KAF deal with the threat. He could tell from the expression on the general's face that this was not about to happen, so Hope offered another alternative: he could stay an extra month to help his successor, Lieutenant-Colonel Omer Lavoie. Fraser looked even less pleased at this recommendation, so Hope wound down his report, then looked his general in the eye. "Sir, this is your job," he said bluntly. "This needs a brigade, not a battle group."

Fraser left the meeting thoughtful and more than a little concerned. He had been planning a large operation to begin in early October, tentatively code-named Operation Medusa, to quell insurgent activity in the Panjwayi. Now, he wondered if that might be too late.

The general walked back to his office in the nearby National Command Element building, headquarters for the entire Canadian contingent in Afghanistan and the same place where Ian Hope had given Major-General Freakley his unwelcome briefing on the Taliban build-up in the Panjwayi. When he got into his office he pulled two books off his shelf, both required reading for officers serving in Afghanistan: *The Bear Went Over the Mountain* and *The Other Side of the Mountain*. The two volumes are collections of articles on the Soviet's long occupation of

Afghanistan, the first from the Russian point of view and the second told by the mujahedeen fighters who eventually evicted the Soviets from the country.

Fraser carefully reread two articles that had sprung to mind when Hope had told him about the strength and unusual boldness of the Taliban his soldiers had fought the day before. The first described a 1982 attempt to encircle and destroy a large guerrilla band in the Panjwayi—an attempt that failed when the mujahedeen slipped sideways instead of retreating and counter-attacked a company-headquarters unit. The second laid out details of an attack on a major centre led by a small group of mujahedeen who snuck into the town and almost literally opened the gates for a much larger force of insurgents, who swarmed in and overwhelmed the Soviet-trained Afghan-government defenders.

The mujahedeen were only able to hold the town for a couple of days in the face of a concerted Soviet counterattack, but the victory demoralized the Russian-sponsored Afghan-government forces and raised the mujahedeen's stock among the local population immeasurably.

"So that's what they're up to," Fraser said to himself.

Spin Boldak
August 5
1700 hrs

Ryan Jurkowski was almost the only officer left in Spin Boldak when the flag-draped coffins carrying the bodies of the four soldiers killed at the White Schoolhouse were loaded onto an air force transport in Kandahar for the journey back to Canada. Fletcher had taken most of the soldiers with him to the farewell ceremony, leaving his second-in-command with only a skeleton crew at the base and one more difficult job to do. Someone had to go through the dead men's personal effects and pack them away to be shipped home to their families. Reid, Dallaire and Keller's fellow privates and corporals had taken care of their effects, but the sergeants and warrant officers who were Vaughn Ingram's closest comrades had gone to Kandahar for the ramp ceremony.

Jurkowski sat in the base's command post most of the day, putting off the difficult chore for as long as possible. Finally, he realized he couldn't do it alone. He stood and abruptly turned to Warrant Officer Ron Gallant. "I need you to come help me clean out Vaughn's room, Ronnie," he said. A surprised Gallant reluctantly nodded.

The two walked slowly to Ingram's room—as a sergeant he had rated his own quarters. Light-headed with emotion, they stared at the door for a moment. Neither had stopped to think that it would be locked. No one on the base had Ingram's key, so Jurkowski was forced to kick down the door, splintering its flimsy wood under his combat boots.

Without a word the two began sorting through Ingram's belongings, separating civilian clothing and personal items from his military-issued kit, which would eventually be turned in to the regimental quartermaster.

Under Ingram's bunk, Jurkowski found a collection of pictures of the sergeant's five-year-old daughter, Brooke, along with some of her artwork, neatly lined up awaiting his return from the operation in the Panjwayi. Jurkowski stared at the row of pictures for several minutes, embarrassed by his reluctance to put them away. Somehow, he felt that as long as the child's pictures were still looking up at him, waiting for her daddy to return, Ingram wasn't really, completely gone. "It killed me to have to put them into his barrack box—I wanted his daughter to keep seeing and not be forced into the blackness," he said later. "Some childish notion, I suppose, but it was there nonetheless."

After a long while, Jurkowski stacked the photos and the paintings, carefully placed them in the box, and gently closed the lid.

EPILOGUE

Task Force Orion's August 3 assaults on the White and Yellow Schoolhouses killed three Taliban commanders and wounded several others. Dozens of fighters were killed or captured, and the rest scattered to avoid the Canadians' follow-up sweeps through the Panjwayi and the coalition air and artillery strikes that accompanied the task force's LAVs.

Mullah Dadullah—the mastermind of the Taliban offensive in the region—was reportedly furious at the setback. In intercepted cellular or radio calls, he berated his sub-commanders and urged them to gather their fighters for fresh attacks. But the Canadians had done too much damage. Reluctantly, Dadullah called off the carefully planned Independence Day attack and instead ordered his cell commanders to prepare an assault on the Panjwayi District Centre for mid September.

Once again, though, the Canadians would throw a wrench in Dadullah's plans. On September 3, one month to the day after Charlie's 9 Platoon and Jon Hamilton's Recce Platoon held off the Taliban in the White Schoolhouse, the soldiers of the Royal Canadian Regiment (RCR) stormed the same cluster of buildings. The attack was one of the opening moves of Brigadier-General Fraser's Operation Medusa—a large sweep through almost the entire Panjwayi region involving more than 1,400 coalition and Afghan soldiers.

The schoolhouse, along with the cluster of nearby complexes that made up the village of Bayanzi, was still a Taliban stronghold, and in the weeks since Hamilton and Ingram had led their small band into the battered white building the insurgents had been busy. When about fifty troops of Charles Company, 1 RCR, rolled into the schoolhouse from across the Arghandab River, following almost exactly the same route used on August 3, the Taliban was more than ready. The insurgents had dug trenches, fortified buildings, walls and tree lines, and lined up arsenals of RPGS, mortars, machine guns and deadly 81-mm recoilless rifles—Soviet anti-tank weapons that were much more effective at penetrating armour than the ubiquitous RPGS.

The Canadians, most of whom had arrived in Afghanistan only two weeks earlier, swept into the school in an early morning attack, but were greeted by ferocious fire when they tried to press forward into the buildings beyond. The Taliban fired into the advancing RCR soldiers from three sides and pinned down most of them almost immediately. Planned air strikes and artillery barrages that were supposed to precede the attack were cancelled at the last minute. Four Canadians died in the day-long battle that erupted around the schoolhouse and it took coalition forces more than a week to finally clear the area of Taliban.

But Operation Medusa fell like a hammer blow on the Taliban forces gathering for Dadullah's mid-September attack, forcing them to scatter once more. By September 14, Operation Medusa was declared over, and NATO commanders were claiming a major success, with more than one thousand Taliban killed. The White Schoolhouse, virtually destroyed by several days of bombing and artillery strikes that followed the RCR assault, was later destroyed. By then, the last soldiers of Task Force Orion were already back in Canada.

In May 2007, a year after his fighters opened their offensive in the Panjwayi area, Mullah Dadullah was killed in a special forces raid on a compound in Helmand Province. His desire to be in front of the camera proved his downfall. Dadullah gave a videotaped interview in Quetta on the day before he died. Shortly after finishing the interview, he was tracked by coalition forces as he crossed the Pakistan border into Afghanistan. The next day, his compound was surrounded by helicopter-borne commandos. Because of Dadullah's legendary status and reputation for cheating death, Kandahar governor Assadullah Khalid had his body retrieved from Helmand and put on display for reporters.

—◦◦◦—

Operation Archer had taken its toll on Charlie Company. During their seven-month tour of duty in Afghanistan, Charlie had lost eight soldiers: Rob Costall, Nichola Goddard, Tony Boneca, Chris Reid, Bryce Keller, Kevin Dallaire, Vaughn Ingram and Andrew James Eykelenboom.

The last fatality came after the costly fight at the White Schoolhouse. On August 11, a convoy on its way from the company base at Spin Boldak to KAF was attacked by a suicide bomber. The explosives-laden pickup veered into the path of a G Wagon in the middle of the convoy, killing Corporal "Boomer" Eykelenboom in the resulting explosion. The twenty-three-year-old—a medic from the Edmonton-based 1st Field Ambulance who had been attached to Charlie for the entire tour—was less than two weeks from boarding a flight home.

Captain Marty Dupuis retired from the Canadian Forces just over a year after returning from Afghanistan. He now lives and works in Ottawa, running the local operations of the business service multinational Cintas. He left the army when he realized he would be assigned to train other soldiers in Canadian Forces Base Gagetown and would have to wait years before being allowed to return to Afghanistan in command of soldiers like those of Charlie Company. "It was the best time of my life and the worst time of my life," he says of his tour in Kandahar. "I don't regret it: it's made me a better person. But I'd trade it all to have the friends we lost back again."

Master Corporal Kiwi Parsons was promoted to sergeant a few months after his return from Afghanistan, along with his friend Tony Perry, and is still serving with the 1st Battalion PPCLI in Edmonton. Looking back on his summer of battling the Taliban, Parsons says simply: "I reckon we did all right. We won ninety-nine percent of the gunfights. We won over some people and converted some Taliban. But what exactly is winning in the big sense? It's a lot more than gunfights and killing the enemy. My war had us as winning, but the generals and politicians don't see the war from my point of view.

"My war was seven months of hunting the enemy, finding him and trying to kill him, succeeding in killing him and keeping my crew alive. That's it in a nutshell. On the side, I tried to make everyday life better for people in Kandahar. I guess I am lucky to see it so simply.

"Canadians may not like the war and what is happening and the dead soldiers, but they sure as hell should feel proud of their soldiers. I am proud to serve with them, have watched them do many gallant things, and seen their emotions up close. But you know what? They still woke up every morning, picked up their helmet and rifle, and continued to advance on an armed enemy knowing full well they may not see lunchtime."

Kiwi Parsons is scheduled to return to Afghanistan in February 2009, as LAV crew commander for the Canadian task-force commander.

When Captain Ryan Jurkowski returned to Edmonton, a military doctor and a staff officer gathering "lessons learned" advice for the army asked, "Did you leave at the right time?"

Jurkowski shook his head emphatically. "No. We should have stayed longer," he replied.

Jurkowski remains convinced that Task Force Orion won the Battle of Panjwayi—"if that's what it's going to be called," he adds wryly—and that the seven months Charlie spent fighting halfway around the world was worth the cost, however painful the losses were to bear.

"Everything we did, regardless of the cost, was worth our efforts for every ounce of blood lost, Taliban or ours. We all knew what we were doing there and, although there were frustrations and fears by all, we knew that through the kinetic defeat of the insurgents, we could do what we had deployed to do—bring stability and humanitarian assistance to the people of Afghanistan," he says now.

"On leaving, we had achieved much in denting the ability for the Taliban to mount anything resembling success, minor or massive, wherever we roamed." One year after his return, Jurkowski was promoted to major. He remains in the army.

Two days after Sergeant Pat Tower landed back in Edmonton, he bumped into Vaughn Ingram's brother, Stacy, in the West Edmonton Mall. "Pat," Stacy told him quietly, "Vaughn left us a package. It's his will, and it's got something for you. He said to give $2,000 to Pat and tell him to throw a party for the platoon."

Stacy Ingram paused. "He said if you weren't alive to give the money to the platoon warrant."

Tower smiled in spite of himself. "Just like Iggy: planning for me not being alive."

The next week, the members of 9 Platoon and several other members of Charlie gathered at an Edmonton bar, hoisted their glasses and proceeded to get riotously drunk in Vaughn Ingram's honour.

Tower was awarded the Star of Military Valour—the highest award for bravery after the Victoria Cross—for his mad dash across the open ground to rescue the soldiers trapped in the

White Schoolhouse. The citation for the award listed his "valiant actions taken on August 3, 2006, in the Pashmul region of Afghanistan," and concluded that "Sergeant Tower's courage and selfless devotion to duty contributed directly to the survival of the remaining platoon members."

Pat Tower is still in the army, posted to Calgary. He has volunteered for a second tour in Afghanistan.

Sergeant Mike Denine was awarded the Medal of Military Valour—the third-highest award for bravery in the Canadian Forces—for his one-man fight with the Taliban in Bayanzi on May 17. The citation reads, in part: "Completely exposed to enemy fire, he laid down a high volume of suppressive fire, forcing the enemy to withdraw. Sergeant Denine's valiant action ensured mission success and likely saved the lives of his crew." Mike Denine is still serving in the army.

Major Bill Fletcher believes firmly that his company's two-and-a-half-month running fight with the Taliban was worthwhile in the end. "The boys did their job and we accomplished our mission. I truly believe we improved the overall situation and did a hell of a lot for Canada's reputation both militarily but also on the world stage."

Still, he admits that the seven soldiers under his command who died during Charlie's tour haunt him. "There is, of course, that part of me who mourns daily for our lost brothers. I cannot help but believe that they died doing their duty and moving forward, taking the fight to the enemy. I take comfort in that, but still wish I could have brought everyone back alive," he says.

"I recall an officer speaking on my Phase [basic officer's] training who said 'Gentlemen, you will live with the ghosts of the men you kill.' I have replayed our operations countless times in my head and do not believe anyone died from a mistake I made, but I do live with their memories. My take on it is that I need to live better to make up for their absence. The Taliban will not have another success on my account."

For his front-line leadership of Charlie Company, Fletcher, too, was awarded the Star of Military Valour. According to his citation for the decoration, he "repeatedly demonstrated extraordinary bravery by exposing himself to intense fire while leading his forces, on foot, to assault heavily defended enemy positions. On two occasions, the soldiers at his side were struck by enemy fire. He immediately rendered first aid and then continued to head the subsequent assaults. On these occasions and in ensuing combat actions, his selfless courage, tactical acumen and effective command were pivotal to the success of his company in defeating a determined opponent."

Soon after returning from Kandahar, Fletcher was sent to study at the Canadian Forces Staff College in Toronto, a prerequisite for promotion to lieutenant-colonel or higher.

Ian Hope left Afghanistan after his offer to remain in Kandahar to help his successor was turned down. Hope stepped onto a Hercules transport plane and off Afghan soil for the final time on August 20, 2006. His remaining soldiers had left a week earlier and, as he had always promised himself, his boots were the first of his battle group to hit the ground, and the last off.

Hope was awarded the Meritorious Service Cross for his command of Task Force Orion, "the Canadian battle group that experienced the first major land combat operations since the Korean War," according to the citation.

"Leading from the front, Lieutenant-Colonel Hope worked tirelessly under difficult conditions to achieve Canada's strategic aims in Afghanistan. A dynamic leader, he assembled an effective combat team that was instrumental in expanding the Canadian presence throughout the region and in achieving considerable success in suppressing enemy activities."

After his return, Hope was posted to the U.S. Army War College in Carlisle, Pennsylvania, where he is working on his doctorate in history, studying the American Civil War. In 2007—almost one year to the day after the opening of the Battle of Panjwayi—he was promoted to full colonel.

He has threatened on several occasions—only half-jokingly—to resign his commission and re-enlist as a corporal in order to get back to Afghanistan.

ACKNOWLEDGEMENTS

As this book was going to print, Charlie Company suffered one more belated casualty in the Panjwayi. Captain Jonathan Snyder, the 8 Platoon leader during the long, hot summer of 2006, died on June 7, 2008, during a routine patrol of Zhari district. Snyder, whose platoon led the attack in the opening skirmish of the Battle of Panjwayi on May 17, fell into a well while conducting a night security patrol with ANA troops. Rescuers pulled him out of the deep hole and he was evacuated by helicopter to the hospital at Kandahar Airfield, where he was pronounced dead upon arrival.

This book would not have been possible without his help and the time and generosity of the other officers and men of Charlie Company, who were fulsome in their praise and admirably restrained in their corrections of my all too numerous mistakes or misinterpretations. I owe a particular debt to those members of the brotherhood of the northern star, who helped enormously with my attempts to shed light on the organization, methods and plans of the Taliban. They know who they are and what they have done.

I'm also indebted to three historians, whose writing in my opinion rivals the best authors that this country has to offer, fiction or non-fiction: Donald Graves, for taking the time to offer criticism that may have been unsparing and often caustic but that was always to the point; Dr. Sean Maloney for his invaluable insights into the nature of counter-insurgency warfare, the war in Afghanistan and the history of the modern Canadian military; and the incomparable Jack Granatstein, whose kind words and encouragement were a great inspiration.

Sergeant Kory Fisher, Sergeant Steve Powell and Master-Bombardier Sebastien Perreault and the members of 2 section,

16 Platoon, Common Army Phase Course 0613, deserve my thanks for pounding the subtleties of the section attack, navigation and patrolling into my skull. Still working for the ma'am guys. Master Corporal Trent Vail, of the Prince Edward Island Regiment, and Jay Conroy, of the Queen's York Rangers, showed me how difficult a job it is to command an armoured vehicle and how effortless it can appear when done well.

The many members of the Canadian Forces public affairs branch are to be commended for tolerating my endless queries and SFQs and for chasing down so many tidbits of information needed to make this book accurate, in particular Captains Mark Peebles, Brian Owens and Michael Wiesenfeld. My thanks as well to Major Chris Stewardson, Captains Aaron Paronuzzi and Scott Plumley, Lieutenants Gord Scharf and Leith Coghlin and the inimitable Warrant Officer Ingo Herbst for their comradeship and often cheerfully contradictory advice.

John Cotter, my once and future canoe partner, offered his unstinting advice, friendship and several days worth of room and board during trips to Edmonton to conduct research and interviews. And as a charter member of the Afghan Old Boys network, his memories of Charlie Company and several of its members were invaluable.

My agent Linda McKnight, my editor Linda Pruessen of Key Porter and my good friend Derek Raymaker, of Charlatan alumnus fame, were valuable sounding boards for the initial drafts and occasional shoulders if not to cry on, then to suffer my occasional whining, complaints and frenetic second-guessing.

My daughter Ariel and son Thomas deserve much credit for tolerating Daddy's long absences, hours in front of the computer screen typing furiously or pacing back and forth, and occasional outbursts of un-parental language.

This book would not have been finished without the help of one person in particular. Without the unstinting support, praise and encouragement of the beautiful and talented Lisa

Zaritzky I might never have written a single page. Her belief in the book and my ability to do justice to the soldiers of Charlie Company and their story helped me overcome many hurdles and nights of writer's block. This book is as much hers as it is mine.

INDEX

1st Battalion PPCLI, 47–48, 291
2nd Battalion PPCLI, 49, 60
3rd Battalion PPCLI, 191
1 Combat Engineers Regiment, 50
1st Field Ambulance, 290
1st Regiment, Royal Canadian Horse
    Artillery, 49–50, 119, 124
2-87 Infantry Battalion (U.S. Army),
    195
2 Platoon (Alpha), 207, 220, 224
7 Platoon (Charlie), 89, 104, 110, 122,
    163, 207
8 Platoon (Charlie), 88–89, 102, 107,
    110, 122, 163, 172, 173, 207, 219,
    221, 224
9 Platoon (Charlie), 134, 138, 144–45,
    163, 166–67, 171, 172, 175, 179,
    239, 240, 242, 248–49, 251, 256,
    257, 263, 279, 284, 288, 292
12é Régiment Blindé du Canada, 49

Adair, Jay, 107, 130
Afghan National Army (ANA), 81, 106,
    112–13, 125, 126, 135, 172–73,
    179, 192, 203, 208, 217, 221–22,
    229, 230
Afghan National Police (ANP), 81–84,
    91, 94, 125, 157, 163, 167, 168,
    194, 192, 203, 270, 212, 252, 257–
    58, 257–58, 259, 270 (See also
    Massoud, Captain)
Akhund, Mullah Obaidullah, 43–44
al Qaeda, 120, 191, 201
Alcock, Craig, 134, 135, 139–41, 150–
    51, 240
alcohol restrictions, 117
Alizi (village), 164–66, 174–75
Alpha Company (Red Devils), 56, 72,
    74, 195, 205–8, 211, 219, 228–29,
    255, 274–75, 276, 277 (See also 2
    Platoon)

Ambush Alley, 91, 134, 141, 146, 162,
    241, 246, 247
ambush patrols, 148–49
American army: tactics compared with
    Cdn., 145; view of Canadians, 52,
    202
Apache helicopters, 162, 203, 223,
    226, 229, 252
Arghandab District, 74
Arghandab Mountains, 44, 75, 78, 195
Arghandab River, 21, 75, 76, 80, 84,
    95, 129, 159, 163, 202, 239, 289
Arghandab wadi, 95, 128–29, 146, 149,
    163–64, 208, 246, 265–66, 282
ASIC (All Source Intelligence Cell), 40
Atwell, Hugh, 163–64, 167–68, 171,
    172

B1 bombers, 277–78
Bagram (air base), 80, 120, 188, 195,
    201, 202, 203, 238
Baluchistan, 31–32
Bamiyan Province, 35
battle stress, 60–61
Bayanzi (village), 16, 95–96, 102–17,
    120, 122, 123, 239, 265, 280, 282,
    283, 293
BDA (battle-damage assessment), 123
Bear Went Over the Mountain, The
    (essays), 48, 285–86
"beaten zone," 225
"bed down" position, 132
Berry, Glyn, 72
Berube, Calvin, 103
bin Laden, Osama, 43
Bison armoured vehicles, 252
Black Hawk helicopters, 143, 159,
    180, 252, 282
blocking forces, 128
body armour, 64, 132
Boneca, Tony, 219–20, 221, 231, 232
Bosnia, 60

Bravo Company, 16, 25, 49, 72, 75,
  80, 96, 102–3, 107–8, 109, 110,
  112, 118, 122, 124, 127–28, 161,
  168, 186, 192, 195, 201–2, 207–8,
  209, 210, 212–13, 206, 211, 217,
  238, 239, 241, 246, 247, 255, 264,
  278
British Army, 48–49, 190, 203
British Household Cavalry, 203
British Special Air Service, 120
British 3 Parachute Regiment (the
  "Paras"), 49, 203
BTE (Brigade Training Exercise), 62
Burdge, Mike, 106
Burger King, 121, 240
"button-hook," 163

Camp Julien, 39
Camp Mirage, 117–19, 123, 124
Canadian Airborne Regiment, 25, 49,
  55, 58–59, 279
Canadian Army Reserve, 48
Canadian Forces, 48, 50, 57, 117, 123,
  207, 225, 290, 243
Canadian Forces Base Gagetown (NB),
  55, 290
Canadian Forces Base Wainwright
  (AB), 61–65, 148
Canadian Forces Staff College
  (Toronto), 294
Canadian International Development
  Agency (CIA), 50, 72, 202
Canadian Technical Operations Centre
  (TOC), 188
CanCon show, 117
Canex compound, 116–17
Caron, Marc, 64–65
"caterpillar" attack, 258
cell-phone networks, 85, 128, 206, 245
  (See also informants)
Chaisson, Peter, 177
Charchuk, Andrew, 215–16, 223–24,
  225–26, 227, 228
Charlish, Mike, 220
Chechnya, 213
Cintas (multinational), 290
Civil Military Co-operation (CIMIC),
  50, 53
clan hierarchy, 126

coalition forces, 52, 83, 116, 120, 130,
  131, 173, 188–89, 191, 193, 204,
  206, 223, 237–38, 283, 288, 289
  (See also NATO)
Cold War, 145
Cole, Tom, 271–72
concerts, 117
"cook off," 228
Corrections Canada, 50
Costall, Rob, 73, 290
Croatia, 24, 60

Dadullah, Mullah, 33–46, 288, 289–90
Dallaire, Kevin, 25, 262–63, 267–68,
  276, 278, 281, 287, 290
Denine, Mike, 57, 88–91, 92–93,
  95–106, 109–10, 113–15, 116–17,
  128–29, 160, 174, 175, 179, 180–81,
  182–83, 184, 208–9, 210–11, 213,
  214–15, 218, 231, 293
Dept. of Foreign Affairs and International Trade (DFAIT), 50, 72
"developing the battle space," 122–23
Dostun, Abdul Rashid, 36
"double tap and drop," 176
Dowrey River, 75
Dubai, 117, 118
Dupuis, Marty, 88–89, 91–92, 93, 95,
  107–8, 110–11, 115, 125, 138, 139
  166–67, 174–75, 179–80, 181,
  184–85, 221, 290

"early warning groups," 211
Electronic Warfare (EN), 206 (See also
  cell-phone networks; informants;
  walkie-talkies)
EOD (Explosive Ordnance Detach-
  ment), 255
Eykelenboom, Andrew James
  ("Boomer"), 290

530 Compound, 125–26, 131, 133,
  134, 138–39, 141, 146, 149, 152
Fehr, Jeff, 215, 225–26
Felix, Shawn, 24
Ferguson, Tim, 177
First World War, 56
Fletcher, Bill, 55–58, 61, 62, 63–64,
  73, 88, 117–18, 160–79, 182,

183–85, 186, 189, 204–5, 209–11,
   212–31, 239, 249, 255, 258,
   259–60, 280–81, 286, 293–94
"floppy hats," 133
"flying squad," 132
Force Protection Company, 48
Former Yugoslavia, 13, 24, 62
Forward Observation Officers (FOOS),
   63
Forward Operating Base Wolf, 73
France, 52
Fraser, David, 51, 189–90, 284–85
Freakley, Benjamin, 189, 190–95, 201,
   202, 237–38, 285
Froude, Jason, 80
Furlong, Rob, 191

G Wagons, 21
Gallagher, Steve, 265, 275
Gallant, Ron, 89–90, 103–4, 117, 172,
   287
Gallinger, Kirk, 205, 216
General Dynamics Land Systems, 53
Germany, 52, 116
ghost towns, 127
Ginther, Brent, 175–77, 178, 180
"go kit," 124
Goddard, Nichola, 63–64, 94, 102,
   107–9, 110, 112, 117, 118–19, 121,
   124–25, 139, 171, 215, 290
Gomez, Francisco, 238
Gorman, Andy, 262–63, 267–68, 276
Governor General's Horse Guards, 11
grenades, malfunctioning, 64, 221,
   224–25, 242, 271
Grimshaw, Nick, 80, 118, 201–2,
   205–6, 216, 264
Grossman, Dave, 60–61
Gundy Ghar feature, 81, 84, 93

Hamilton, Jon ("Hammy"), 243–45,
   248–50, 252–59, 261, 262–63,
   266–67, 268–69, 270, 272, 273–74,
   275, 282–83, 288–89
"hard-core Taliban," 45, 85–86
Harrier jets, 182, 183
Hazzaras, 35
Health Services Support Company, 50
helicopters, 141, 143, 223, 277

Hellfire missiles, 223, 224, 225
Helmand Province, 41, 51, 73, 75,
   121, 122, 162, 195, 203, 232, 237,
   238, 244, 289, 290
Helmand River valley 203, 232
Highway One, 78, 83, 84, 91, 93, 95,
   110, 111, 113, 115, 125, 130, 134,
   144–48, 159, 162, 207, 246, 251
Hillier, Rick, 48, 51, 64–65
"hit-and-run" attacks, 85, 241–42
honors, medals, 292–93, 294
Hope, Ian, 12, 13–14, 15, 21–26,
   47–55, 58, 59, 61–65, 71, 74–85,
   87, 89, 93–95, 109, 112, 120, 122,
   125, 128–30, 131, 145, 157–60,
   161–62, 188–95, 201–6, 230, 237,
   238–39, 243, 245–48, 249, 254–56,
   259, 264–66, 274–75, 277, 278–80,
   283–85, 294–95
HumInt, 205 (See also informants)
HVT (high-value target), 120
Hydra missiles, 223

IEDs (Improvised Explosive Devices),
   45, 195–96
Independence Day (Afghan), 238, 288
informants, 85, 126, 128, 152, 192,
   205, 217, 239–40, 242–43, 245,
   248, 254
Ingram, Brooke, 287
Ingram, Stacy, 292
Ingram, Vaughn, 24–25, 58–59, 139–41,
   166, 185–86, 251, 256–57, 261,
   262, 264, 266–67, 269, 270, 273,
   279, 281, 287, 288–89, 290, 292
International Security Assistance Force
   (ISAF), 12, 39, 41, 48, 238
Iran, 130
Iraq, 39, 51, 52, 54
Islam, 13, 43
Ivanko, Sean, 207, 224

Janek, Mars, 259, 283
jihadist emblem, 186
"jingle," 42, 258
Joe, Jason, 254
Joint Task Force 2 (Canada), 120
Jurkowski, Ryan, 57–58, 63–64, 73,
   88, 118–19, 123–25, 130, 131–33,

138–39, 144–52, 159, 178, 180, 237, 286–87, 291–92

Kandahar Airfield (KAF), 50, 71, 88, 115, 116–17, 120, 143, 160, 162, 201, 204, 205, 228, 238, 240, 241, 255, 265, 275, 283, 285, 288
Kabul, 12, 34, 39, 49
Kandahar City, 15, 42, 59, 71, 72, 74–75, 84–85, 91, 115, 189, 193, 238, 244, 247, 283, 285
Kandahar Province, 11, 12, 34, 41, 51, 238
Karachi, 46
Karzai, Hamid, 36, 82
Keller, Bryce, 25, 266–67, 269, 270, 278, 281, 287
Khalid, Assadullah, 292
khameez, 33
"kill zones," 127, 148, 149, 191
Koran, 43
Korean War, 14, 15, 65, 149, 284, 294
Kosovo, 57
Kunduz Province, 36
KIA (killed in action), 118

Landstuhl (Germany), 116
laser range finders, 130
LAV (Light Armoured Vehicle), 53–54
Lavoie, Omar, 285
"leaguer," 162
"leap frog" attack, 258
"line of departure," 209
Loewen, Mike, 78

MacDonald, Willy, 70, 245, 264, 268–70, 272–73, 279, 283
madrassas, 33, 132, 185
marijuana, 77, 84, 85, 133
Martin, Paul, 47
Massoud, Captain, 81, 82–84, 87, 94–95, 115, 126, 152, 157–58, 159, 192, 205, 217, 238, 245, 257–58
Masum Ghar (ridge) 211
Mavin, Chris, 175, 176–77
Meade, Bob, 171, 182, 183
Medak Pocket (Croatia), 24, 60
Medal of Military Valour, 293
medevac. See helicopters

medical outreach program, 202–3
Meritorious Service Cross, 294
military tactics, Cdn. compared with Amn., 145
Mirage fighter bombers, 278
"mobility kill," 111
Mooney, Keith, 165, 166–67, 171, 176, 177–78, 183, 215, 219, 226–28
Moores, Gerry, 98, 99, 100, 101
mujahedeen, 32, 145, 157, 158–60, 286
Mushan (Punjwayi), 202

Nalgham, 16, 89, 90, 95, 160 (See also Seyyedin)
National Command Element building, 285
National Defence HQ (Ottawa), 207
NATO, 12, 15, 34, 41, 43, 48, 51–52, 62, 193, 206, 237–38, 241, 265, 289 (See also coalition forces)
night ambush patrols, 132–33
night-vision equipment, 63, 130, 150
"nine-liner" (casualty report), 251
Niner Tac, 22, 71, 73, 78, 80, 83, 93–94, 121, 129, 211, 243, 247, 248, 283
Nolan, Tony, 270–71
Northern Alliance, 35–36, 82
North Vietnam, 193
Northrup, Randy, 80, 121–22, 143, 280
Nyala patrol cars, 21, 71

Objective Puma, 204–5, 208
Officer Commanding (OC), 55
"O group" (orders group), 128–29
Omar, Mullah Mohammed, 35, 37, 38–39, 43, 44–45, 84
On Combat (Grossman), 61
Operation Anaconda, 191
Operation Archer, 60, 290
Operation Bravo Guardian, 87, 89
Operation Enduring Freedom, 41, 51, 80, 120, 238
Operation Iraqi Freedom, 190
Operation Jagra, 160
Operation Medusa, 285, 289
Operation Mountain Thrust, 188–89, 194, 195–96, 201, 202, 203

Operation Zahar, 203, 206–10, 217
opium, 77, 84, 85
Osmani, Mullah Akhtar Mohammad, 43
Other Side of the Mountain, The, 285–86
Ozerkevich, Kory ("Oz"), 93, 96, 98–99, 100, 104, 176, 177, 178, 180

Pajhwok Afghan News, 46
Pakistan, 31, 72, 85, 130, 132, 159, 213, 289
Pakistani Inter-Service Intelligence, 32, 38
Panjwayi, 14, 15–17, 71–87, 244
Panjwayi District Centre, 25, 129, 130, 208, 247, 277, 288
Parsons, Matthew ("Kiwi"), 57, 110, 111–12, 121–22, 124, 132–37, 141–43, 240–41, 249–51, 247, 261–62, 271, 273–74, 275–76, 283–84, 291
Pashmul, 16, 129–30, 131–33, 157, 158–59, 160, 197–232
Pashtuns/Pashtun culture, 32, 78
Patrol Base Wilson, 207, 225, 241, 243, 244, 247
Patton (film), 248
Payendi, 205, 207–11, 218, 231, 232
Perry, Tony, 135, 142, 261, 274, 275, 276–77
Persian Gulf, 117
Peterson, Sean, 240, 249, 250–51, 252
Pizza Hut, 121, 240
Predator (unmanned drone plane), 223–24, 226
Princesss Patricia's Canadian Light Infantry (PPCLI), 11, 12–13, 16, 51
"Priority Four" (wounded), 139
"professional jihadists," 45
professional soldiers, 13
Provincial Reconstruction Team (PRT), 50, 72

qalas (village compounds), 76
Qualtier, Tim ("Q"), 269–60
Quetta (Pakistan), 31, 289

Rachynski, Paul, 137–38, 169–70

rahbari shura (ruling council), 37
Rashid, Ahmed, 38
RCMP, 50, 59, 81
Recce (Reconnaissance) Platoon, 127, 208, 211, 214, 216, 239, 243, 244–45, 246, 247, 248, 249, 251, 253–54, 256, 260, 279, 283, 288
reconstruction projects, 50, 72, 202
recruits, Taliban, 45–46
Red Army, 32, 145 (*See also* Soviets, Soviet occupation)
Redford, Dave, 138–39
refugee camps, 209
Reg Desert, 42, 75
Reid, Chris, 251, 252, 260, 281, 287, 290
Reid, Tony, 135–36, 141, 143
Richards, David, 238
right flanking attack, 172
Royal Air Force (RAF), 182
Royal Canadian Horse Artillery, 25, 49–50, 94, 119, 124, 141
Royal Canadian Regiment (RCR), 238
Royal Military College (Kingston), 55, 88
RPGs (rocket-propelled grenades), 23
Russian military tactics, 145
"RV" (rendezvous), 150

Saigon, 193
sand fleas, 218
schoolhouse battles. *See* White Schoolhouse; Yellow Schoolhouse
September 11, 2001, 36, 82
Serbia, 57
Seyyedin, 16, 153–87, 189, 202, 195
shabnamas (anonymous notes), 84
Shahi-Kot Valley, 191
Showali-Kot District, 74
shura, 37, 126
Siah Choy (village), 127–28
Smith, Randy, 180, 181
snakes, 148
SNC Technologies Inc., 225
Snyder, Jon, 104, 113–14, 207, 219–20
Social, Andy, 257
"soft contact," 127
South Vietnam, 193

Soviets, Soviet occupation, 13, 44, 77, 85, 145, 157–59, 285–86
special forces, 120, 122, 201–2, 289
Spin Boldak, 204, 237, 239–40, 259, 280–81, 286–87
spy planes, 223–24
Star of Military Valour, 292–93, 294
Stevens, Sean, 281
Strickland, Tod, 80
"Strykers" (armoured vehicles), 53
suicide bombing, 25–26, 39–40, 42, 43, 44–45, 46, 72, 74, 78, 228, 238
"sunray," 108
Sutherland, "Suds," 181, 209–10, 212

"3D" approach, 50, 72
Taliban (Rashid), 38
Tarnak River, 75
Task Force Bayonet, 51
Task Force Orion, 11, 12, 15–16, 47–65, 145, 194, 206, 207, 208, 238, 285, 288, 294
TCCCS (Tactical Command and Control Communications System), 22
Tet Offensive, 192–93
thermal sites, 134
Thorlakson, Doug, 25–26
Tim Hortons, 121
Tower, Pat, 24–25, 59–60, 64, 134–345, 137, 141, 143, 144, 169–70, 171–72, 239–40, 242–43, 248, 270–73, 278–79, 284, 292–93
"triggers" (ambush), 133
Trowsdale, Jeff, 98, 99
Turner, Tim, 179

UAVs (Unmanned Aerial Vehicles), 50, 203
United Arab Emirates, 117–19, 123–24

United Nations Human Rights Watch, 35
United States Agency for International Development (USAID), 50
Uruzgan Province, 36, 51
U.S. Air Force, 277–78
U.S. Army, 51, 52, 60, 193, 195 (*See also* American army)
U.S. Army War College, 295
U.S. Black Hawks. *See* Black Hawk helicopters
U.S. Command, transition to NATO, 237–38
U.S. Delta Force, 120
U.S. special forces. *See* special forces

Vachon, Alain, 253, 254
Van Mol, Glen, 136, 142
Vernon, Chris, 190, 192, 193, 194
Victoria Cross, 292
Vietnam War, 193
villages, typical, 76–77
VSA (Vital Signs Absent), 139, 251

walkie-talkies, 128, 130, 206
Warren, Jason, 238
Weir, Ben, 247
West Nova Scotia Regiment, 48
White Schoolhouse, 16, 112, 233–87, 288, 290, 293

"X" (target area), 111

Yellow Schoolhouse, 239, 246, 278, 288

zap numbers, 108, 139
"zap straps," 184